HISTORIC COURTHOUSES OF NEW YORK STATE

For Ed and Dale
Merry Christmas 1977
Barbara and Jim

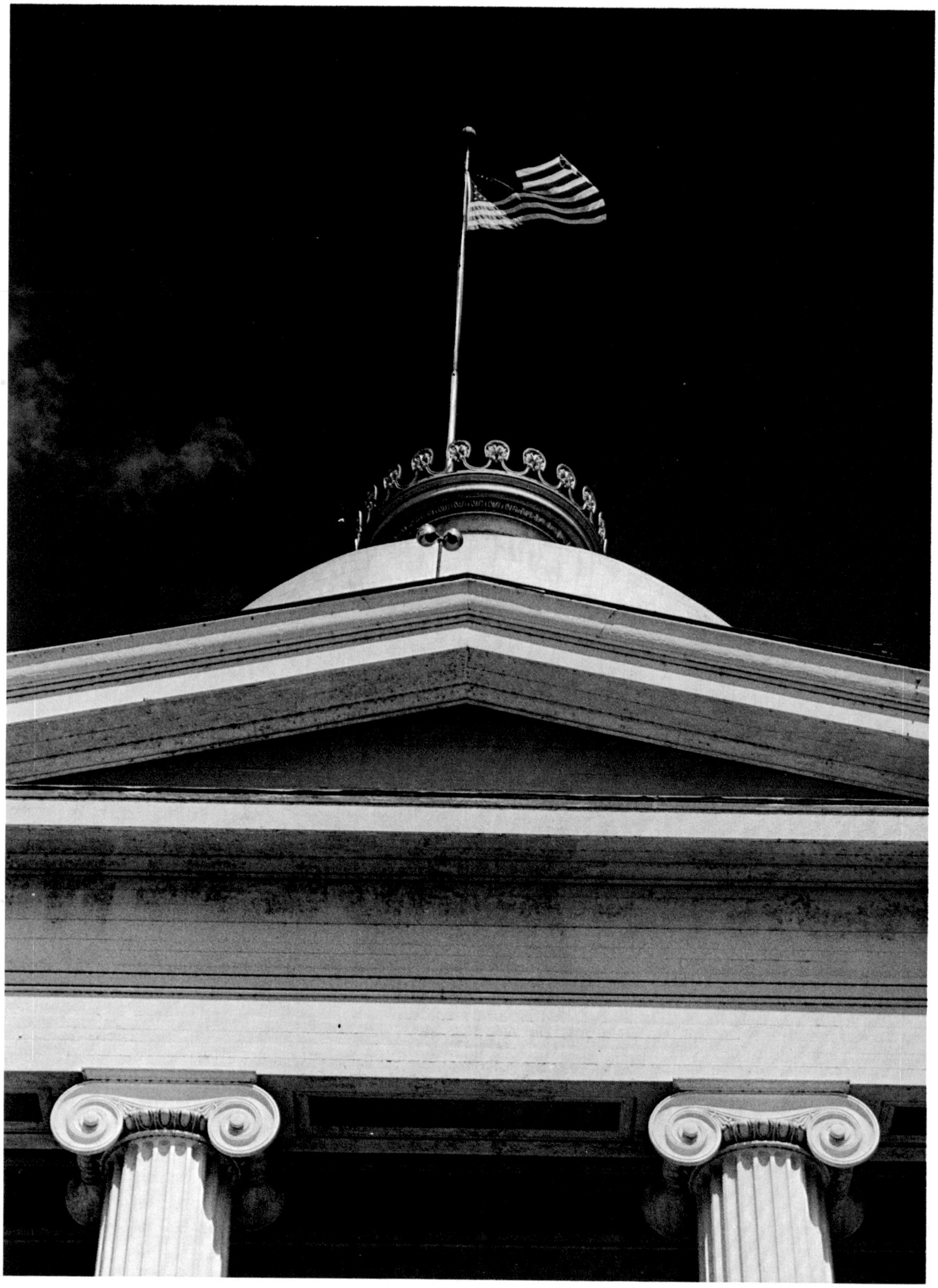

HISTORIC COURTHOUSES OF NEW YORK STATE

18th and 19th Century Halls of Justice Across the Empire State

By Herbert Alan Johnson and Ralph K. Andrist

With a Foreword by Charles D. Breitel Chief Judge of the Court of Appeals

Photographs by Milo V. Stewart

Columbia University Press   *New York 1977*

Printed in the United States of America

Library of Congress Cataloging in Publication Data

Johnson, Herbert Alan.
Historic courthouses of New York State.

1. Court-houses—New York (State)—Pictorial works. 2. New York (State)—Buildings—Pictorial works. I. Andrist, Ralph K., joint author.
II. Title.
F120.J64 974.7 77-23962
ISBN 0-231-04432-1

Columbia University Press
New York / Guildford, Surrey

Designed by Ron Gordon of The Oliphant Press
Printed in "Stonetone" process by
the Rapoport Printing Corporation
Production supervised by
the Publishing Center for Cultural Resources
This volume has been published
under the joint sponsorship of
the New York Bar Foundation and
the William Nelson Cromwell Foundation.

Frontispiece: Wayne County Courthouse,
Lyons (1854)

This book is dedicated to the memory of

ORISON S. MARDEN,

a dedicated and soft-spoken leader of the New York bar who served as president of the New York City, New York State, and American Bar Associations, and who encouraged plans for publication of this work to help preserve the traditions of the bench and bar at a time when the book was little more than a spark.

CONTENTS

ACKNOWLEDGMENTS

Many people have helped make this volume possible, not only by aiding its actual preparation but also by promoting the preservationist philosophy that it presents.

Clarence R. Runals, of Niagara Falls, established in 1957 the Committee for the Preservation of Historic Courthouses in the New York State Bar Association; this was the first organized attempt to halt senseless destruction of sturdy, useful, and tradition-filled halls of justice and their replacement with something "modern"— and often ugly.

Whitney North Seymour, Jr., was chairman of the committee founded by Mr. Runals, and he and other members of the group have worked hard—and with considerable success—to stir up interest in courthouse preservation. Mr. Seymour has also been responsible in large part for conceiving this book and for finding a way through the difficulties of production and financing.

Photography, research, and the writing of the book were made possible by grants from the New York State Bar Association and from the Historical Activities Committee of the National Society of Colonial Dames in the State of New York, and were conducted under the auspices of that committee and of the Committee for the Preservation of Historic Courthouses of the New York State Bar Association. The photographs of the interiors of courthouses and courtrooms were taken with the approval of the presiding justices of the four Appellate Divisions of the Supreme Court of the State of New York.

Publication has been aided by grants from the William Nelson Cromwell Foundation and from the New York Bar Foundation and has been coordinated by the Publishing Center for Cultural Resources.

The authors wish to express their thanks for assistance to W. Harold Calderwood and Mrs. Nina Sloan Bovee, both of Johnstown; E. Ritzema Perry of Bedford; Lewis C. Rubenstein of Albany; Louis C. Jones of Cooperstown; Willis Barshied of Palatine; John E. Becker, John S. Genung, and Judge Jerome Wolff of Waterloo; Charles J. Sauers of Oswego; Lynn H. Carpenter of Penn Yan; Miss Dorothy Facer of Lyons; Cary Lattin of Albion; Miss Charlotte

Reed of Batavia; Professor Harley J. McKee of Syracuse; David F. Lane of Watertown; John Addeo of New York City; and Mrs. Barbara A. Johnson of Williamsburg, Virginia.

Thanks are also due to Joseph H. Murphy of Syracuse, who reviewed the manuscript, and to the following persons who provided additional factual material, checked portions of the text for accuracy, or made other valuable contributions: Frederick L. Rath, Jr., and Doris Manley of the New York State Office of Parks and Recreation; William J. Herron of Malone; J. Boyd Mullan of Rochester; Anna E. Patchett, County Historian, Livingston County; Hon. Edmund L. Shea of Ogdensburg; Mrs. Mary H. Biondi, County Historian, St. Lawrence County; Hon. Liston F. Coon of Watkins Glen; Hon. James A. FitzPatrick of Plattsburgh; Mrs. Frank W. Williams of Cuba; Mae Smith, Historian, Chenango County; Bernard Amell, Clinton County Clerk; Donald G. Tkacy, Columbia County Clerk; Harold D. Owens, Jr., Delaware County Clerk; H. Sass, Senior Librarian, Buffalo and Erie County Historical Society; Alice Wood Gough, Essex County Clerk; E. S. Tattershall, Historian, Town of Malone; John M. Kasson, Fulton County Clerk; Neal Brandon, Greene County Clerk; H. Paul Draheim, Historian, Herkimer County; H. Ben Mitchell, Jefferson County Clerk; A. Einhorn, Historian, Lewis County; Margaret McCaughey, Livingston County Clerk; Mrs. Violet D. Fallone, Senior Clerk, Montgomery County; Benjamin F. Banta IV, Public Information Director, Oswego County; Joseph L. Peloso, Jr., Putnam County Clerk; Chilton Latham, Steuben County Clerk; Pamela Vogel, County Historian, Warren County; Leon D. Putnam, Washington County Clerk; L. H. Carpenter, Yates County Clerk; Thomas G. Elred, County Historian, Cayuga County; Virginia M. Barons, County Historian, Genesee County; William E. D. Barlow, Broome County Clerk; Gloria Bilotta, Cattaraugus County Clerk; Clyde Maffin, County Historian, Ontario County; June B. Hotaling, Otsego County Clerk; Hon. George Boldman, Owego, N.Y.; Mrs. Lucille Grinnell, Tompkins County Clerk; Sharon Wiles of New York City; and the indefatigable Hester B. Coe, who has served as unofficial coordinator on the project throughout its development.

Finally, we are most grateful to M. J. Gladstone and Francis F. Dobo of the Publishing Center for Cultural Resources—a unique and remarkable institution in itself—for the guidance, enthusiasm, and good taste they have contributed to the design and production of the book itself.

FOREWORD

Charles D. Breitel

Chief Judge of the Court of Appeals

A courthouse is not a court. Even judges do not make a court. A court is a social, historic, and cultural institution. Not only tradition but also the essence of its function makes a court a unique and special resource of a society. In the Western world, quite independent of the constitutions or statutes that create and govern its structure and function, a court expresses a continued wellspring of tradition, principles, concepts, and attitudes to the governance of man in an organized society. There is no appropriate comparison with the legislative and executive branches of government. In contrast to those two branches, the courts stand for a neutrality, a disinterestedness, a morality, if you will, and the dignity without which courts would disappoint, and properly so, the deepest expectations of the people.

It is perhaps in the Jewish tradition that the earliest origins of judges' especially high dignity are found. It occurs, perhaps due in some degree to the Jewish tradition, in the latter, Christian period of our history. There are roots in Rome; there are roots in ancient Greece. It is in the Anglo-American system of justice that one finds the flowering of that high dignity. The development of the several courts of England is, of course, the primary source of the Anglo-American legal tradition. The source of

the high dignity of judges and courts is best exemplified in the common religious-secular origin of the powers of the chancellor and the development of the courts of equity.

This dignity and the deep-rooted tradition of the courts are reflected in the special role that the bar holds in Anglo-American society. Despite some modern cynics, it is still true that the legal profession is, to an extent matched by no other profession except perhaps that of the clergy and teaching, one that carries a social responsibility of the highest degree.

If this backdrop to the situation and predicament of the courts is accurate, it is understandable that the courthouse has always been a special kind of place in Anglo-American history, reflecting the social, historic, and cultural significance of the courts.

Man thinks and speaks in symbols. These symbols are not only the words of the language. The symbols man uses are so frequently images— things of art, of architecture—images that gain an evolving connotation, although they may lose part or all of their original meaning over the centuries. This is not peculiar to any one part of our culture. It is especially well demonstrated in houses of worship. Spires of the country church, like the steeples and arches of a medieval cathedral, express most effectively man's striving toward the ineffable in the universe. They express his aspirations; they express his humility; they express his respect for his forebears and the progeny to come. No less do courthouses when they are beautiful courthouses.

Indeed, although no man has ever succeeded in expressing the essence of the aesthetic, we do know that the aesthetic is a reflection of man's soul.

As one looks at the courthouses of a nation, small or large, low or high in judicial rank, old or new, one sees a reflection of the culture's feeling for this very important part of man's life, in the buildings he has constructed in which the rule of law is developed and applied.

Men do not too falsely believe that if a court-

Court of Appeals Hall, Albany (1824)

house is fouled by dirt and disrepair, by ugliness and inadequacy, there is something lacking in the dignity and nobility of the justice that is rendered there. So, too, if a courthouse is magnificent, whether simple, like some of the courthouses in the rural areas of the state or the nation, or grand, like some of the great courthouses of the nation or the state, the quality of justice that is rendered there may partake in some degree of the magnificence of the surroundings. The same is true of houses of worship and schools of education. True, a great courthouse will not make a great court, even as a group of great judges will not alone make a great court. Involved always is a continuum of tradition, culture, history—and the capacity of men, seemingly, to surpass themselves.

A simple anecdote may illustrate just a small corner of what I am trying to say. Many years ago, grand juries of New York County used to hold their sessions in the old criminal court building just north of the old Tombs prison. There was an elevated bridge, a Bridge of Sighs, between the two buildings. They were old buildings. They were in disrepair. They were not too clean. Coming before the grand juries, when they were in session, were the witnesses in criminal cases—routine criminal cases—cases that arose from the terrible events that brought about criminal prosecutions. In the waitingrooms outside the grand jury rooms the witnesses from all walks of life, usually from the most humble levels, would assemble and wait. (Witnesses, like soldiers and jurors, spend most of their time waiting.) While waiting the group would be noisy, engaging in voluble conversation, eating and drinking, and littering the room with the newspapers with which many of them sought to occupy their waiting time. Those waiting rooms were not places of dignity, let alone of comfort.

In 1941 the new criminal court building, the one that still stands across the street on an angle from the site of the old building, was completed. It was then, as it is not now, a shining-clean, even immaculate, building. The quarters for its occupants were furnished with elegant paneling, benches, and chairs that were not only new but were appropriate to a building devoted to so important a purpose. It was a great building— then.

The change from the old building to the new building was a quick transition. The thing that

Appellate Division Courthouse,
First Judicial Department,
Manhattan (1899)

was remarkable to me (I was then a prosecutor handling matters before the grand jury) was the strange change in the behavior of the witnesses while they waited, as they always had waited, to appear before the grand jury. Voices were subdued. Newspapers were read, but they did not become the ugly litter of an earlier or later day. Food and drink were not consumed by the waiting witnesses, because they feared to sully the quarters in which they were waiting.

No one told these people that they should keep their voices subdued. No one told them that they should not litter the quarters. No one told them that they should abstain from food and drink while waiting. They just did so.

The significance was not lost on any observer of the conditions before and after the transfer from the old building to the new. People, most of them humble, not of any particular elevation in standards or training, had merely reacted to their surroundings.

Extrapolate the principles that derive from that simple illustration from a corner of a house of justice. For the more decisive, more formal, more significant doings that occur in a house of justice, what the magnificence, even simple magnificence, of a courthouse means is inevitably inferable.

That is why the idea of collecting, in this handsome book, photographs of the great courthouses of New York State is so happy a one and so appropriate. Of course, these buildings are of historic and architectural interest. But they are so much more. They show us, through pictures, through beautiful photographs, the striving of man throughout our history for courthouses of justice as architectural symbols of man's endeavor, his ideals, and his effort to surpass himself. They tell us that the human beings of our society, for all of their failings, the grave and the venial, have nevertheless dreamed of what in their souls they hoped would be.

No one can look upon these pictures and not feel deep pain at the tawdry, dirty, inadequate, and ugly structures, parts of structures, and debasing surroundings in which so many of our courts must do their work. The affront is not so much to the permanent occupants of those buildings. The affront is to those who come to those buildings as transients, whether as litigants or witnesses or lawyers.

The reader who goes through the pages of this book should enjoy it. He should have a rich aesthetic experience. He should also suffer pain that what ought to be does not exist everywhere in the handling of law and justice, without which there is no society.

Perhaps there should be another book of photographs, a book of photographs of the courthouses that should not be, a book of disgrace.

But for now we are grateful for the beauty of this book's contents, and for the symbol it is of the courthouses, as they are the symbols of a great tradition.

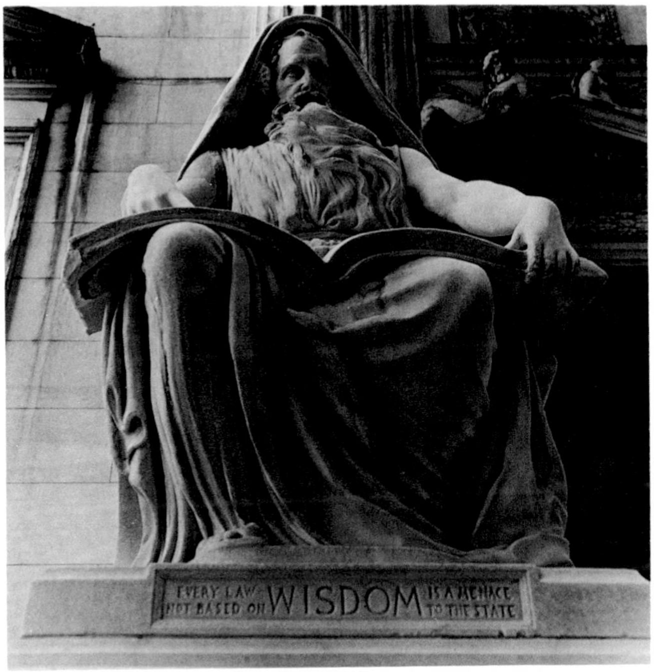
EVERY LAW NOT BASED ON WISDOM IS A MENACE TO THE STATE

Appellate Division Courthouse, First Judicial Department, Manhattan (1899)

INTRODUCTION

The county courthouse occupies a unique and revered place in American life. More than any other structure, it symbolizes the formative and unifying influence that law and the tradition of constitutionalism have played in the history of the United States. As outposts of our young republican states, the first courthouses stood at that intangible frontier of human progress and civic order where legal process attempts to resolve society's conflicts and to secure the safety and dignity of mankind.

From its earliest days Anglo-American law has been administered locally to secure a more effective prosecution of crime and to ensure that justice is done at the hands of informed judges and juries. In more recent times, American rules for the selection of grand and petit juries, as well as the widespread practice of electing the judiciary, have brought the influence of local public opinion into the judicial processes.

This localism of the courts in the American states is reflected in governmental legislation and administration at the local level. Although considerable amounts of statute and case law emerge from central tribunals and legislatures, the regulations that touch everyday life most intimately tend to emanate from city councils and county boards of supervisors. Popularly elected county officials have taken the place of the ubiquitous justices of the peace of Tudor England, but these officials—by maintaining order in the community and establishing local ordinances—have just as much effect as the justices once did on the quality of life of the citizenry. Because American local governing bodies have traditionally held their legislative and executive sessions in the county courthouse, and the activities of officials such as sheriffs, tax assessors, county clerks, and registrars of wills and deeds have also centered in the courthouse or its neighborhood, the county courthouse has been the focal point of local political and governmental life.

A century ago the courthouse was the scene of most local entertainment, including concerts, theatrical performances, and various exhibitions. More often, though, it was court trials and political debate that drew crowds into the building. When a major criminal case or an exciting civil matter came to trial, courtrooms were packed. Men and women knew at first hand how the law was administered, and they had a sense of security in knowing that their neighbors sat on the jury and their elected representatives made the laws that protected the community. This familiarity with the processes of the law did not diminish regard for it; citizens who took part in forming the local government and were themselves prospective jurors felt respect for the law and responsibility for upholding it.

Such widespread participation in government bred a nation of citizens well acquainted with public affairs, who took a proprietary pride in their local public institutions and in the ideals of individual liberty. This pride, along with American optimism for the future, played an important role in the design of new courthouses. With few exceptions, county courthouses were much larger than was necessary to satisfy current needs.

Courthouse architecture reflected the esteem in which law and local government were held. The records indicate a general sentiment that proposed courthouses should reflect the "latest" in style and accommodations. Courtrooms were graced with large windows and lofty ceilings, and those on the second floor were often reached by long and impressive staircases. The judge's bench, jury box, and witness's chair were usually placed on elevated platforms so they could be seen clearly from anywhere in the courtroom.

Even though courthouse design was influenced by a wish to be modern and an inclination to plan expansively for the future, it also reflected the conservatism of local taste and a frugality in authorizing "nonessential" expenditures. Horatio Nelson White, a popular Syracuse architect in the post-Civil War period, preferred to work in cut stone, but two of his three Anglo-Norman courthouses were built of brick with stone facing as a concession to his clients' parsimony. Local materials not only kept costs down, but also demonstrated the quality and beauty of local products, and their use benefited suppliers and builders in the area. Committees appointed by county governing boards spent months visiting and studying courthouses in the state in a search for ideas that might be used in their proposed

structure. Architects and builders were chosen for demonstrated competence and were carefully supervised while they worked. All these factors limited the freedom of the architect and injected public taste and local requirements into design. Even when architects were distinguished (and in early New York State, few were), the pervasive influence of local citizens and officials would produce a courthouse embodying compromises in style and design. For that reason the courthouses of New York, though charming and significant as examples of public taste, are seldom examples of groundbreaking architectural design.

But if New York's older courthouses are not masterpieces of architecture, they are monuments to the rich local history of the counties they have served. For that reason, the text of this book centers on local history as it was reflected in county courthouses. New York has a rich legal and constitutional history, and though some of it has been lost through the destruction of records, most is recoverable through careful research. This is especially true where county and city records have remained neglected in old courthouses, awaiting discovery and study by historians and archivists. The survival of a historic courthouse has frequently also meant the survival of county archives tucked away in its crannies.

While the movement for preservation at first depended on nostalgic appeal and antiquarian sentiments, respect for history and appreciation of the economic practicality of continuing to use durable old buildings have given it a stronger base. Courthouses are among the least adaptable structures in America, and so they are extremely vulnerable to demands for progress and utility. Nostalgia will rarely bring about the preservation of a courthouse if a demonstration of the historical significance of the building is lacking. Nor can a wistful hearking back to the amenities of the past outweigh arguments of practical economics in the use of county buildings. Courthouses can best be saved through their continued use for judicial and governmental purposes, and most of the state's older courthouses are still so used. Some, however, are supplementing the overtaxed facilities of newer courthouses; others have been converted to use as museums or college halls, or have been adapted to other purposes far removed from the intent of their builders. While the historical associations of these buildings have usually contributed to their survival, it has been the discovery of new usefulness that has really saved them from destruction.

New York's local history is scarcely a provincial theme. Events that occurred in its small communities are intertwined with national developments. Colonial New York lay astride the Hudson and Mohawk rivers, the early path of water-borne trade and migration to the Great Lakes and the West. The construction of the Erie Canal strengthened this geographical advantage and ensured a major role for New York in continental expansion and the development of the Old Northwest.

The development of law and legal institutions within early New York courthouses set a model for other states. The restatement of substantive law in the New York statutory revisions of 1830 and the enactment into law of the Field Code of procedure in 1848 have had a pervasive influence on the development of American law. So too have the evolution of the legal concept of criminal intent and the related defense of innocence by reason of insanity. Also, from colonial times onward, New York has been a leader in the growth of a new and enlightened view of the law of criminal libel.

It is interesting that despite New York's leading role during the westward movement, large areas within the state remained undeveloped and remote. Though historian Frederick Jackson Turner noted that the Western frontier had disappeared in the 1890s, New York's vast Adirondack region during that same period was still a frontier community in both a demographic and a cultural sense. Boom towns of one era, like Johnstown, were bypassed by changing trade patterns, and their early courthouses were preserved because there was no need to replace them with larger facilities. Streams of immigrants once passed through Batavia and Albion; the proud courthouses built then remained more than adequate during the quiet decades that followed.

Variety and diversity in the legal history of New York provide background for a study of the state's historic courthouses. No single volume can tell the whole history of law and justice in the Empire State, and this book is only a modest step in that direction. It is admittedly selective in its scope and directed toward encouraging the study of local history as a means toward the preservation of historic courthouse buildings. It is hoped that the work will encourage other legal historians to examine their own communities.

Included in this book are all the known county courthouses built before 1900 that were still standing in 1976. Every effort has been made to identify, photograph, and discuss all extant structures that at one time or another served as county courthouses, regardless of their current use. Local city courthouses and the chambers of justices of the peace and magistrates are not included. While every effort has been made to make this a comprehensive survey, it is possible that some county courthouses have been inadvertently omitted. The authors would greatly appreciate corrections from readers so that a complete list may be maintained.

Though all known courthouses have been visited and photographed, lack of records has at times frustrated efforts to provide a detailed sketch of the history of each building. Fire, flood, and the destruction of old records to make room for newer files have wreaked havoc with New York county records. Consequently, extended discussion is given only to those courthouse buildings for which considerable material is available. Other courthouses have been treated more briefly in thumbnail histories.

The genesis of this book is of sufficient antiquity and complexity to deserve some comment. It was launched by the joint efforts of two organizations, the National Society of Colonial Dames in the State of New York and the Committee for the Preservation of Historic Courthouses of the New York State Bar Association. Mrs. Eugene Stetson, chairman of the historical activities committee of the Colonial Dames, and Whitney North Seymour, Jr., chairman of the bar association's historic courthouse committee, agreed to work toward a book-length study of the historic courthouses of New York. Herbert Alan Johnson, then teaching at Hunter College of the City University of New York, was commissioned to research the background of extant courthouses and to prepare a photographic survey of the buildings. That work was begun in June 1965 and continued into 1967 until Mr. Johnson

moved to Virginia to assume editorial duties on *The Papers of John Marshall*. A first draft of the book was completed in August 1968, and since then has undergone a series of revisions, the last by the co-author, Ralph K. Andrist of New Canaan, Connecticut. Mr. Andrist has completed research on historic courthouses built in New York between 1890 and 1900, which were not included in Mr. Johnson's survey. In 1973 Milo V. Stewart, associate director of the New York State Historical Association, was enlisted as photographer, and he has produced the brilliant illustrations contained in this volume. Although Mr. Stewart served principally as photographer, he has also helped provide the authors with historical material. Coordinating this multifaceted activity has been Whitney North Seymour, Jr., who despite heavy official duties in both state and federal offices has continued to direct the work to its completion.

In the final analysis, this book could not have been written without the people of New York who built and preserved these historic courthouses. Their artistic preferences and tastes and their aspirations for the future are expressed in the fabric of the buildings. Their local history—which sometimes became national history—took place in these structures and endows the courthouses with a significance that transcends their beauty or their ugliness. Without the custodianship of local officials and the interest of local citizens, the records on which the authors have drawn would no longer exist. All who have had a part in preparing this book hope that it will serve as a source of pride and satisfaction in the historical and artistic heritage that New York is preserving for future generations.

ALLEGANY COUNTY

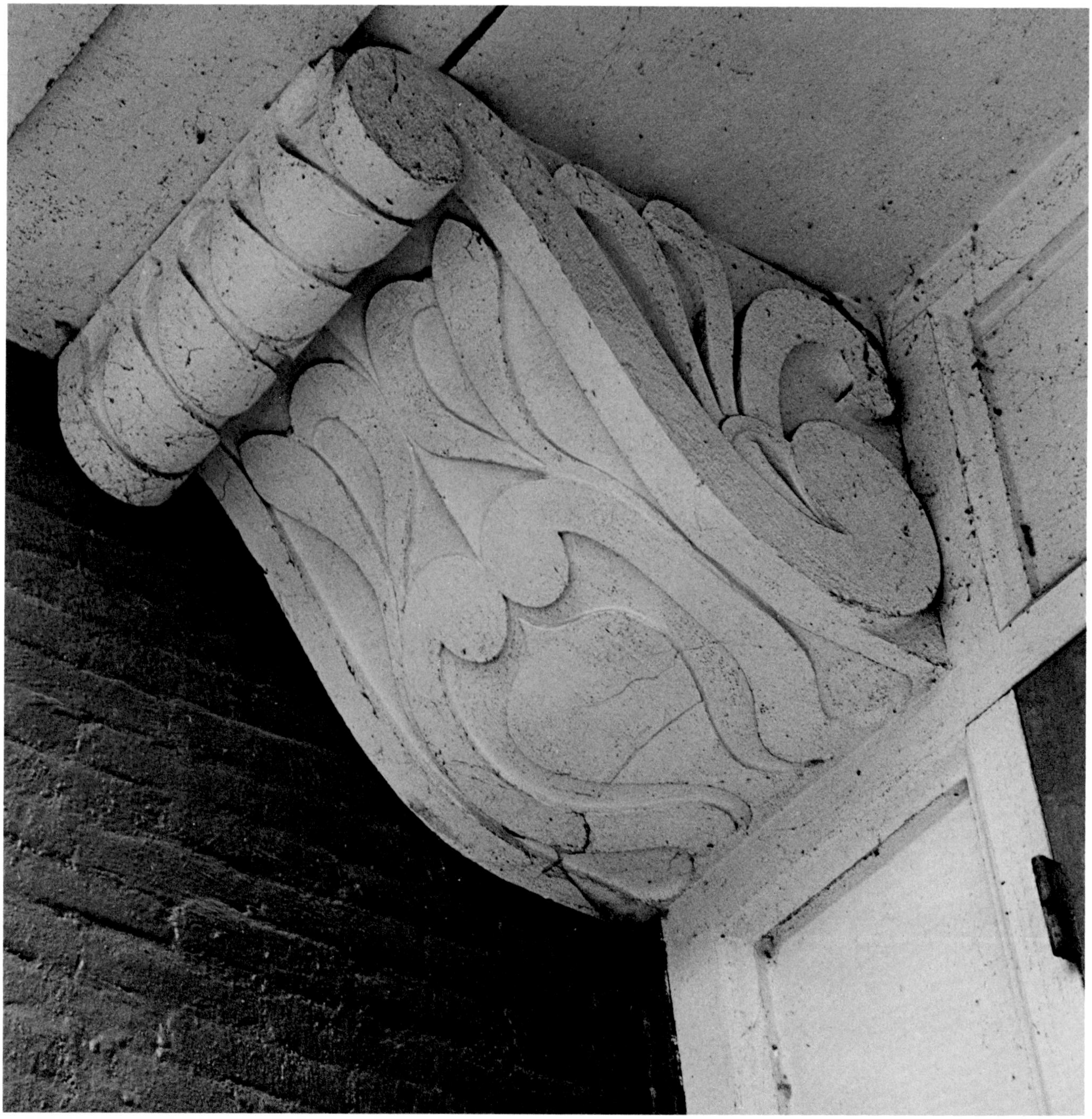

Angelica is no longer the county seat of Allegany County—has not been for a long time. But the county's first courthouse still stands in Angelica, though converted to other uses; it is now the community's town hall.

When Allegany County was established in 1806, the legislature decreed that Angelica should be the county seat. For a time courts were held in private homes or offices, but in 1819 a courthouse was built, and the people of the county remained, by and large, well satisfied for several decades with their county seat. But time eventually brought changes; the routes of commerce in the county shifted. The Genesee Valley Canal was constructed east of Angelica and diverted much traffic from the town; the Erie Railroad bypassed it on the south. The town languished while the trade that it had once handled went on other roads.

By the late 1850s the demands for a change in the county seat had become so insistent that the legislature acted, and in 1858 it chose Belmont as the site of a new courthouse, which was completed in 1860. At the same time the Angelica courthouse was repaired and refurbished, and for the next thirty-some years Allegany County was divided into two jury districts, with court being held alternately at Belmont and Angelica.

In 1892 all courts were consolidated in Belmont, which was declared the sole county seat, and the Angelica structure ceased to be a courthouse. The simple, unadorned little building was taken over by the community, and still serves well as the Angelica Town Hall.

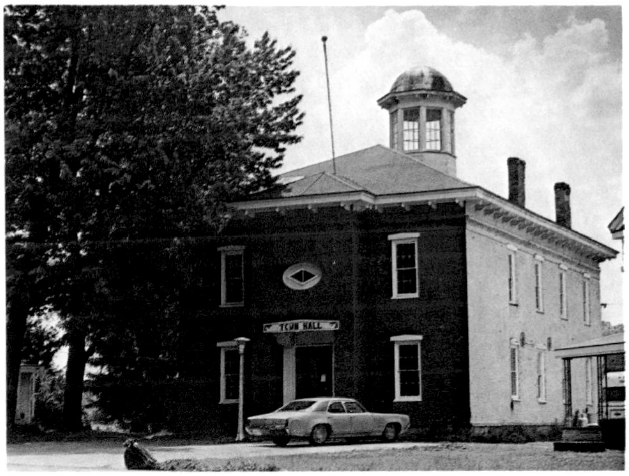
TOWN HALL

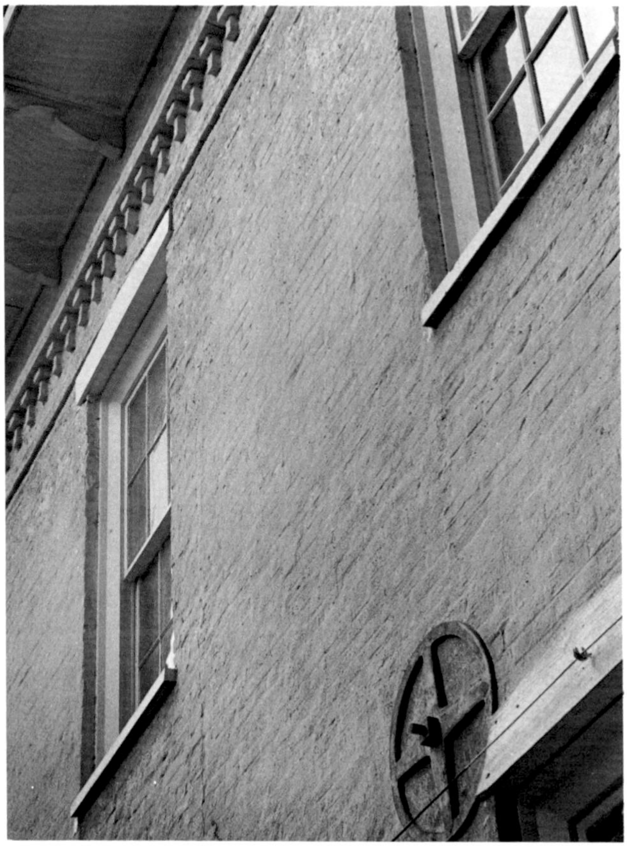

BROOME
COUNTY

The Broome County Courthouse, old though it is, is only the latest in a long line of court meeting-places at Binghamton that goes back to a time when there was no Broome County, Binghamton was known as Chenango Point, and court was sometimes held, weather permitting, outdoors under the trees.

In 1791 Tioga County was created from a portion of Montgomery County. The new county's boundaries encompassed today's Broome, Chemung, and Tioga counties, and small parts of four other counties. Probably because of its large size, the legislature made it a half-shired county, with seats at Newtown (now Elmira) and at Chenango Point (now Binghamton). A courthouse was built at Newtown Point—as it was first called—in 1796, but Chenango Point went without one until 1802. In the interim, court sessions were held in private homes and occasionally, at first, under the trees.

Broome County was formed from a part of Tioga County in 1806, and soon after it was organized, the 1802 courthouse was moved across the street to a site on a knoll that became known as Courthouse Hill. This first building, a twenty-four- by thirty-six-foot structure, was replaced in 1829 by a new courthouse, which in turn gave way in 1858 to another building, a massive brick structure ornamented by a portico that ran the ninety-six-foot length of the build-

ing; its four pillars were each six feet in diameter and thirty-six feet high. It was said to be one of the most beautiful courthouses in the United States.

This architectural gem, unhappily, was destroyed by fire late in December 1896. Although both county and town were in straitened financial circumstances at the time, plans to rebuild went ahead at once. The foundation walls of the destroyed courthouse were used wherever possible for the new building, whose exterior was made of Ohio sandstone trimmed with bluestone. The burned-out courthouse also served as a pattern for the new one; the main changes were in widening the portico and enlarging the stone columns. Construction was completed in 1898, and the building has remained essentially unchanged since.

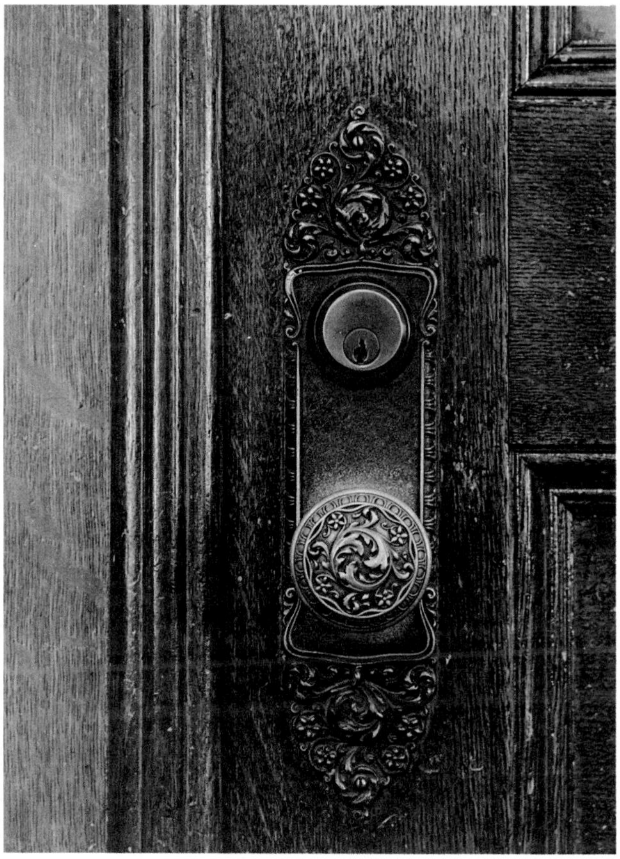

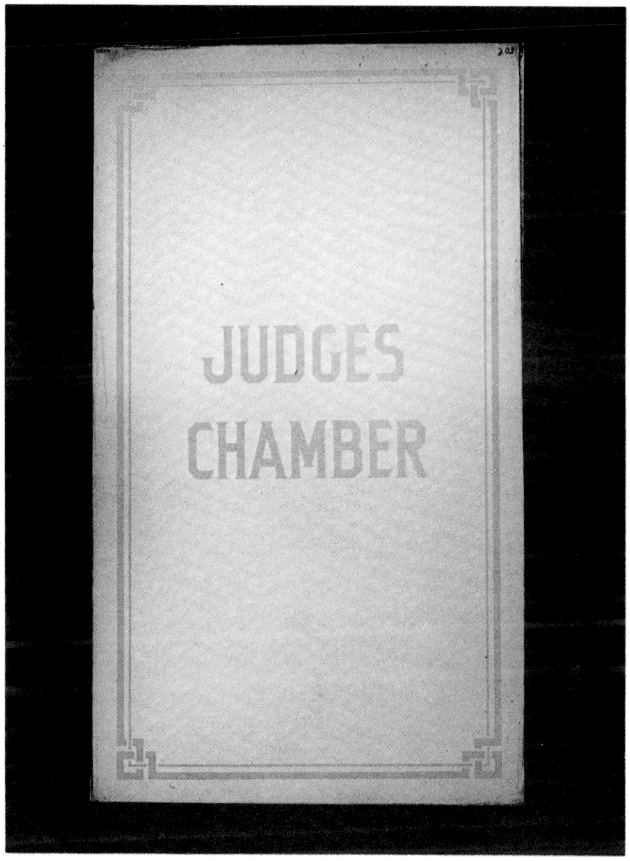
JUDGES
CHAMBER

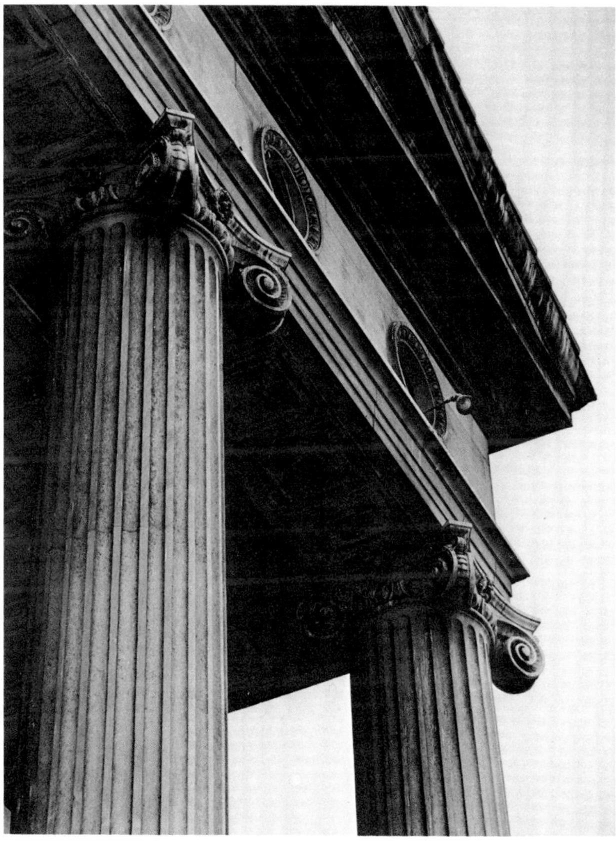

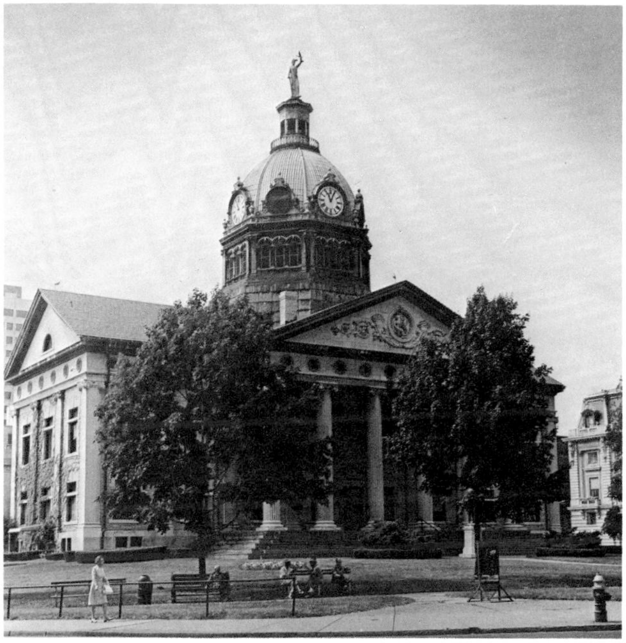

CATTARAUGUS COUNTY

A decade ago Cattaraugus County had two courthouses worth preserving. The wrecking ball and the bulldozer have been there since, and now only one remains. The loss was an urgent argument on the need for preserving our remaining historic courthouses.

The county of Cattaraugus was created in 1817 by the legislature, which in the next year directed that the courts of the new county should meet "at the house of Baker Leonard, in the village of Ellicottville." These homey quarters were replaced in 1820 by a courthouse, with jail, built on the Ellicottville public square. It was apparently a sturdy but unsophisticated building; the jail was built with inner and outer walls of logs, the space between packed with stones to frustrate escape attempts. Above the jail, on a second floor, were offices and a courtroom. This first courthouse burned in the winter of 1829 and was replaced by a stone building, simple but handsome, which was ready for the June term of court in 1830.

In 1865 the legislature decided to move the county seat to Little Valley, because the track of the Erie Railroad passed through that town, while Ellicottville had been bypassed by the railroad builders. The changeover became effective in 1868, when a courthouse in Little Valley was finished, and county offices, prisoners, and court sessions were all moved there from Ellicottville.

The Little Valley courthouse, a red-brick structure with cut-stone trim and a white wooden porch, was demolished and replaced in the winter of 1965–66 in the name of progress. The old courthouse at Ellicottville, however, continues to serve, but now as the town hall.

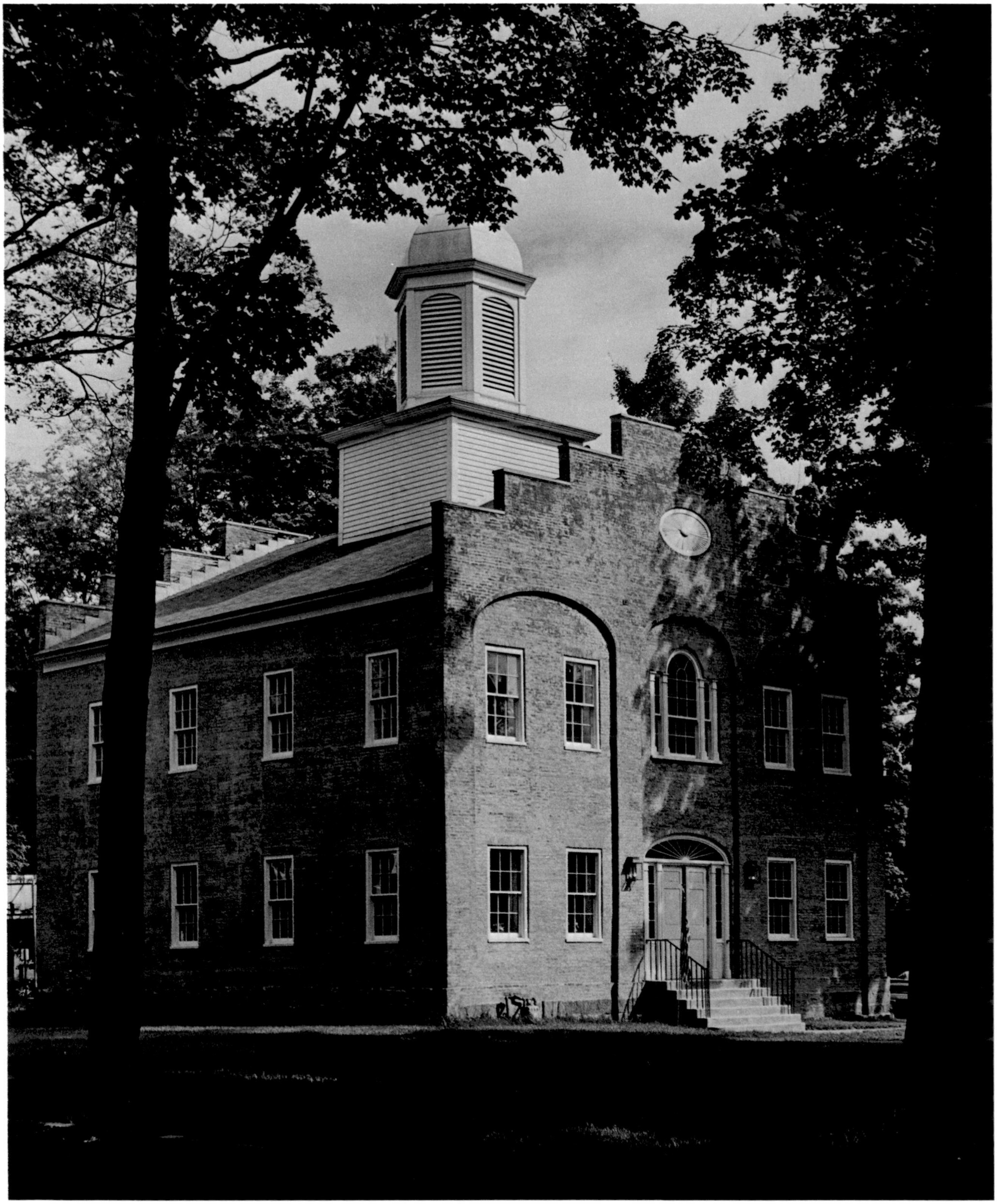

CAYUGA COUNTY

The Cayuga County Courthouse at Auburn is not the oldest of the surviving Greek-Revival courthouses in the state—its walls were put up in 1836—but between the fluted columns of its portico have passed the actors in one of the great dramas in the legal history of upper New York State. It was there that William Seward, best known as the United States secretary of state who negotiated the purchase of Alaska, proved himself a man of courage and principle, qualities he exercised during his long career in politics.

The story begins with one Bill Freeman, who had been sent to Auburn State Prison for five years for stealing a horse, although he continued to insist that he was innocent. The prisons of the day were completely brutalized, and Freeman, half-Indian, half-black, probably was treated even worse than most of the other convicts. One day, when he argued with a prison guard, he was beaten over the head with a board until, as he later put it, "The marbles dropped out of my ears." Soon after, he began to lose his hearing. When he was released from prison and began to look around his hometown of Auburn for odd jobs, those who knew him noted other changes besides the hardness of hearing. He had become slow of wit, his conversation was muddled, and an empty smile almost constantly spread over his face.

On rare occasions, and only when he was talking about his imprisonment, Freeman's smile would fade, he would become earnest and intent in his conversation, and he would say that he would "have to get his pay." One day he went to the office of a justice of the peace, demanded a warrant for the arrest of those who had put him in prison, and went away bewildered when informed the justice could do nothing. He stopped in at the law offices of the former governor, William H. Seward, and asked the clerk there to obtain an arrest warrant. And again he went away empty-handed.

By the beginning of March 1846, Bill Freeman had made preparations for getting his pay in another fashion. A kindly blacksmith let him shape a knife blade in his shop. Someone else, sympathetic to Freeman's poverty, sold him a second knife at a bargain rate. On the evening of March 12, Freeman took his two knives and a spear he had made and walked south along the shores of Owasco Lake to the farmhouse of John Van Nest.

A few hours later Freeman took an old mare from the Van Nest barn and rode away. Behind him Van Nest, his wife, and their two-year-old son lay dead. The farmer's aged mother-in-law lived long enough to make her way through the snow to a neighbor's farm to ask for help. Freeman was quickly captured; his confused mind seemed to recall the murder of not four but five persons, and he insisted that he had not harmed the slain baby.

Feeling ran very high in the community, with

the usual demands for immediate lynching. And, by a weird kind of distorted logic, the townspeople were holding former Governor William Seward to blame for the Van Nest murders. A few months before, one Henry Wyatt had killed a fellow convict at Auburn State Prison. His victim had informed guards that Wyatt had committed a crime in Ohio, and when Wyatt denied the allegation, guards whipped and tortured him and finally tossed him into the dank hole used for solitary confinement. After he had continued to insist on his innocence through several weeks of this mistreatment, Wyatt was finally returned to the company of the other prisoners. There he revenged himself on the man who had informed on him by killing him in one of the prison shops. Seward had defended Wyatt and had unsuccessfully attempted to persuade court and jury that the inhuman treatment Wyatt had received had made him an insane man bent on revenge.

During the arguments on Wyatt's case, a constable had told a black man in the back of the courtroom to get down from a chair on which the man was standing to get a better view of the proceedings. As the policeman later recollected the incident, the man resembled Freeman, but as he told and retold his story, his tentative identification became fact. Soon most of Auburn was convinced that Freeman had committed his murders after hearing Seward argue that insanity was a defense against a murder charge. And so, their reasoning went, Seward was directly responsible for the Van Nest murders, and it was suggested that he had better not try to use insanity as a defense for Freeman.

Governor Seward (the title was honorific, for after serving as governor of New York he had returned to Auburn to resume law practice) was away on a business trip when the Van Nest murders occurred, but his wife, Fanny, wrote and warned him of the incredible connection made between his defense of Wyatt and Freeman's homicides. When Seward returned to Auburn his wife and friends met him at the station and escorted him to his home, where he was told of the feelings of the town against him and the resolve of community leaders that he should not defend Freeman. Actually, Seward had not been asked to undertake the defense, but several weeks later, when a friend suggested that he visit Freeman in his cell, he did so, and came away troubled and saddened by the physi-

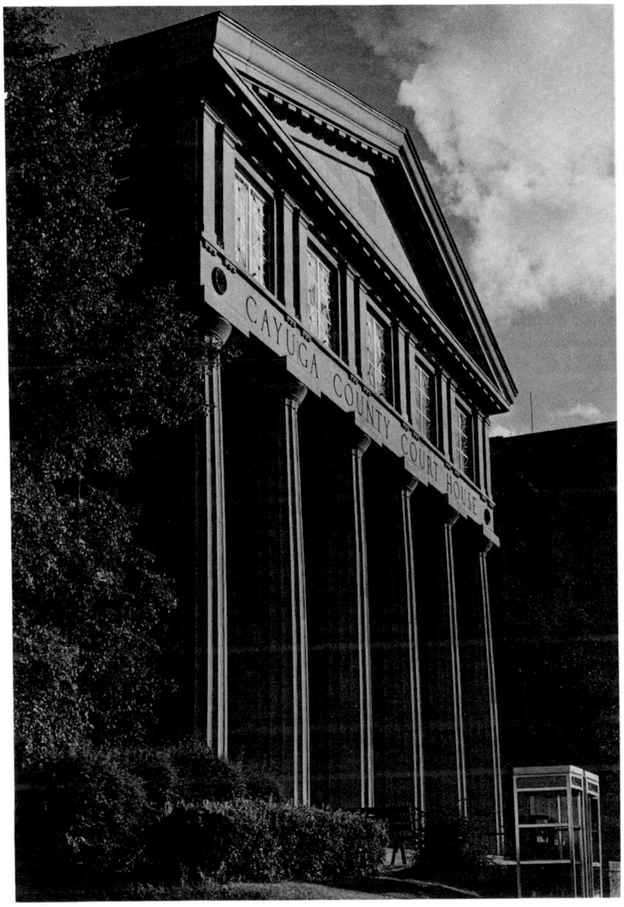
CAYUGA COUNTY COURT HOUSE

cal and emotional state of the accused murderer, especially the constant, empty smile on the man's face and the earnestness with which he discussed "getting his pay." Inevitably, Seward ended up acting as counsel for Freeman.

The law of New York in 1846 did not recognize that a person could be not guilty of a crime by reason of insanity, although there was a considerable body of medical literature to support this thesis. Seward reasoned that the defendant's sanity was an issue that should be resolved at the very threshold of criminal trial proceedings. Seward at once pleaded Freeman "not guilty by virtue of insanity," and the battle of the experts began. Medical men who had served in New York mental institutions testified about the prisoner's state of mind; they were followed by Auburn residents who had known Freeman both before and after his term in prison; and several amateur psychologists who had questioned and tested the accused in prison gave their opinions. After all witnesses were heard, the judge left the decision of sanity up to the jury, which after considerable deliberation, returned the ambiguous verdict that the prisoner was "sufficiently sane to stand trial." Seward objected to the finding as inconclusive of the issue of sanity, but his objection was overruled and the trial was scheduled to proceed.

The trial had become more than a criminal proceeding; with a prominent Whig like William Seward involved, it had strong political overtones. The case had gained such wide publicity that it was strategically wise for the Democratic administration to clip Seward's wings lest he use the trial as a new springboard for his political career. So, rather than depending on the local district attorney to handle the prosecution of the Freeman case, Governor Silas Wright sent State Attorney General John Van Buren to conduct the state's case. "Prince John" was the son of former President Martin Van Buren and greatly admired in the New York Democratic party.

The trial began on July 4, 1846; that day the good citizens of Auburn hanged Seward in effigy. For the most part, the trial was a more elaborate restatement of the evidence submitted in support of and opposition to Seward's request at the arraignment that Freeman be discharged because of insanity. Van Buren's experts argued that the defendant was perfectly sane, that his slowness of speech and unemotional behavior were due to his descent from African slaves and savage Indians. Seward countered that his mannerisms were indeed due, at least in large part, to heredity, because there was a history of insanity in his family.

Seward had first come to Auburn as a young attorney in 1822, marrying the daughter of a local judge; he had settled down to raise a family there and earn his place in the community. This he placed in jeopardy when he took on the defense of Bill Freeman, and a letter to editor Thurlow Weed, written on May 29, 1846, several days before Freeman's arraignment, testifies to Seward's moral courage: "There is a busy war around me, to drive me from defending and securing a fair trial for the negro Freeman. . . . He is deaf, detested, ignorant, and his conduct is inexplicable on any principle of *sanity*. It is natural that he should turn to me to defend him. If he does, I shall do so. This will raise a storm of prejudice and passion. . . ."

The trial was short; the jury went out to deliberate on July 6, while the crowd outside shouted that Freeman should be crucified and

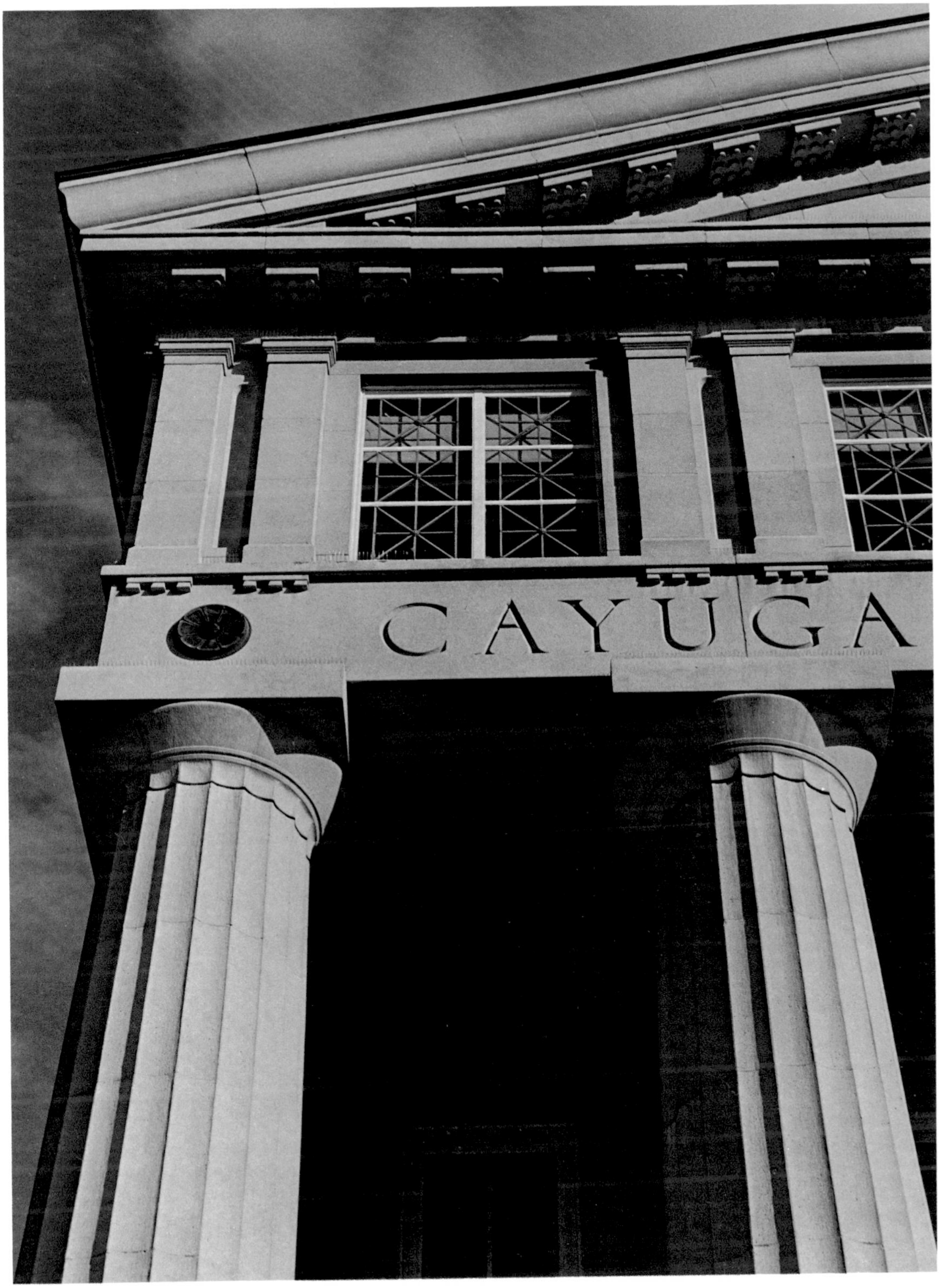
CAYUGA

IN 1846
WILLIAM H. SEWARD
IN CAYUGA COUNTY COURT HOUSE
DEFENDED A MAN ACCUSED OF
MURDER AND BASED HIS PLEA ON
THE UNPRECEDENTED GROUNDS
OF INSANITY. ALTHOUGH SCORNED
AND HUMILIATED BY MANY FOR
HIS STAND AT THAT TIME, HISTORY
HAS SINCE VINDICATED HIM AS
A MAN OF PRINCIPLE, COURAGE,
AND FORESIGHT.
ERECTED IN 1958 BY THE CITIZENS
OF CAYUGA COUNTY

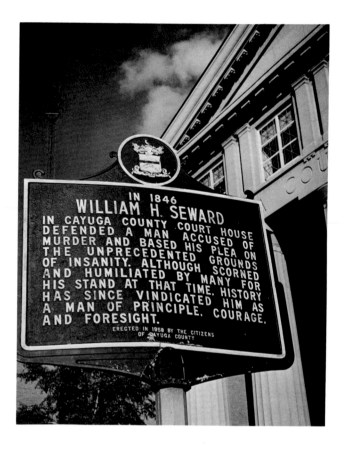

Seward stoned. It was not surprising that the jury soon returned with a verdict of guilty. But it was not the temper of the town or the verdict that was memorable, but rather Seward's speech in summation to the jury.

He commenced by observing that he spoke for society, not for Freeman, and said that mankind would be shocked to see a maniac tried as a malefactor. For that reason he was there to argue for a man who could not break through the veil of his own insanity to defend himself. He pleaded with the jury to remember Freeman's smile, and recalled how the man had smiled through the preliminary hearings, at his trial, and now, as his fate was about to be determined, he continued his senseless, vacant smiling. "Follow him to the scaffold," Seward said. "The executioner cannot disturb the calmness of the idiot. He will laugh in the agony of death. . . ."

And Seward justified his dogged defense of the miserable and helpless man, a justification voiced in the lush rhetoric of the day, but completely sincere: "In due time, gentlemen of the jury, when I shall have paid the debt of nature, my remains will rest here in your midst. . . . Perhaps, years hence, when the passion and excitement which now agitate this community shall have passed away, some wandering stranger, some lone exile, some Indian, some Negro, may erect over them a humble stone, and inscribe thereon 'He was Faithful.' "

Seward did speak his own epitaph, for after his term as United States senator and then his tenure as secretary of state in Lincoln's and Johnson's cabinets, he died and was buried at Auburn, and on his tombstone was inscribed "He was Faithful."

In spite of the jury's verdict of guilty, Freeman did not face the executioner. Seward took an appeal from the conviction and won a reversal and new trial on the ground that the preliminary finding of "sufficiently sane to stand trial" was improper. But in the interval, imprisonment in the Cayuga County Jail had had its effect on Freeman's health, and when Seward went to tell the prisoner of the reversal, he found Freeman physically weak and completely incoherent. Freeman died a short time later, awaiting a new trial, and an autopsy showed that there was advanced deterioration of his brain—a finding that caused many Auburn residents to reconsider their former violent stand against Seward. The case of *People* v. *Freeman* also went far toward establishing insanity as a defense in the criminal procedure of the state of New York.

A plaque in front of the Cayuga County Courthouse today reminds visitors of the historic trial. The walls that witnessed Seward's eloquent defense in 1846 still stand, and the columns on the portico between which he passed on his way to and from the trial look down now on a much later generation of lawyers, earnestly involved in the problems of today. But not much else is the same.

The first Cayuga County Courthouse on the premises was a frame building, erected in 1809 to the rear of the present courthouse. By the time the county decided to replace its wooden courthouse in the 1830s, the Greek-Revival movement was sweeping the country, and Cayuga County went along with the tide; the six fluted columns and pediment of its courthouse are suggestive of the Parthenon—the most jarring note is a line of windows between the top of the columns and the roof pediment.

In spite of such anachronisms, the courthouse was a handsome building. Then, in 1922, it became a victim of fire. The interior was completely gutted, the roof went, the domed cupola was destroyed. But the solid walls and the neo-Greek pillars were saved, and the courthouse was rebuilt within them during 1922–24. So the old courthouse, though well over a century old, continues to serve the people of Cayuga County.

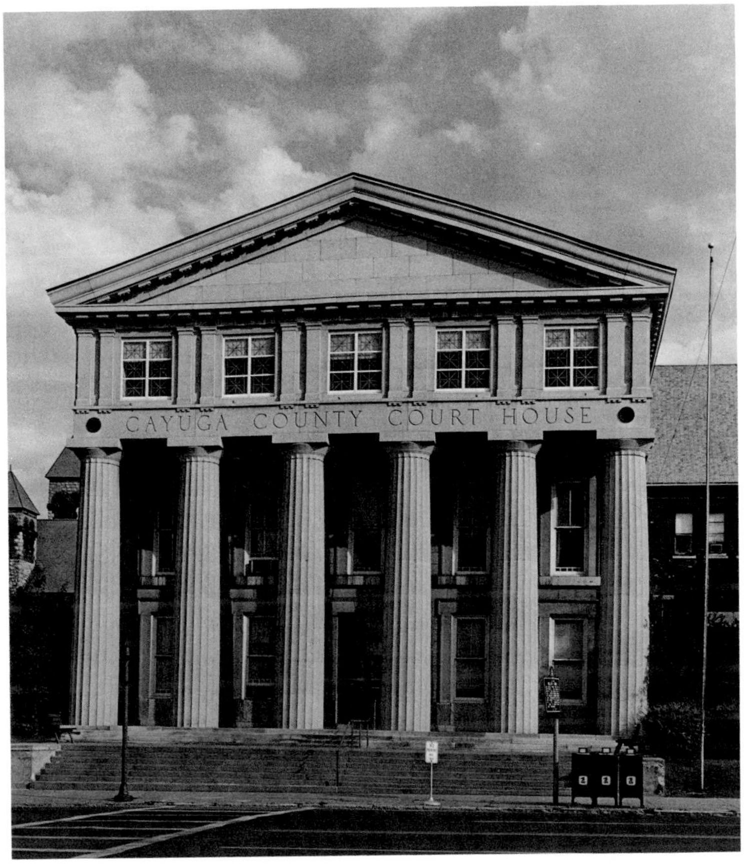
CAYUGA COUNTY COURT HOUSE

CHEMUNG COUNTY

The Chemung County Courthouse at Elmira was designed by Horatio Nelson White, a prolific self-taught architect who at one time had a strong impact on building styles in the Syracuse area. White, a New Hampshire carpenter, came to Syracuse in 1843 to practice his craft, set himself up in Brooklyn four years later as an architect, went out West when that venture failed, but returned to Syracuse in 1851 to become an eminently successful architect.

White designed residences, armories, and courthouses. He popularized a style described as Anglo-Norman; it was characterized by towers topped with stonework suggestive of the battlements of medieval castles. The courthouse at Elmira is so like the one White designed for Jefferson County in Watertown that the identity of architects is inescapable.

Elmira has been a county seat since 1791 when—then named Newtown Point—it became one of the two centers of newly formed Tioga County, and it remained a county seat when

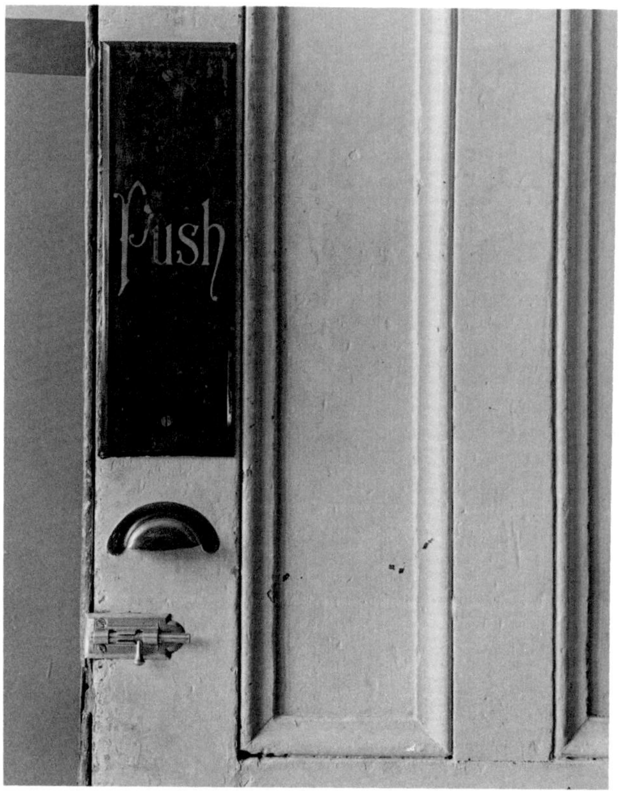
Push

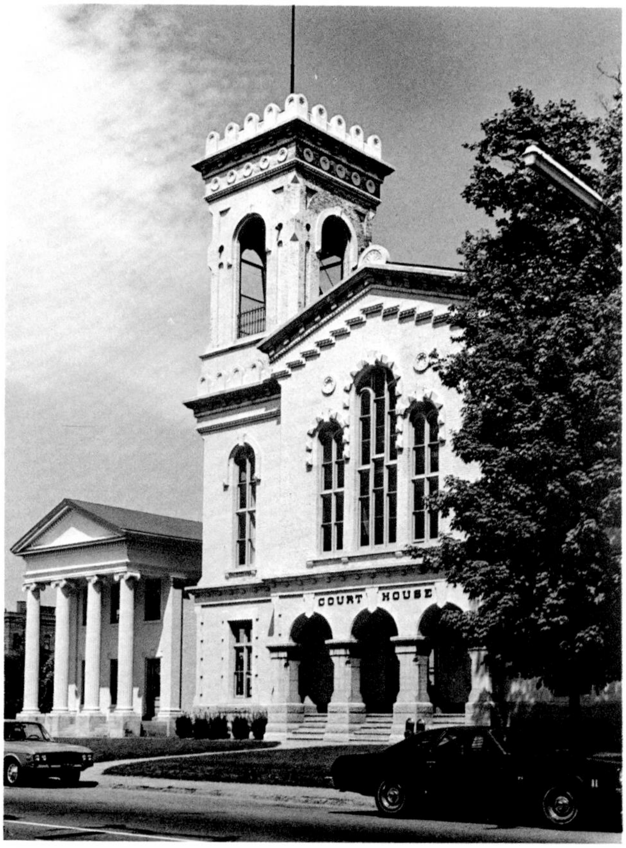
COURT HOUSE

Tioga successively lost parts of its territory to other counties. Then, when Chemung County was detached from Tioga in 1836, Elmira was in the detached portion and became the seat for the new county.

During its long career as a county seat under changing jurisdictions, Elmira has seen a number of courthouses, beginning with a log building put up in 1796; before that courts had been held in a tavern. The most recent of Elmira's courthouses is Horatio White's towered and battlemented structure; it has been serving Chemung County since 1862.

CHENANGO
COUNTY

Chenango County was separated from Herkimer in 1798, but Norwich did not become its county seat until almost a dozen years had passed; Hamilton and Oxford both served as county seats until 1806. Then the legislature made Norwich the new seat, though the act did not become effective until 1809 (where courts were held and county business transacted between 1806 and 1809 is unexplained).

The first courthouse in Norwich, a two-story, "substantially built" wooden structure, was ready for business in 1809, when Norwich took over as county seat. The building was soon outgrown as court activities increased, and talk about a new courthouse roused Oxford's ambitions to become the county seat again. The rivalry between Norwich and Oxford was sharp, and their contention was carried to the legislature, which in 1837 acted in favor of Norwich and authorized a new courthouse there.

That building, made of stone quarried near Oxford, was described in an early book as "a plain but sightly and imposing structure, built in the Grecian style of architecture, with a portico supported upon four Corinthian columns." It is the same simple, well-proportioned courthouse that stands on the Norwich village green today, more than a century and a quarter later.

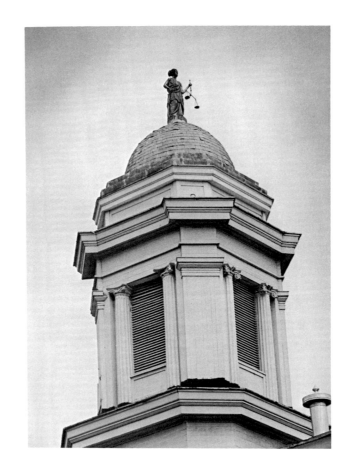

CLINTON COUNTY

Clinton County was established in 1788—a much larger entity then, for it included the present Essex and Franklin counties. The first courthouse was a log blockhouse, built originally as a jail but soon enlarged and used as courthouse, schoolhouse, and religious meetinghouse. Its site, then a farm, now lies within the city limits of Plattsburgh, the county seat.

The blockhouse continued to serve until 1803, when a real courthouse and jail were built—at a total cost of $2,751. This structure served for eleven years; then, during the War of 1812, the courthouse was struck by shot from the cannon of American forces attacking British-occupied Plattsburgh in 1814 and was burned to the ground. It was replaced by a new structure in 1815–16; this, too, burned (in 1836) but was rebuilt on the surviving outer walls.

No other catastrophe occurred; it was age and inadequacy that finally decided the Clinton County Board of Supervisors in 1888 to build again. The new courthouse, the substantial structure pictured here, was completed in 1890, and served as Clinton County's courthouse until October 1976, when it was replaced by a much larger building. It now houses the county jail and several county offices.

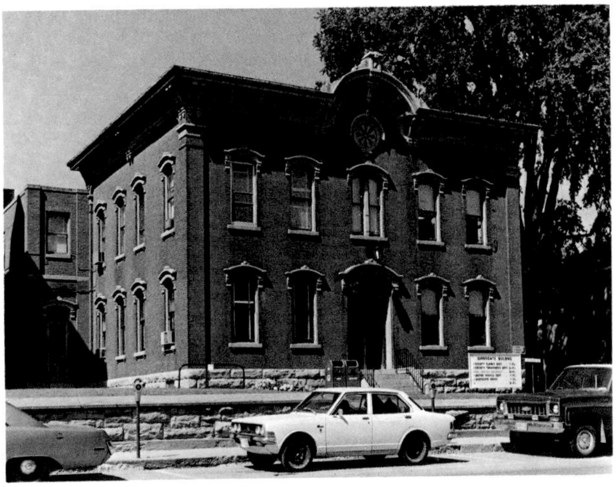

Surrogate Building

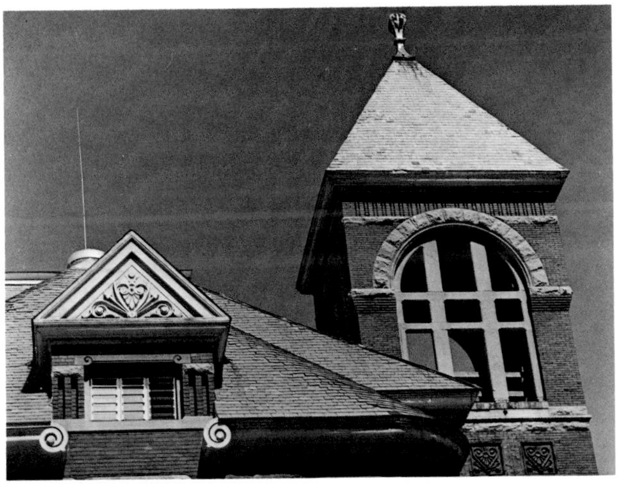

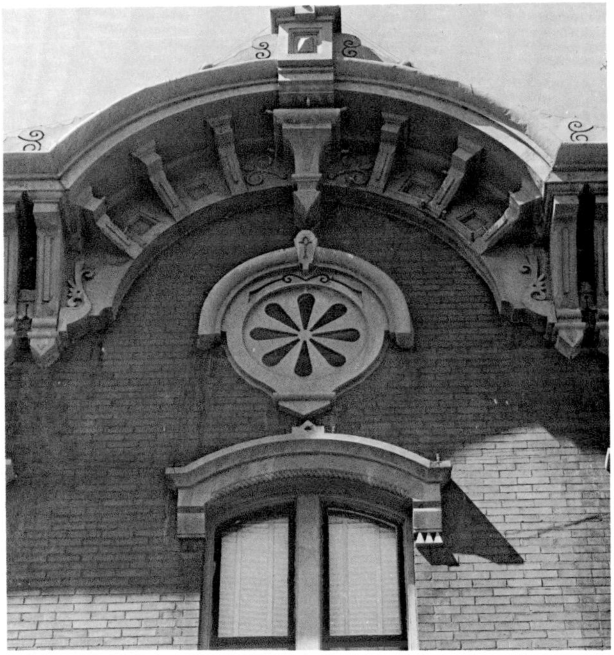

Surrogate Building

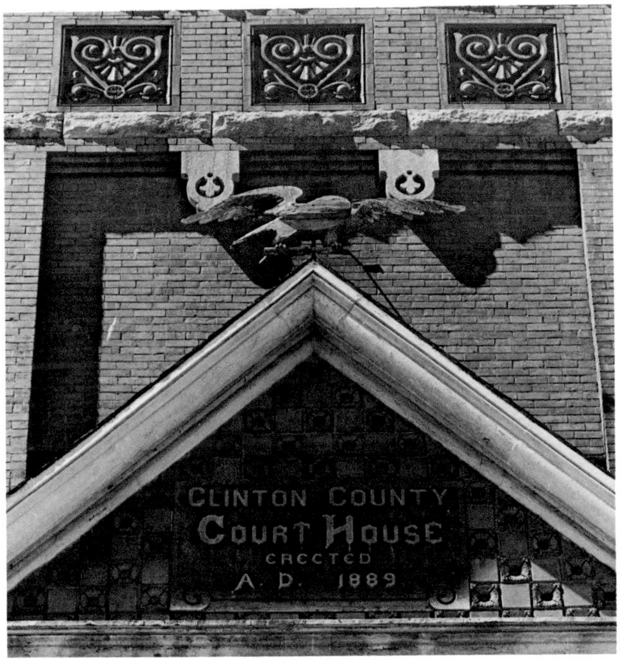
CLINTON COUNTY
COURT HOUSE
CRECTCD
A. D. 1889

COLUMBIA COUNTY

The one-time Columbia County Courthouse, in excellent condition and apparently good for at least another century or two, stands on the main street of Claverack. Unfortunately, the casual visitor has no chance to see the inside of the fine old structure, and even if he did, he would see no traces of its courtroom past, for the building is in private hands and has served as a residence for many generations.

The courthouse was authorized in April 1786, not quite a month before the one in Bedford, Westchester County, and construction on the two seems to have begun at about the same time. But the builders at Claverack were faster in completing their work (the first session of the Columbia County Court of Oyer and Terminer was held in the courthouse in March 1788), and so the Claverack building ranks as the second oldest New York courthouse. It is also the place where a landmark case affecting freedom of the press was tried.

That case involved Harry Croswell, editor at nearby Hudson of *The Wasp,* a Federalist newspaper. Croswell had regularly attacked President Jefferson in doggerel and in prose, but in 1802 he was charged with seditious libel when he stated that Jefferson had abetted James Callender, a political writer patronized by the president, in making scurrilous attacks on John Adams. After some delay, Croswell was ultimately brought to trial before the circuit court at Claverack on July 7, 1803.

The critical issue of the case was raised by the defense counsel's request for an adjournment so that Callender could be brought in to testify to the truth of the statements published by Croswell. This request was denied by Chief Justice Morgan Lewis, who based his refusal on the traditional legal view of libel, under which no evidence except the fact of publication was admissible. Truth could not be raised as a defense, the chief justice explained, nor proven to the court and jury, in a prosecution for criminal libel. The only issues to be decided, said Lewis, were whether the defendant printed the words, and if so, whether the words printed were intended to have a harmful effect. With these instructions the judge submitted the issues to the jury, and the jury returned a verdict of guilty.

Croswell was released on bail pending the entry of judgment and sentencing. After a series of postponements the matter finally came before the Supreme Court in February of 1804. Croswell's attorneys, now joined by Alexander Hamilton, proceeded to argue a motion for a new trial. Among the errors they claimed was the court's refusal to delay trial so that Callender might appear as a defense witness. Thus, the

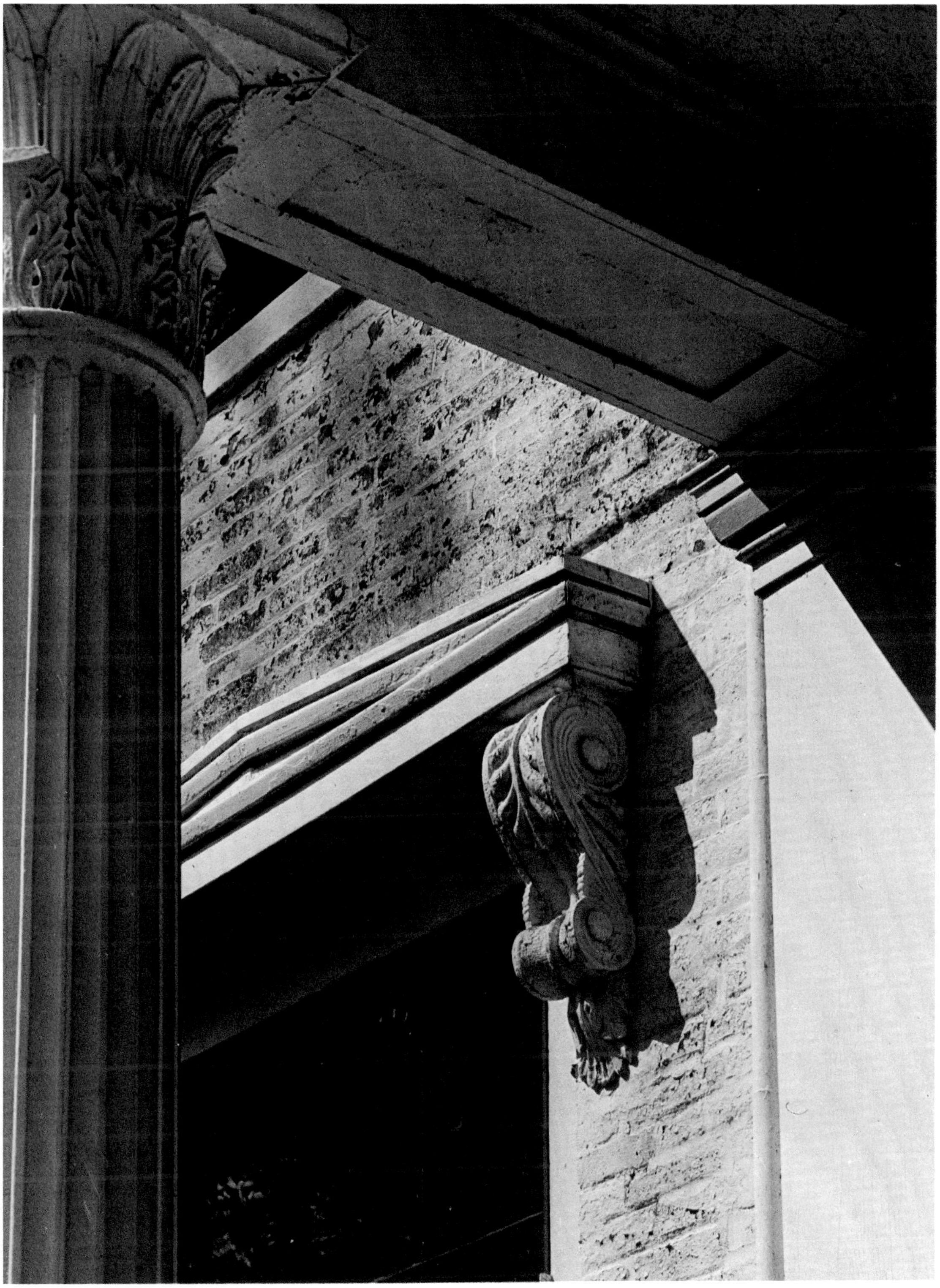

issue of truth as a defense in criminal libel was brought before New York's Supreme Court, which then consisted of Chief Justice Lewis, Justice Henry Brockholst Livingston, and Justice Smith Thompson, all Jefferson Republicans, and one Federalist, Justice James Kent. Hamilton argued that the libel laws should be liberalized, that truth should be acceptable as evidence in a trial for libel. In deciding the motion for a new trial, the court split evenly, Justice Thompson joining Federalist Kent in voting for a new trial.

As a result the motion did not pass, and the way was open for a prosecution motion for judgment. However, the attorney general took no further action, and Croswell was ultimately released.

But the case had far-reaching consequences. It made certain people aware of a gap in the guarantee of freedom of the press, and even while *People* v. *Croswell* was pending in the Supreme Court, a bill was introduced in the New York state legislature authorizing the use of truth as a defense to a charge of criminal libel. The bill was passed in April 1804; a number of years later, when the state's constitution of 1821 was adopted, this principle was specifically included in the guarantees of freedom of speech and of the press.

The courthouse in Claverack served Columbia County only until 1805, when the county seat was removed to the growing town of Hudson, on the Hudson River. The courthouse, a sturdy brick building only recently repaired, was sold for $1,500 and the proceeds used to help defray the cost of the new courthouse.

Today the old courthouse is rather difficult to distinguish from the other large and handsome brick houses that line the main street of Claverack, except that in front of it is a historical marker revealing that it was Columbia County's first courthouse, that Aaron Burr, Alexander Hamilton, and "other prominent lawyers" tried cases there, and that Martin Van Buren (later the eighth president of the United States) was admitted to the bar there. Hamilton did try cases in the Claverack courthouse, though in *People* v. *Croswell* he was not present till the case reached the Supreme Court. But there his arguments had a lasting, liberalizing effect on the laws of criminal libel, and so broadened the meaning of freedom of the press.

DELAWARE COUNTY

The Delaware County Courthouse at Delhi is considered one of the two finest examples of late nineteenth-century red-brick courthouses in New York (the other is the Tioga County Courthouse at Owego, built at almost the same time). It is not only a charming building but a practical one as well, built generously, with spacious courtrooms.

The present courthouse is the last in a line that began with one whose foundations were laid in 1798. That first courthouse appears to have been largely a waste of money; it was reported that "the jail was unused for fourteen years, and so little was the courthouse needed that in 1812 the legislature authorized it to be used as a tavern." Yet the courthouse saw such leading members of the New York bar as Elisha Williams, Ambrose Spencer, Aaron Burr, Erastus Root, and Martin Van Buren (who, when state attorney general, prosecuted an important murder case there in 1819 at the request of Governor De Witt Clinton). The courthouse, along with most of the county records, burned in 1820 and was immediately replaced by a new courthouse and jail.

In time the new courthouse became old and inadequate, and when moves to replace it were made in 1866, the town of Walton tried to snatch away the county seat, offering to build a new courthouse if the county board of super-visors would locate it in Walton. Delhi, however, offered a counterbribe and kept the county seat by offering to pay $10,000 toward a new building.

That courthouse—the present one—was designed by Isaac E. Perry, of New York and Binghamton, who had designed the Capitol at Albany. Ground was broken in March 1869, and the courthouse was dedicated in January 1871. Fortunately, the generous scale of the building has made it unnecessary to alter the interior significantly; unlike so many historic courthouses, the inside is as nearly like its original state as the outside, and the elaborate woodwork remains as it was in 1871.

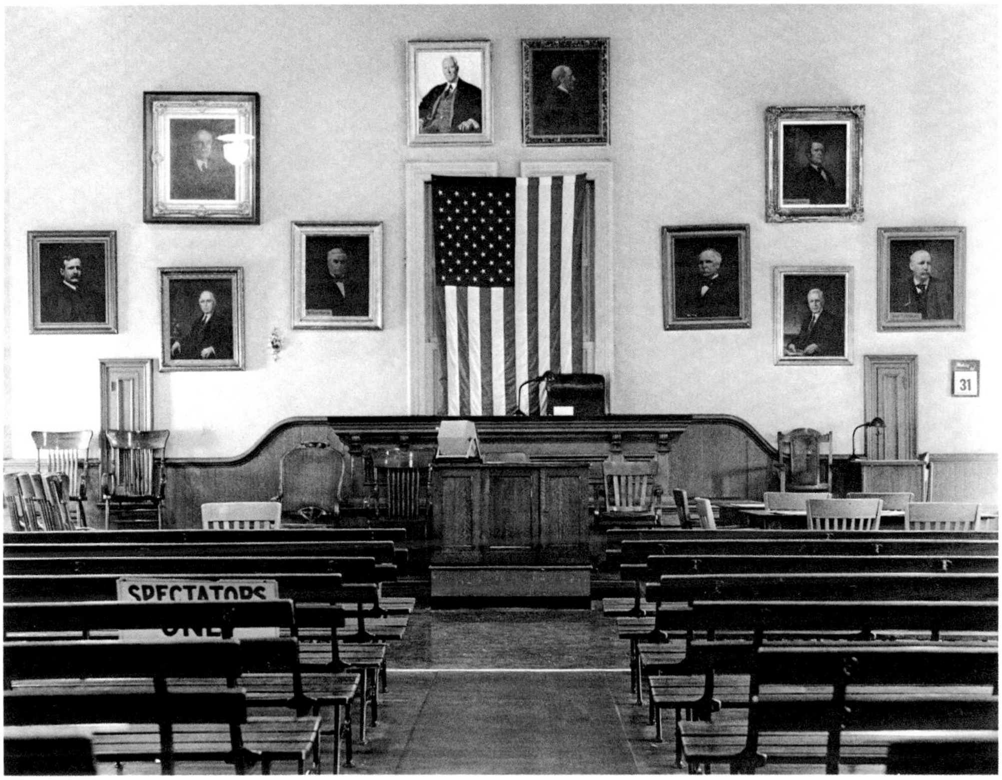
31
SPECTATORS

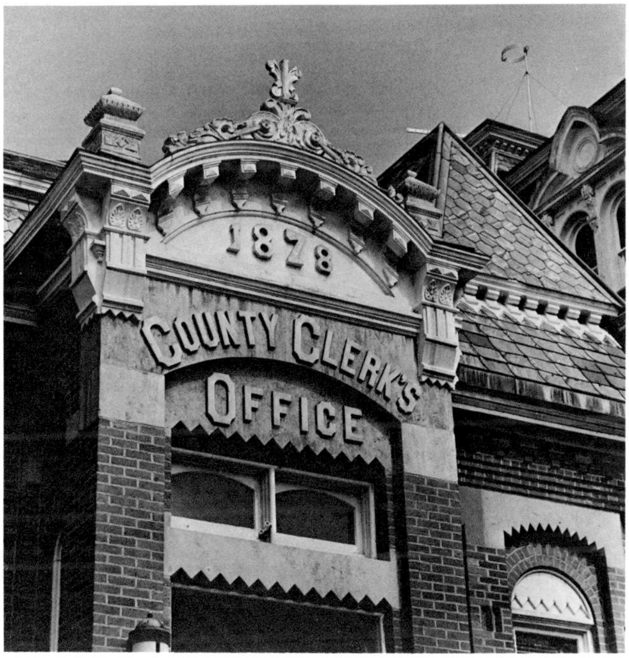
1878
COUNTY CLERK'S
OFFICE

County Clerk's Office

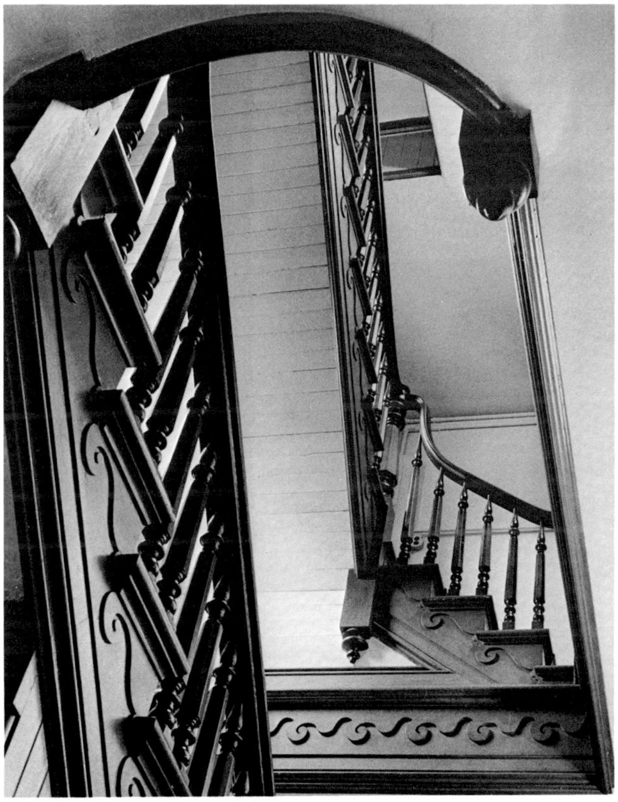

ERIE COUNTY

The courts of Erie County are housed in the Erie County Hall, a large building begun in 1871 but not dedicated till 1876; its aging walls also enclose the many offices of a county whose boundaries include a populous metropolitan area, the city of Buffalo. Courts serving such largely metropolitan counties almost inevitably see more than a fair share of human misery, problems, and felonies. They pass judgment on so many crimes, including murder, that criminal trials become almost routine; but one Erie County court has a distinction—a distinction not to be envied—that it shares with only one other court in the country. It tried a man for the murder of a president of the United States.

Four presidents have been assassinated. The men who murdered two of them were themselves slain before they could be brought to trial. Charles Guiteau, the man who mortally wounded President Garfield in 1881, was one of the two brought to trial and sentenced to die. The other assassin to stand in court was Leon Czolgosz, who chose Buffalo as the place where President McKinley should die.

Czolgosz was an anarchist; his decision to murder the president sprang undoubtedly from the same murky reasoning that had led him to embrace anarchism. His opportunity came when President McKinley visited the Pan-American Exposition at Buffalo in early September of 1901. It was an era when American presidents moved in a more leisurely fashion than they do today; instead of making the kind of hit-and-run visit that is the fashion among harried chief executives now, McKinley spent several days seeing the sights and greeting the public at the exposition.

On Tuesday, September 3, Czolgosz first tried to carry out his plan to kill the president but was turned back by police lines. On Wednesday he stood in the crowd listening as the president delivered a speech, but he was so far off that he was afraid he might miss if he shot. Not until Friday did he get his first real opportunity, when the president shook hands with citizens as they filed by in the exposition's Temple of Music. Czolgosz swathed his right hand, holding the pistol, in a handkerchief, as though it were

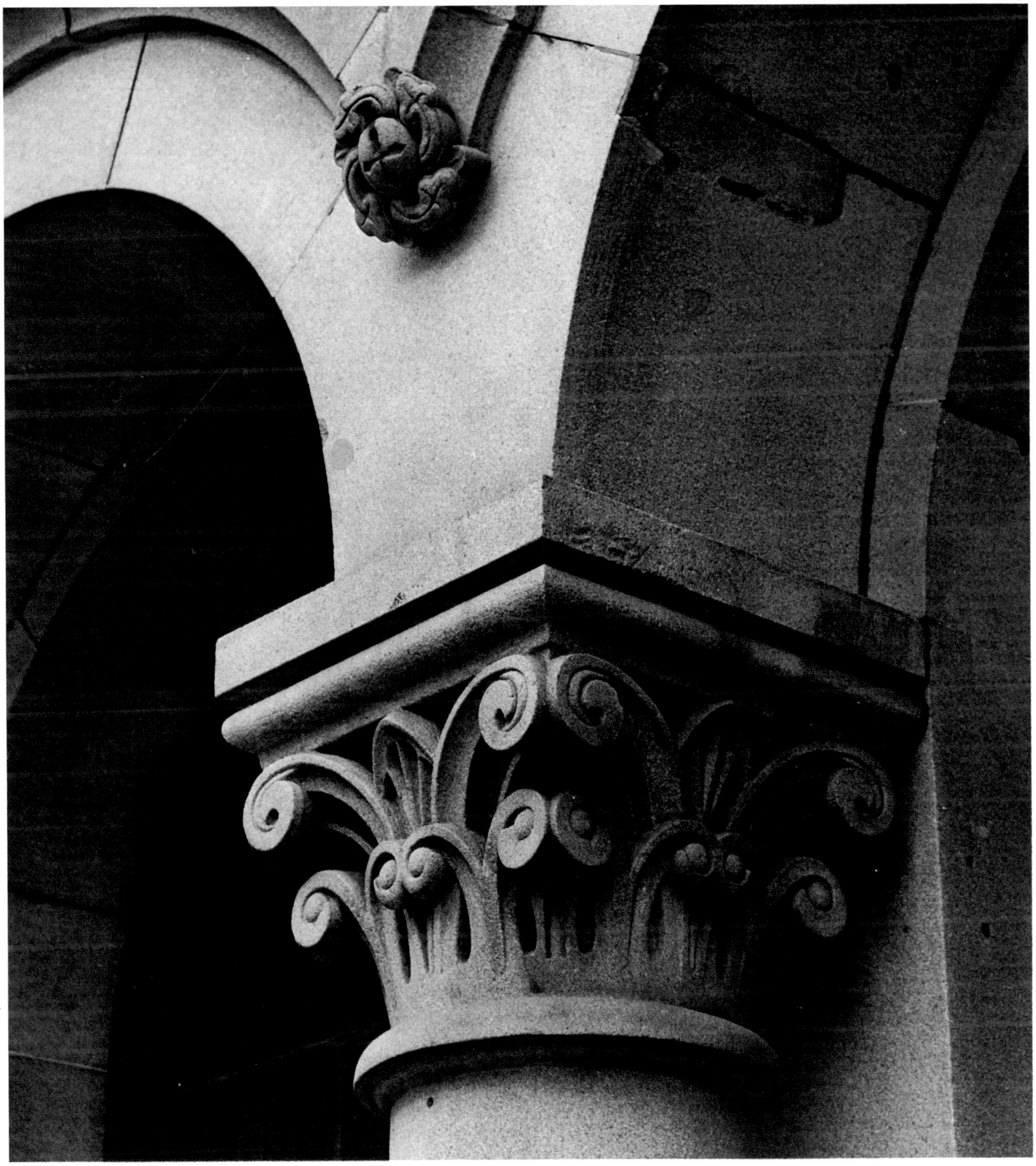

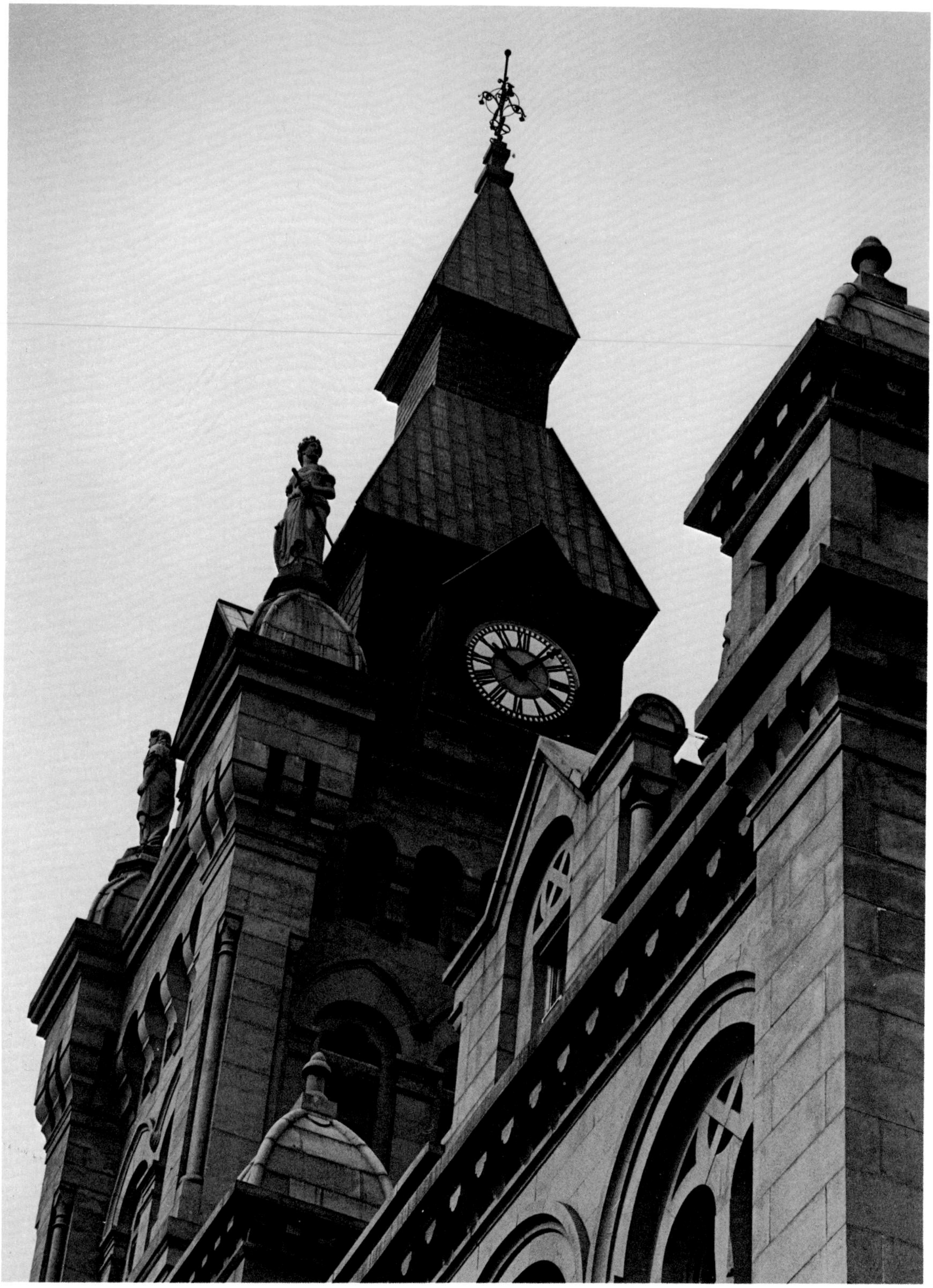

bandaged, and joined the line. McKinley stood in a grouping of potted palms, flanked by George B. Cortelyou, his personal secretary, and by John Milburn, the president of the exposition. It was four o'clock in the afternoon of September 6 when Czolgosz came abreast of the president, who reached out to take the assassin's unbandaged left hand. Two sharp reports of his revolver rang out, and the president staggered back.

Czolgosz was seized by two Secret Service agents and a man who had preceded him in the reception line. In the struggle the handkerchief was ripped from his hand and the revolver grabbed. As soon as the crowd realized what had happened, it surged forward, clamoring for the lynching of Czolgosz, who was taken by the Secret Service agents to the rear of the Temple of Music and turned over to the superintendent of the Buffalo police department. From that time on, New York authorities were charged with the protection and trial of Czolgosz.

Early reports that the president was recovering from his wounds gave rise to speculation that Czolgosz would probably escape with a relatively short prison sentence for first-degree assault; this, contrasted with the enormity of his crime, caused nationwide murmurings. There was also a prevalent belief that the assassination attempt was only part of a worldwide conspiracy to slay all heads of state throughout Europe and America. In his first statements to the police Czolgosz said that Emma Goldman, the firebrand anarchist editor, propagandist, and lecturer, was his inspiration, and Goldman was arrested in Chicago on September 10 and held several days for questioning. In New York City, an obscure citizen named Alfonzo Stutz was arrested on sus-

picion of complicity in the assassination; the arrest was made on such flimsy grounds that Stutz brought suit against the city of New York for false arrest. Public opinion against anarchists was so violent that the libretto of a popular musical play, "The New Yorker," was abruptly revised to remove three characters from the plot who were anarchists.

In the early hours of September 14, 1901, William McKinley died, with one of Czolgosz's two bullets still embedded in his body. The physicians in attendance had been able to remove one, but the other, deep in his abdomen, had evaded all their probings. Nevertheless, for a time the president's physical condition had improved, and on September 10, four days after he had been shot, the physicians near him felt justified in issuing a press bulletin saying that the president would soon recover from his wounds. But three days later a change for the worse came, and in a few hours McKinley was dead. His death has since been blamed on the negligence of his doctors, but given the medical knowledge of the time, it seems unlikely that they could have saved his life.

The public outcry and the demands for immediate lynching that arose when the president was first shot multiplied many times when he died, and some of the demands for Czolgosz's execution had a medieval savagery. A man in as high a position as United States Senator Thomas C. Platt proposed: "I would advocate a drumhead court-martial and let the man be taken off at once. This is one of the instances where I think lynch law would be justified!" A Kentucky colonel gave his prescription for justice to the press, saying that "if the thing could be done out of the public view, the assassin ought to be burned up inch by inch." Riots resulted in Chicago and Pittsburgh when speakers were foolhardy enough to say that McKinley's death was a good thing for the country, and in Casper, Wyoming, a man who expressed sympathy for Czolgosz was tarred, feathered, and ridden on a rail.

In this inflamed atmosphere it was difficult to ensure the safety of Czolgosz, much less give him a fair trial. He was moved from police

headquarters to the city jail, which was connected to the combined courthouse and city hall (both municipal and county offices were then housed in the same building) by a network of tunnels. Buffalo police had been made aware of the need to take special precautions to guard their prisoner on the night of the assassination, when a crowd of some fifty thousand persons had gathered outside police headquarters, shouting for the lynching of Czolgosz; the police had been able to disperse them only by calling in reserves. Thereafter a large part of the Buffalo police force was held in a state of readiness to prevent any attempts at violence to the prisoner, and two regiments of the New York National Guard were put on alert status in their armories in case they were needed to handle any disturbances that might develop.

Immediately after the shooting, the Buffalo police had begun investigating the background of the assassin. During preliminary questioning Czolgosz had claimed that his name was Fred Nieman and that he lived in Detroit. At this time he was so talkative that the police were suspicious of what he was telling them, and in fact, only part of the six-page statement he signed on September 6 was later verified. A search of the hotel room where he had been staying turned up documents that quickly identified him as Leon Czolgosz, of Toledo, Ohio. Police also found another pistol in the room, but nothing that answered their most urgent question: Did Czolgosz have the help of any accomplices in his act?

To uncover any possible conspirators, the police questioned Czolgosz for another six hours on September 7, without learning anything. The next day they arranged to put the plumbing in his cell out of order, in the hope that a police-man disguised as plumber sent in to repair it might gain Czolgosz's confidence. The attempt was unsuccessful. Despite the failures to uncover any accomplices, there was a widespread feeling in the country that Czolgosz was just not smart enough to have planned and carried out such a crime on his own. On September 9, two psychiatrists examined Czolgosz for half an hour and then announced that they had found him sane. All these steps had been taken while McKinley still lived—while optimistic doctors' reports predicted that he very likely would recover.

But McKinley did not recover. Upon his death, the prosecution at once announced that his assassin would be indicted on September 16. Counsel would be assigned to defend him if help came from no other source. And so the Erie County grand jury returned its indictment to County Judge Edward Emery on September 16, and the judge assigned two former state Supreme Court justices, Loran Lewis and Robert Titus, to act as defense counsel.

On the day following the return of the indictment, Czolgosz walked through the tunnel under Delaware Avenue and up a narrow staircase to the courtroom in the courthouse–city-hall, where the indictment was read to him. In the days ahead this trip along what was called the Tunnel of Sobs would become very familiar to him, as would the hisses from the spectators in the courtroom. At his arraignment Czolgosz remained mute, and his attorney Judge Lewis entered a provisional plea of not guilty on his behalf. The defense was given a week to prepare its case, which was scheduled for trial before Justice Truman C. White on September 23.

The building in which Czolgosz's trial took place was the third courthouse to serve Erie County. Construction had begun in 1871, when the county outgrew the three-story building it was then using, but for economy and other reasons, the new courthouse was made large enough to take care of the municipal needs of Buffalo as well as house the county offices and courts—a combined courthouse and city hall. It is an Italianate-style building, with a tall central clock-tower flanked by allegorical statues, and the entire building is an excellent example of the detailed stonework of the period. The cost, shared almost equally between city and county, was $1,170,965.29 for the building, with an additional $125,000.00 requested for furnishings.

The courtroom of the trial was on the south side of the building, on the second floor. Light entered from "latticoe'd" windows directly behind the judge's bench and witness stand. The jury's chairs were on the right side of the courtroom, on a platform about six inches higher than the rest of the floor. The *New York Times* noted: "The room is high, studded with drab walls, seamed with the cracks of time, and showing the need of a scrubwoman's brush."

Czolgosz appeared on the first day of his trial dressed in a new, dark gray suit, white shirt, and a light blue bow tie. Though he had been unkempt when arraigned, he was now clean-shaven and had combed his hair. When the indictment was read, he spoke for the first time and asked that it be read again. He then pleaded guilty, but Judge White ordered a plea of not guilty entered, as required by law. At the request of defense counsel, it was ordered that the trial should proceed from 10:00 A.M. to noon, and then adjourn until 2:00 P.M., when the court would reconvene for another two hours. This request was granted because of the advanced age of both defense attorneys.

Testimony on the first day began with Dr. Harvey R. Gaylord's statement of his findings in the course of an autopsy performed on the president's body. Gaylord and the doctors who attended McKinley were closely questioned by Titus, who tried to develop some doubt as to the cause of death. Since the president had not died immediately as a result of his wounds, there could be a possibility that some organic weakness unrelated or ancillary to the gunshot wounds was responsible for his death. This question of proximate cause was really the pivotal issue of the case, and Titus showed considerable acumen in concentrating his defense tactics around it.

Lewis, the other defense counsel, spent his efforts on attempting to establish insanity as a justification. During his closing statement to the jury, Lewis argued that although both attorneys and psychiatrists agreed that Czolgosz was sane while being held for trial, it was unbelieveable that a sane man would commit such a heinous crime. This was an attempt to justify the crime on the basis of temporary insanity or irresistible impulse. Extensive examination of the accused by both state and defense psychiatrists had found no trace of mental disease in Czolgosz. As District Attorney Thomas Penny stressed in his summation, the justification by insanity put forward by the defense was based entirely on mere supposition as to the state of the accused's mind at the instant of the assassination. The jury clearly agreed that the defense had not presented a convincing case. After hearing a total of eight hours of testimony over two days, the jury retired to consider the evidence at 3:51 P.M., September 24, and returned in just slightly more than half an hour with a verdict of guilty of first-degree murder.

Two days later Czolgosz was brought back to the courtroom, to be sentenced to die in the electric chair. He was removed to Auburn State Prison that same evening, and in spite of efforts at secrecy, an angry mob was at the Auburn railroad station, and guards had to hustle their prisoner into the prison yards to avoid a lynching. While he waited in his cell, Czolgosz was the object of morbid curiosity, and promoters put forth ghoulish plans for gaining commercial advantage from his execution. The press faithfully reported his eating habits in detail. Private citizens wrote for his autograph and asked for tickets to his execution. An eastern museum offered the warden five thousand dollars if he would deliver either Czolgosz's body or his clothes. A motion picture photographer offered two thousand for permission to photograph the condemned man entering the death chamber. However, prison authorities protected Czolgosz from all such pressures, stopping the flood of mail to him from the outside, and even refused his request that his brother be permitted to witness the execution.

On the morning of the execution Czolgosz refused to see two priests, and when they persisted in visiting him, he remained mute in their presence. He went stoically to the death chamber and told witnesses that he was not sorry for his crime. He was pronounced dead after three surges of electricity had been sent through his body and was buried in an unmarked grave in the prison yard.

The combined courthouse and city hall in

which Czolgosz was tried is now simply Erie County Hall. When the ever-increasing functions of both city and county crowded the old building beyond capacity, the city of Buffalo built its own city hall in 1932 and turned the 1876 building over to the county. A great many changes have undoubtedly been made inside the building, but except for the grime of the years, on the outside it looks largely as it did a century ago.

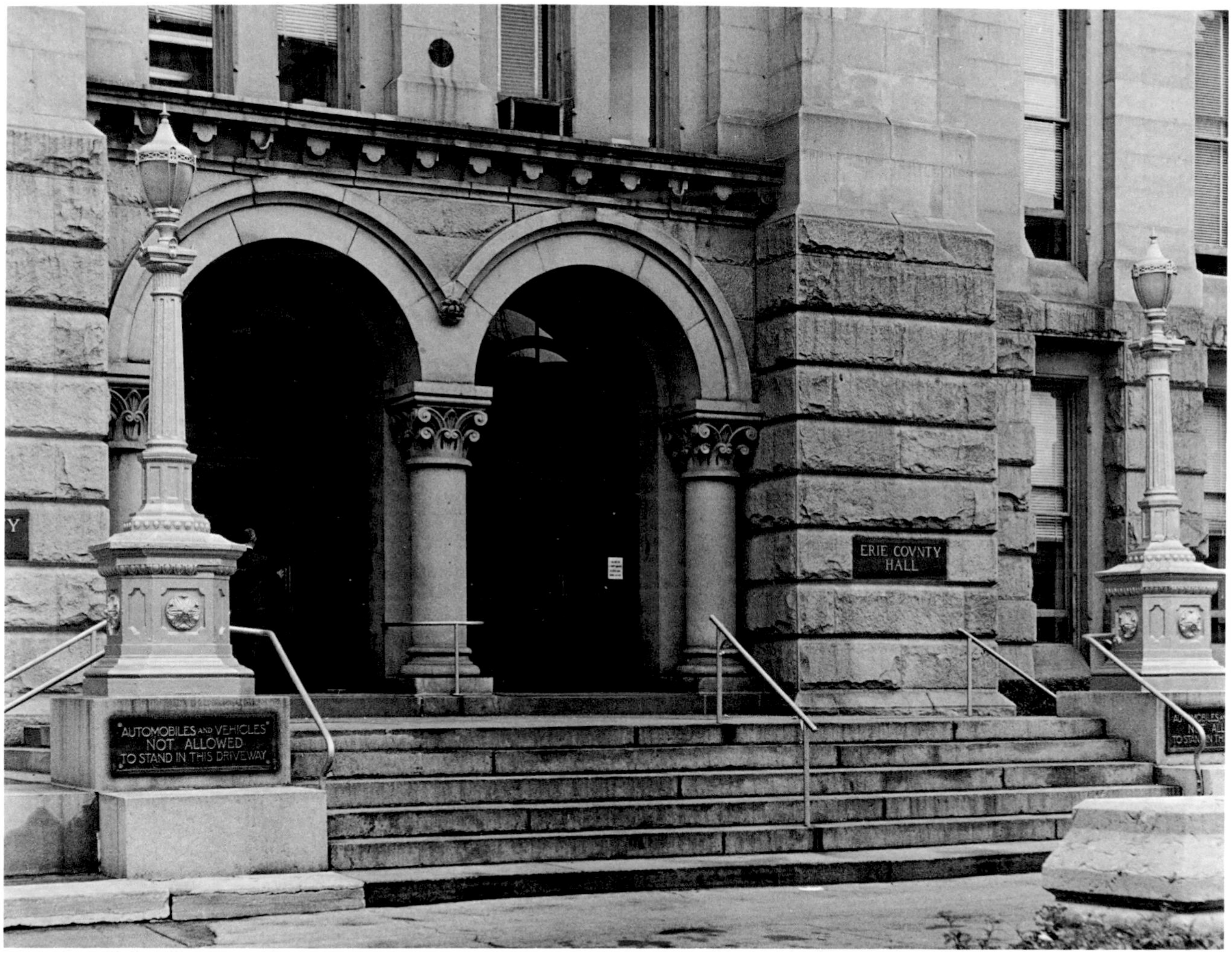
ERIE COVNTY HALL
"AUTOMOBILES AND VEHICLES" NOT ALLOWED TO STAND IN THIS DRIVEWAY

ESSEX COUNTY

The tidy brick Essex County Courthouse in Elizabethtown, with its pillared portico, has every appearance of having been designed and built in a piece. However, the 1824 date on the transom window above the main entrance is somewhat misleading, for the two stories of the structure were built years apart.

The first county seat of Essex County, from its establishment in 1799 until about 1811, was the town of Essex; court was held and prisoners confined in a small blockhouse that had been built as protection against Indians in that Adirondack mountain region. Then the county seat was moved to more centrally located Elizabethtown, although the courthouse there was not ready until 1814.

That first courthouse burned down not long after it was completed and was replaced by another built on much the same plan. This too burned, in 1823. After the second loss it was decided to build a larger structure, and the first part of the present courthouse was built. That structure, completed in 1824, was only one story high, and it was not until 1843 that a second story was added and the courthouse took its present form. Additional enlargement was made by adding a wing in 1888, but the basic 1824–43 building with its pillared facade remains essentially unchanged.

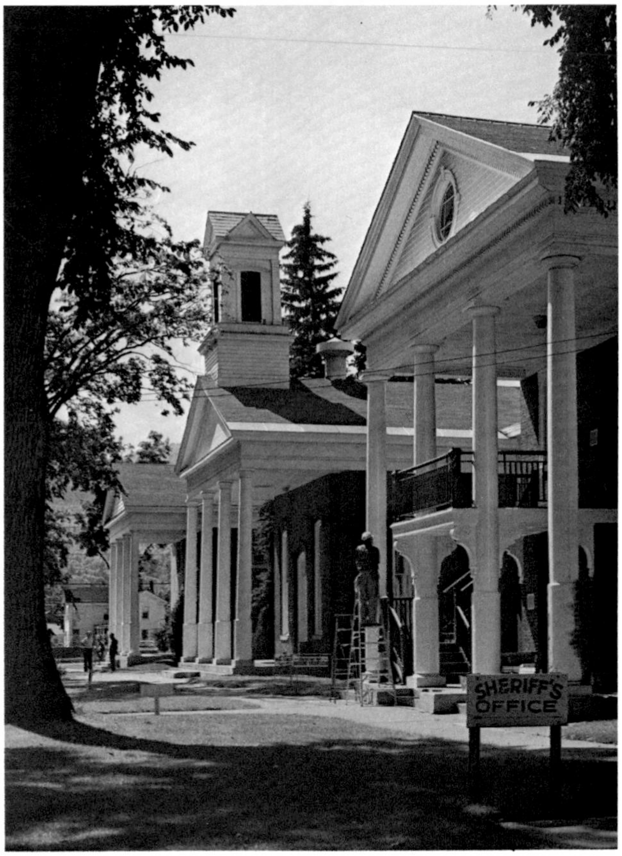
SHERIFF'S
OFFICE

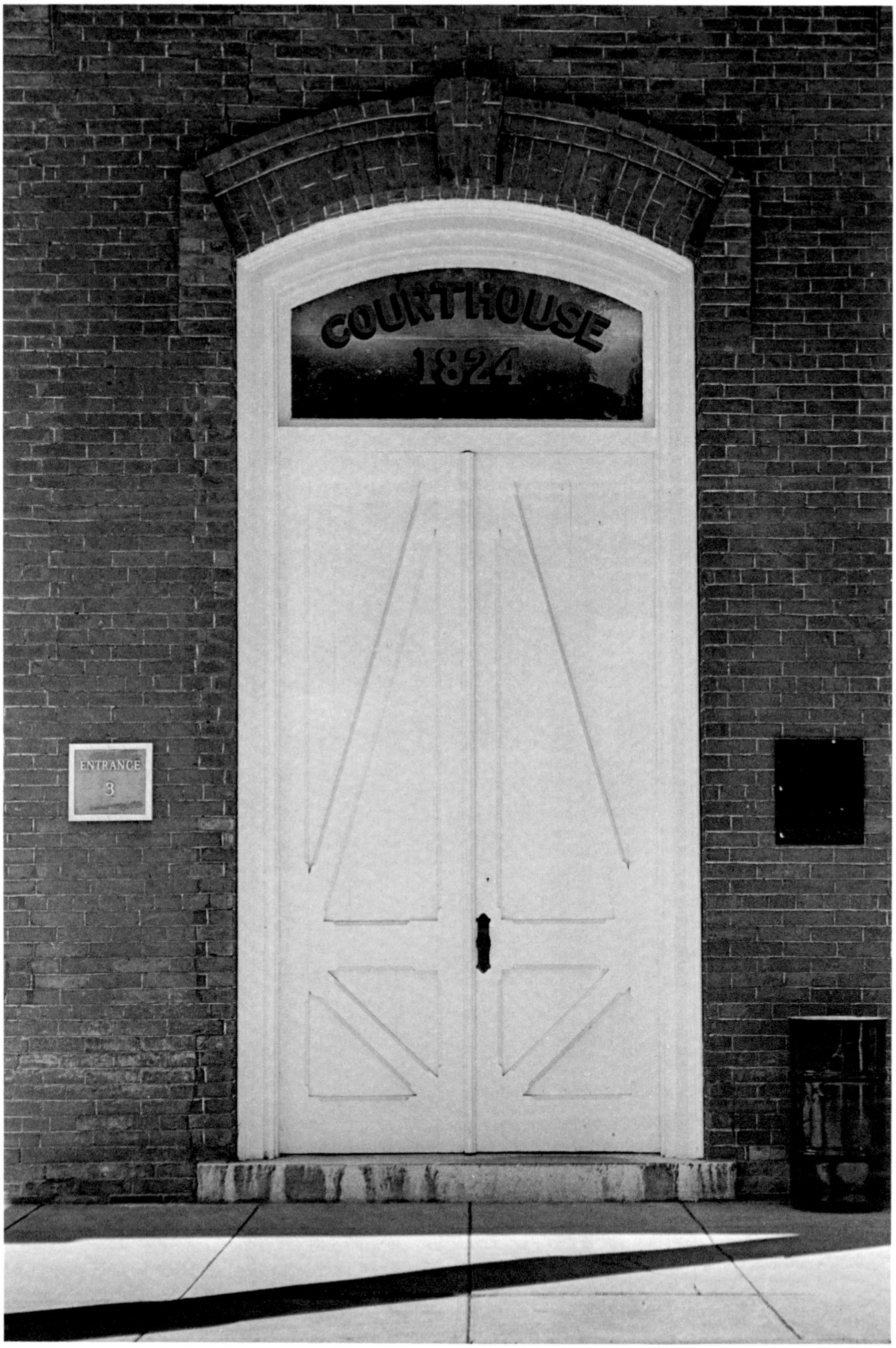
COURTHOUSE
1824
ENTRANCE
3

FRANKLIN COUNTY

was completed in 1812 at a cost of only $4,757.25, including the cost of a "necessary" and $3.00 for "spit boxes." This building lasted almost eighty years before it became completely inadequate (it was also damaged by fire when prisoners in the basement jail tried to escape by burning out, with a red-hot poker, dowels that held the ceiling together). Its replacement,

The old courthouse at Malone is still in use, but no longer as a courthouse. It now serves as the county clerk's office, demoted to that use when a new courthouse was built in 1930–31. Now more than three quarters of a century old, it was the second courthouse to serve Franklin County (not counting various temporary quarters used for court purposes during the first years after the county was created in 1808).

The first courthouse, a hip-roofed structure,

the historic structure that now serves as the county clerk's office, was completed in 1892. The new building, along with a combined jail and sheriff's home, cost approximately $35,000, which gives some indication of the march of inflation over the years—even allowing for the larger size of the new courthouse.

The 1892 structure, in its turn, became too small for increasing court business, and the present courthouse was built in 1930–31. The old courthouse was remodeled inside for its new role as county clerk's office, but from the outside it is much the same no-nonsense, sturdy brick structure that it was back in 1892.

FULTON COUNTY

Of all the courthouses built in New York before the Revolution, the one at Johnstown in Fulton County is the only one that survives. It is not a case of the survival of the best or the most protected; the Johnstown courthouse was the smallest of the colonial courthouses and was one of those most exposed to Indian raids and military action during the Revolutionary War. Yet this simple building is the only link the state has to those distant days when court was summoned by the clanging of an iron triangle and justices wore wigs in imitation of those in His Majesty's courts in London.

The Johnstown courthouse came into being ahead of its time because Sir William Johnson, England's Indian agent in the Mohawk country and one of the great men of the early frontier, was a moving force in the separation of a new Tryon County from Albany County. The population out on what was then frontier did not justify the creation of the new county, but Sir William was a man of considerable political consequence, and he wanted a system of justice more responsive and convenient to himself and the people residing in the vicinity of Johnstown. Moreover, he objected to the predominance of Dutch-speaking inhabitants who served as judges in the Albany County courts.

Tryon County was created with the help of some political log-rolling. Johnson and his group won over enough of the opposition to get the bill through the colonial assembly by agreeing to support in turn the creation of Charlotte County. A final concession was probably made in naming the new county after the colonial governor, William Tryon, a conceited and pompous army officer whom Johnson had little use for. (With the coming of the Revolution, the name was changed to Montgomery County, to honor Richard Montgomery, the patriot general killed at Quebec.) Having brought the county into existence, Sir William helped finance the construction of the courthouse and jail. Construction began in 1772, and a large proportion of the cost was borne by Sir William himself. The date of completion is obscure, but the two buildings must have been virtually finished by the time Sir William died in 1774, for he had written to a friend of his pride in the appearance of the village of Johnstown: "I have laid out a great deal of Money upon it, & the New Church, Court House and Gaol are very decent buildings. . . ." Although Sir William was advised that it was customary to put the jail in the courthouse building to save money, he—wisely, as it turned out—decided on two separate buildings. When fire destroyed the jail in 1849, the courthouse was saved.

In its long existence, the Tryon County Courthouse has seen many cases argued, heard many

verdicts pronounced. And it has served many functions besides judicial ones. As early as 1819 a county and agricultural fair was held on the courthouse grounds—perhaps one of the first county fairs to be held in the United States. Lectures on "Scottish Song," temperance, and an assortment of other subjects were given in the courtroom, singing groups performed there, and on one occasion "Bullard's Panoramic View of New York City" was exhibited there.

These were important events in the life of a small village in the nineteenth century, but they were diversions from the main activity of the courthouse, which was judicial routine. In the records of the courts that have met in the Johnstown courthouse one finds many proceedings that are echoes of national history. In 1799 John Tys Ripson was prosecuted for sedition under the notorious Sedition Act of 1798, passed by the Federalists to muzzle Jeffersonian editors and publications. The jury found Ripson guilty, but the judge showed rare good sense by fining him only two dollars. Ripson was then tried for criminal libel, found guilty, and fined fifty dollars.

Aaron Burr, then a former vice-president of the United States, was present in the courtroom in 1811 as co-counsel for the defense in the trial of one Solomon Southwick, charged with attempted bribery of state officials in connection with the issuance of the Bank of North America charter. Southwick was acquitted.

A case that grates harshly on modern sensibilities is that of *Garlock* v. *Failing,* from 1828. Failing had been on the alert for a bear that was supposedly prowling in the vicinity, and in a tragic mistake, he shot and mortally wounded a black slave, Jack. Failing was freed of criminal charges after a coroner's inquest but was compelled to pay Jack's owner two hundred fifty dollars in civil damages. Gradual emancipation had already become part of the law of New York State, and this was a rare case even for that early date, but it nevertheless is a reminder of the way in which the law was forced to accommodate itself to slavery.

Occasionally cases were more amusing than significant or tragic. In July 1848, Luther and Sophiah Holman filed a summons and complaint against Guy T. Wells, alleging that he had committed an assault and battery upon Sophiah with intent to carnally know her and demanding a judgment of two thousand dollars. Wells entered a general denial. When the case came to trial, Sophiah revealed to her attorney that she believed herself to have been wronged because Wells had taken hold of her and kissed her in a playful manner. Upon learning of this unusually strict interpretation of the term "carnal knowledge," Sophiah's attorney rested his case and the jury returned with a verdict dismissing the complaint.

The official records, however, usually give only the bare bones of a case; even the newspapers of a century and more ago did not often supply what today is called local color. We have one brief but descriptive glimpse of a small-town courtroom in action a century ago in the diary of Donald McMartin, a Johnstown boy who was taken to a murder trial in 1864. It was a rough-and-ready scene. "The floor was covered with sawdust and peach pits, and peanut shells, and old tobacco quids. And there were boys much bigger than I peddling molasses candy, and pears, and peaches and nuts." The accused sat in the prisoner's box and wore leg-irons, Donald

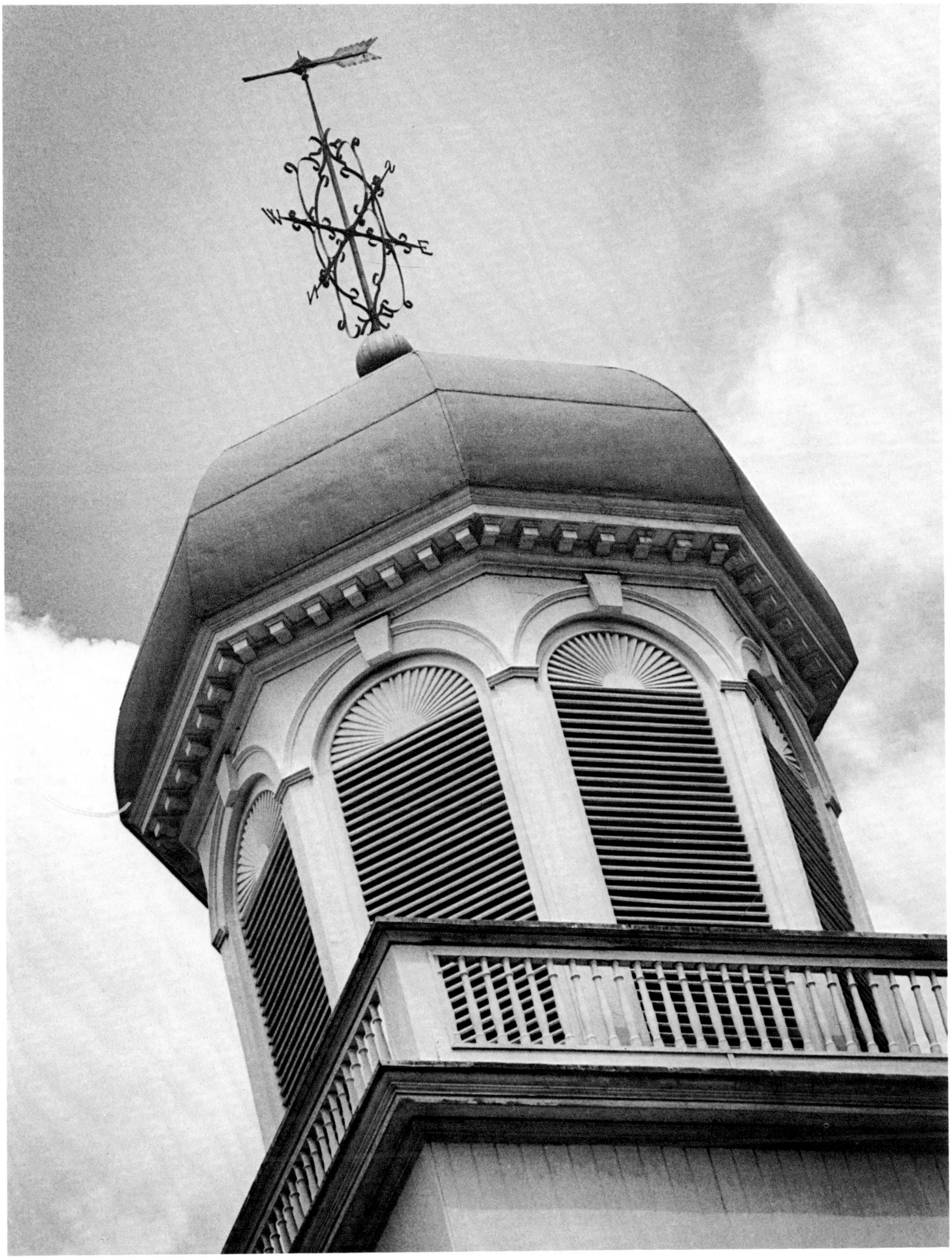

wrote, and several constables called the court to order by banging long black poles on the floor.

Young McMartin was most unfavorably impressed with the lawyers. They were, he wrote, "an ornery looking lot; some were big and fat, and some were thin and skinny-like and wore spectacles. . . . The case dragged along and the lawyers talked and got mad at each other . . . and it seemed, from the way they called each other names, that they were being tried their own selves, instead of the poor prisoner who was the most orderly and best behaved man in the court room."

Probably the best-known trial in the Johnstown courthouse was for murder, and it was notable because the defendant not only was the first woman to be so tried there, but also was executed for the crime. Although the event occurred well over a hundred years ago, it made such a strong and lasting impression on the local residents that even today her case is the one murder trial widely known in the county.

In the spring of 1845 John Van Valkenburgh died in such violent nausea that it was evident he had been poisoned, and his wife, Elizabeth, was indicted for murder in the court of general sessions, pleaded not guilty, and after six months in jail, was finally brought to trial in November. John Van Valkenburgh was Elizabeth's second husband, and no special bargain, a fact that most of the jurors knew before the trial began. Among other things, he drank heavily and often, and while he was away on one of his sprees in mid-December of 1844, Elizabeth bought some arsenic, ostensibly to kill rats, and on her husband's return offered him some tea laced with the poison. He vomited immediately and became so sick a doctor was called. Elizabeth apparently nursed him back to health and restrained herself as long as he remained off the bottle, but when he returned to it in March, she resumed the arsenic. Now she abetted his drinking, each time adding a little of the poison to the liquor.

The grand jury's true bill lists the potables used by Elizabeth: half a gallon of cider, a pint of unspecified liquor, half a pint of brandy, and half a pint of "sweetened liquor"—all consumed by John during his short last illness. Only twice was it necessary for her to use milk to administer her usual dose of three grains of arsenic.

The arsenic inevitably proved fatal, but Van Valkenburgh's last hours were accompanied by such violent nausea that his wife lost her nerve and fled to avoid arrest. She hid in the hayloft of a barn, and just before being apprehended, she fell to the floor, dislocating her hip. The injury never healed and she was crippled to the day of her execution.

The trial was short; it began November 27, 1845, and ended on November 30 at 1:00 A.M., when the jury brought in a guilty verdict after eight hours' deliberation. Supreme Court Justice John Willard, who presided, advised Mrs. Van Valkenburgh that he would not recommend executive clemency, and then sentenced her to death by hanging. Many of the people of Johnstown by then seem to have been filled with misgivings and compassion, and some of them petitioned Governor Silas Wright to grant a reprieve from the death sentence. Wright referred the matter to the chancellor, the justices of the Supreme Court, and the attorney general of the state, but all, in view of Judge Willard's refusal to recommend clemency, advised that the petition be denied.

Elizabeth Van Valkenburgh was hanged on January 24, 1846, in the yard of the Fulton County Jail. Because of her hip injury, she could not stand on the trapdoor of the scaffold, and the sheriff devised a harness that would lift her into a standing position just before the moment of hanging. Although all of the dozen or more witnesses signed the certificate stating she was dead when taken down from the gallows, doubters exhumed the body several years later and asserted that its position in the coffin showed that she had been still alive when she was buried.

In any event, the compassion for her seems to have been largely misplaced. After she had been convicted of murder, she revealed that her first husband had not gone to glory unaided. She had helped him along with arsenic in a drink of rum after he had gone to a social gathering without her and against her will. "I always had an ungovernable temper," she said.

In large part, the continued existence of the relatively small courthouse at Johnstown is due to the declining importance of Johnstown as a center of trade and population. As a result, the old building has remained adequate only for local needs. The village is well off the main avenues of commerce; one does not pass through Johnstown in the ordinary course of travel but must leave the heavily traveled highways and wind into Johnstown on picturesque secondary roads. In the eighteenth century, in contrast, the village was at the crossroads of trade routes and was the place where British authorities met with the leaders of the Iroquois Confederacy. At Johnson Hall, a short distance from the court-house, Sir William Johnson exercised his powers as superintendent of Indian affairs to keep the natives allied with Britain in both trade and

politics. It made sense to build a courthouse at Johnstown in 1772; by 1832 no one would have suggested such a location.

The decline of Johnstown's importance was offset by the growth of the towns along the Erie Canal just a few miles to the south. The nearest of these was Fonda, named after Jellis Fonda, the only Tryon County judge to remain loyal to the patriot cause during the Revolution, and in 1836 a Greek-Revival courthouse was built there. Residents of Johnstown arranged for two villagers to buy the old courthouse for $1,650. Then they began to lobby in the state legislature for the division of Montgomery County, with the northern part to have its shire town at Johnstown.

Under the leadership of Daniel Cady, county judge, they were successful in 1838. The county was divided, and the northern part named Fulton after the steamboat man, who was a distant relative of Judge Cady. The two purchasers of the courthouse then sold it back to the county at the price they had paid for it two years earlier. Judge Cady's portrait hangs in the courtroom today, a fitting recognition of his part in saving the old courthouse.

The interior of the courthouse consists of a large room. Originally there were two small anterooms, to the right and left of the main entry door. Recently two doors have been cut through the back wall on each side of the judge's bench, giving onto a passageway to the county office buildings at the rear of the old courthouse. In 1931 it became necessary to strengthen the roof and repair the cupola; during this work the old iron triangle placed in the cupola in Sir William's time was brought down and exhibited, along with the gallows, which had been stored in the attic. As the courthouse stands today, the brick walls are original, and some of the moldings and support beams may be original. The cupola is undoubtedly in the form it had when the building was erected, but it has been entirely reconstructed. Restored to its place, the iron triangle clangs again to announce court sessions as it did in the reign of George III.

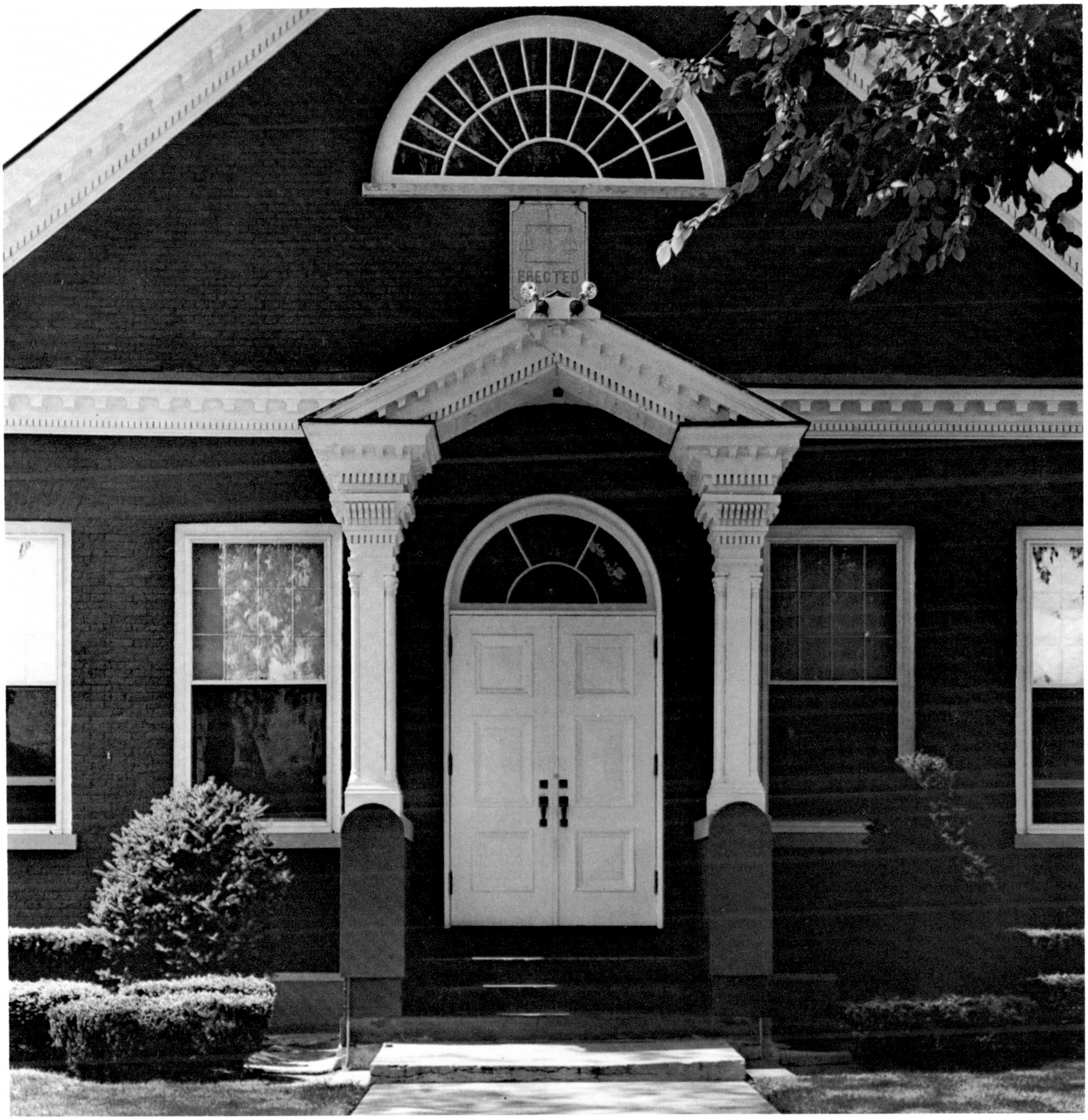
ERECTED

GENESEE
COUNTY

The Genesee County Courthouse at Batavia was begun in 1841 and completed in 1843, at the beginning of the transition period from Greek-Revival architecture to the kind of design we call Victorian. Basically the building is Greek-Revival, but columns and portico have been eliminated, and though there is none of the exuberant gimcrackery so common in Victorian buildings, the pattern of the limestone walls trimmed with granite is typical of the increased emphasis put on the nature of the building material—its color, texture, reflection of light, or pattern—so typical of Victorian buildings.

It is not surprising that a courthouse built in Batavia should reflect new ideas in architecture sooner than those in most of the surrounding counties. Batavia stood in the path of westward migration, and the people who moved through, and sometimes stayed, brought new and fresh ideas from the outside world, everything from politics to moral values—and, of course, architecture. The constant movement in population, too, brought a mixed bag of people to Batavia and the surrounding countryside, and left the names of many of them on the court record, sometimes in homicidal contexts.

There was, for instance, Polly Frisch, who kept a boardinghouse. For reasons now unknown, she developed a dislike for three of her guests, Henry Hoag and his wife and adult daughter, a dislike strong enough to cause her to kill them with arsenic. Polly Frisch apparently was respected or at least well liked in the community, because several hundred talesmen had to be called before a jury could be impaneled. Then, in trials lasting through most of 1858 and 1859, Polly was tried and acquitted of murdering Mr. Hoag, tried and acquitted of killing Mrs. Hoag, but at last found guilty of murdering the daughter, and for this she was sentenced to be hanged.

Another county resident who took to killing was Richard Winn, but his victims were livestock, for which he showed a psychotic hatred. In 1852 he was indicted for killing twenty lambs, twenty sheep, twenty calves, ten cows, and ten steers in a three-month period (the round numbers suggest that the number of his victims was only being approximated). Winn was tried for malicious mischief, fined only twenty-five dollars, and ordered to put an end to his destructive practices. But the next March more livestock were found slain. When a search for Winn failed to find him, his surety for good behavior went to reimburse the owners of the destroyed animals.

Along with the rough-and-ready spirit of a region not too long removed from its frontier days and still preserving a great deal of frontier mentality was a strict and sometimes bigoted sense of religion. Genesee County was in the

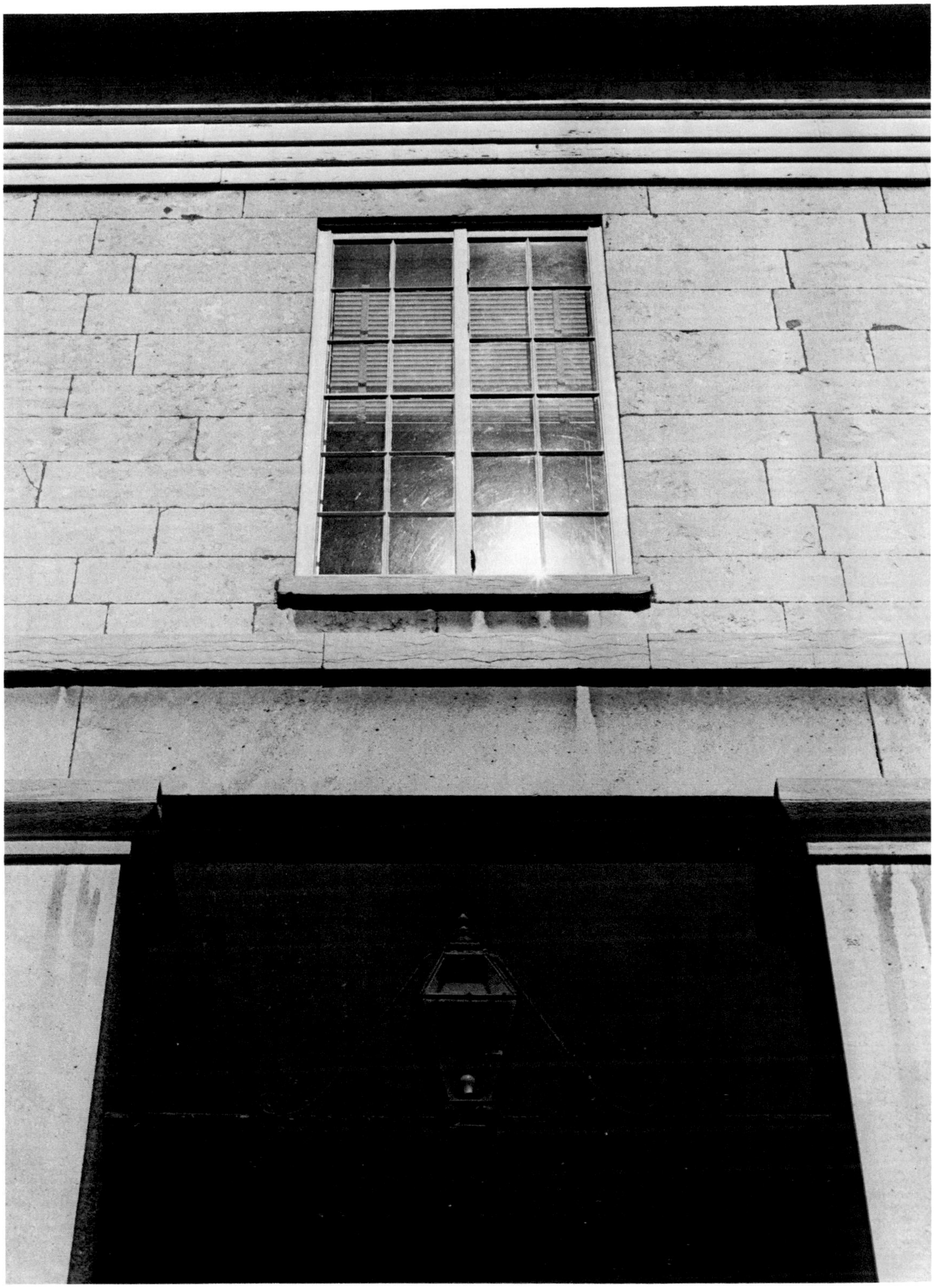

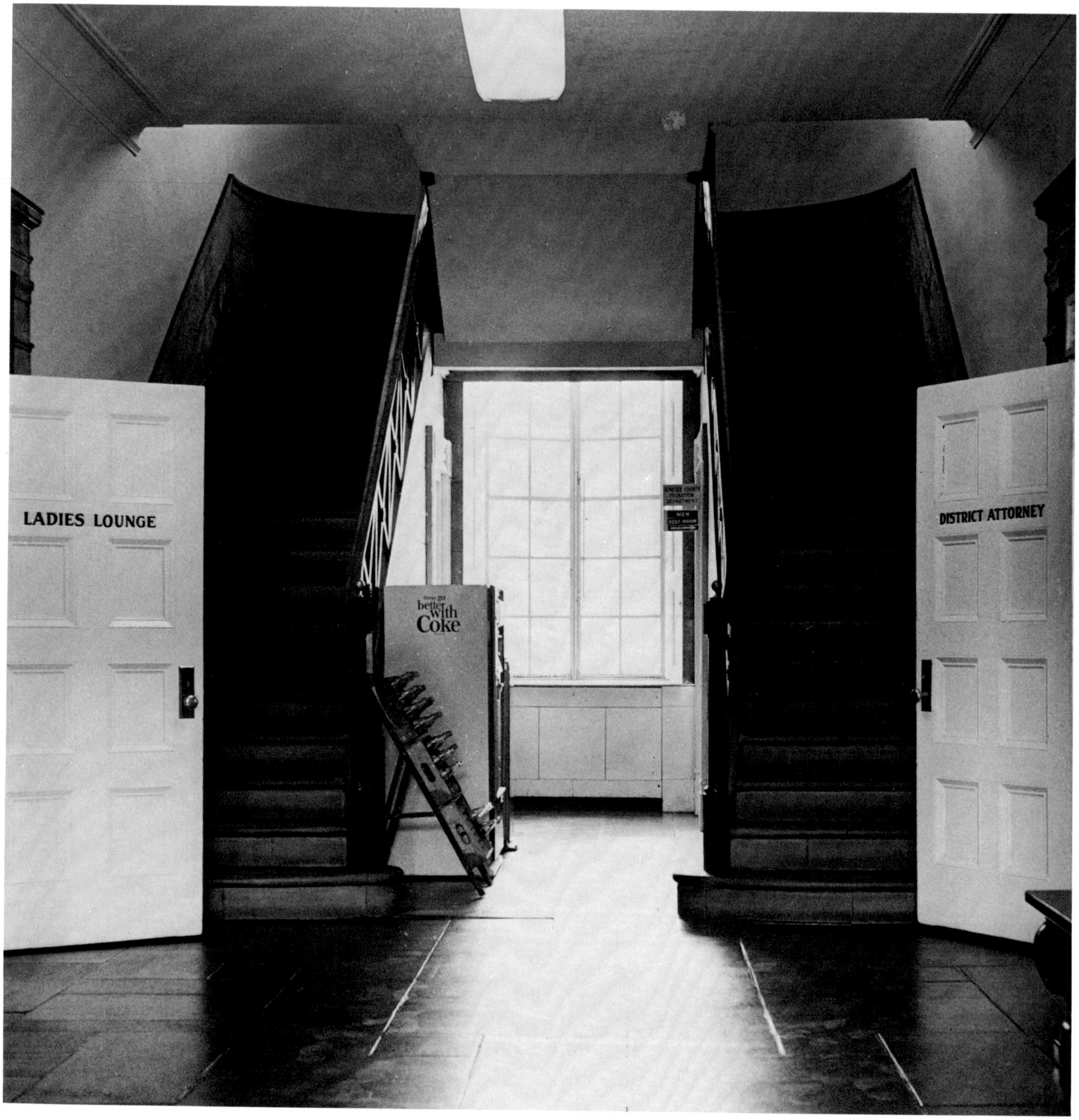
LADIES LOUNGE
go
better with Coke
DISTRICT ATTORNEY

midst of the Burned Over district of western New York, which was the scene of a great religious revival in the early decades of the nineteenth century. Out of this came not only a general heightened religiosity, but also a number of religious sects that were to have a considerable impact upon American life and thought. Those coming from this area included the Mormons, the Seventh Day Adventists, the Millenarians, and the Perfectionists.

However, a very harsh and austere religion can have a backlash, and it did in the case of Benjamin White, who was tried in March 1843 for the murder of his father. Benjamin came from a home deeply affected by the revivalist spirit of the times. His father was a devout man by the standards of that day, but they were not indulgent standards, for the boy was cruelly mistreated by his parent. When Benjamin reached adulthood and married, his father refused him the usual patrimony of a farm of his own, and so Benjamin migrated to new land, which, however, proved to be barren. There his wife sickened and died, leaving the grieving and confused young man with a small son.

Benjamin returned to his father's home, left the child there, and enlisted in the United States Army. By this time he had turned completely against the rigid and chilly faith of his father and had accepted instead the secular writings of the Enlightenment philosophers. The thought of his son being raised in a household where he had spent such an unhappy youth soon led Benjamin to desert the army and return to Genesee County to reclaim his son. There was an argument, and he shot his father to death.

The trial of Benjamin White in the courthouse in Batavia was not especially eventful.

White was indicted in March 1842, a month after the murder, and two days later pleaded not guilty. With delays and the difficulties of selecting a jury, it was the following March before the case came to trial, a year and ten days after the murder; White was found guilty and sentenced to be hanged on April 26, 1843.

The usual scenario is for a condemned man to recant his heresies on the scaffold and ask to be returned to the bosom of the Lamb. Benjamin White, however, had continued to read and to contemplate on the non-existence of God while he awaited his fate, and when the day he stood beneath the gallows came, and the sheriff asked if he had any final words, White had a great many.

He made a long pronouncement, beginning with a description of his miserable childhood and the pinched and cheerless religiosity of his father. From this point he went on to attack the tenets of Christianity, to deny the existence of life after death, and to cite Voltaire, Holbach, and even the Bible in support of his agnosticism. Benjamin White's last words probably gave the few who watched him die some things to think about, but his farewell speech reached beyond the gallows. Someone transcribed it, and it was later published, possibly even to cause some of those who read it to reflect on their own religion and philosophy of life.

The building in which Benjamin White was tried was the second courthouse to serve Genesee County. At their 1839 meeting the county board of supervisors came around to deciding definitely that a new courthouse building was needed; the next year the New York legislature authorized a loan of $10,000 for the purpose, and later the board of supervisors chipped in with another

$2,000. The total was considered a pretty fair amount at that time, and work began, with materials being obtained locally. If nothing else, this use of area materials ensured that local quarries would have a perennial, if small, interest in maintenance and repair of the building, for its soft limestone exterior is easily worn by weather or abrasion. The courthouse steps are a special maintenance problem; they were last torn up for repairs in 1966.

By February 1843 the courthouse was completed to the point that the county courts could hold their sessions in the building—in time to try Benjamin White and condemn him to the gallows. It apparently was an austere courtroom at first—no shades on the windows during the first court sessions, not even any cushioned chairs for the jurors until 1849—but then, it was an era when no one expected much in the way of comfort.

The courtroom appears originally to have occupied the entire second floor of the courthouse, as it does now, but it is most likely that the nineteenth-century position of the judge's bench was at the front of the building, over the front porch, whereas today it is against another wall of the courtroom. For a time various rooms in the building were unneeded and unused, and sheriffs of Genesee County, charged with care of the courthouse, were quite active in obtaining tenants for the empty space. Originally the board of supervisors agreed to the use of these rooms for such public purposes as political caucuses, shows, and exhibitions, but when in 1850 the sheriff rented the grand jury room for use as a writing school, he was ordered to eject school and scholars forthwith. The board of supervisors soon reversed themselves, for three years later they authorized repairs to rooms being occupied by an insurance company. By 1858, though, the demands of county business were so great that the sheriff was directed to prohibit use of the courthouse for any other than county business.

In the meantime the first courthouse, built in the opening years of the nineteenth century, remained in use to house various county offices, but time and wear eventually took such a toll on the ancient structure that in 1912 a county grand jury condemned it as a public nuisance. It burned down in 1918, and a county building was put up on the site. The second—present —courthouse has always been well cared for: painted, exterior sandblasted, and various alterations made from time to time. Major remodeling was done in 1931, and a complete refurbishing of the exterior was completed in 1976.

The Genesee County Courthouse was placed on the National Register of Historic Buildings in 1973. The building still makes use of one item that was part of the first courthouse: the bell that once hung in the cupola of the original courthouse is now in the cupola of the 1843 building, where it is rung on the hour and half hour and when a verdict is reached in the court-room below.

GREENE COUNTY

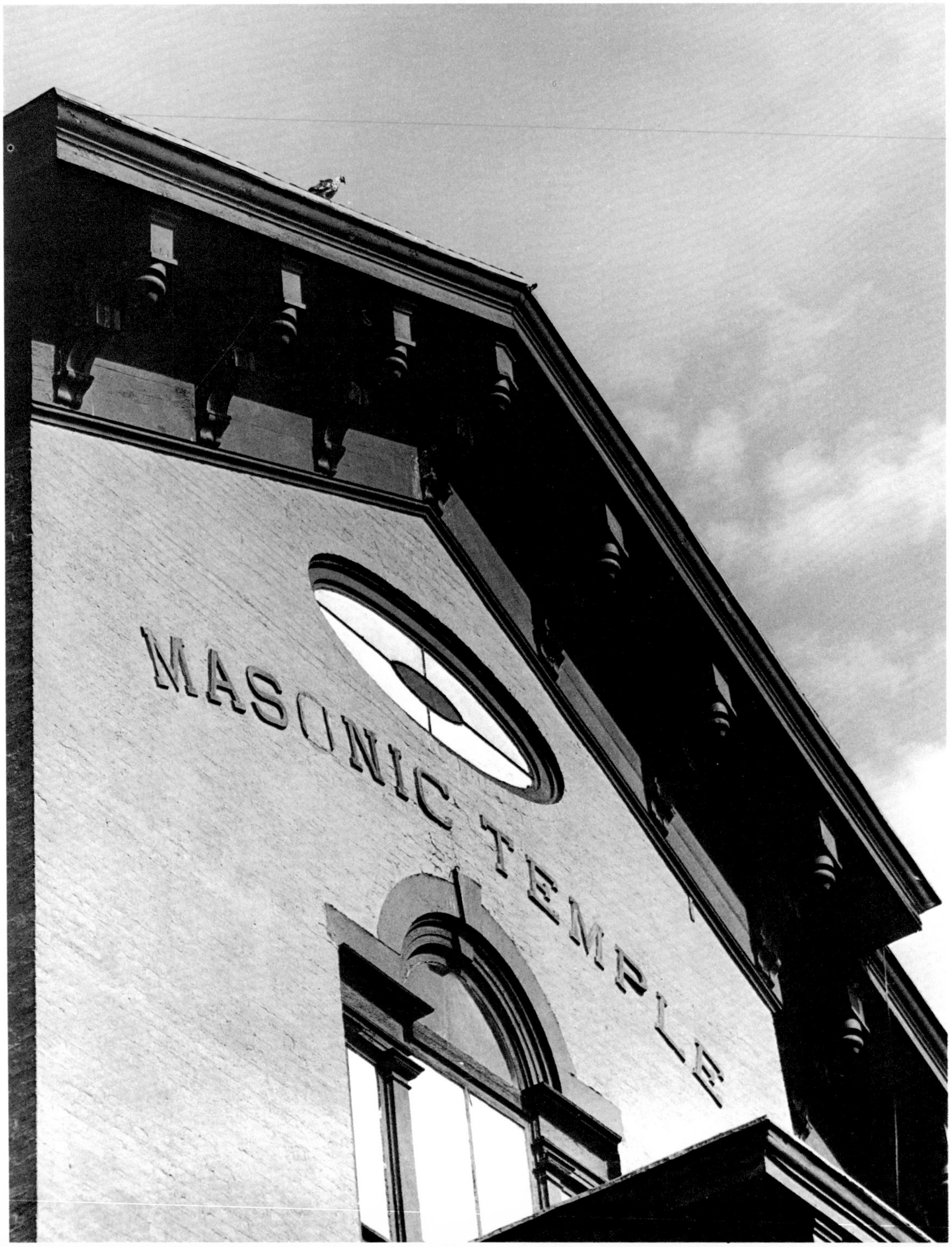
MASONIC TEMPLE

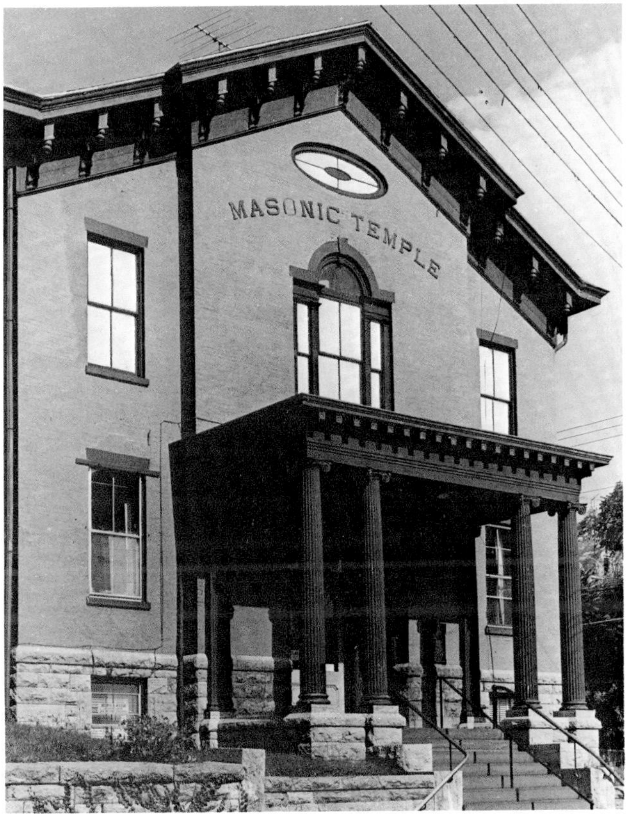
MASONIC TEMPLE

The venerable Greene County Courthouse is one of those that have survived by being converted to other uses. Today it is the Masonic Temple in the town of Catskill; the courthouse that replaced it stands nearby.

The history of Greene County's courthouses is without violence or great drama. After Greene became a county in 1800, court was held for a time—as it was in most new counties—in private homes and other ad hoc quarters. In 1801 the county purchased a school building—called the academy—constructed a stone jail on the academy grounds, and these two buildings became courthouse and county jail.

A new courthouse, authorized by the legislature in 1812, was built on the site of the academy building and soon after inconveniently burned down. It was replaced by a new brick courthouse on a different site in about 1819 (the exact date is uncertain), a building whose architecture today gives little hint that it was once the county's courthouse (originally it had a cupola with bell, which was removed in this century). Now, even without "Masonic Temple" across its facade, one would hesitate to identify it as a courthouse. It deserves preservation, if for no other reason, as one more example of how eclectic courthouse architectural design can be.

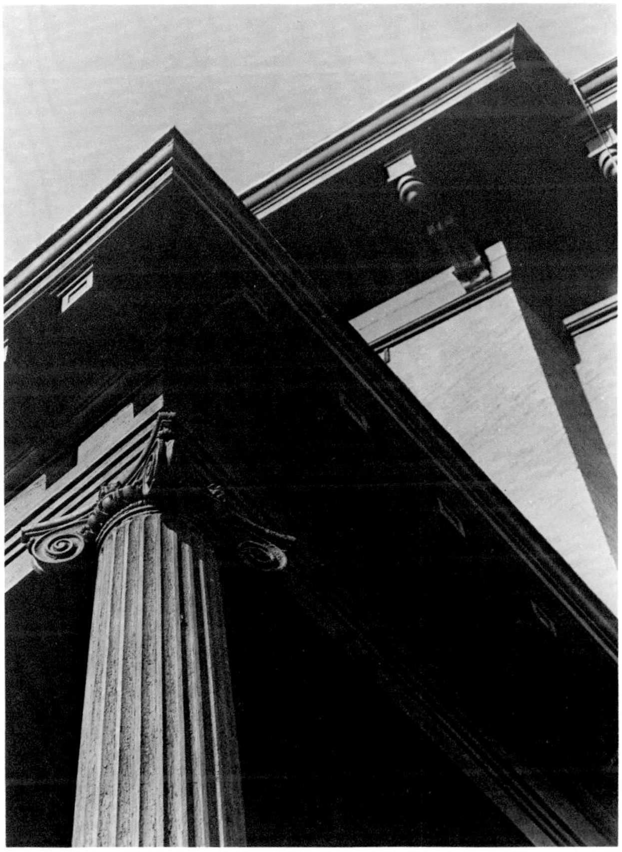

HERKIMER COUNTY

In 1906 Chester Gillette was tried and found guilty of murder and sentenced to die for the slaying. His crime was not a spectacular or unique one—he killed a young woman who had become an embarrassment to his social ambitions after he made her pregnant—but it was one that achieved a kind of immortality because it became the basis for a great American novel, Theodore Dreiser's *An American Tragedy*. The murder occurred in New York's Herkimer County, and the Herkimer County Courthouse, with its distinctive mansard-roofed cupola, contributed its small share to the real-life drama that went into the making of the novel, for it was there that Chester Gillette was tried and condemned to death.

The basic facts about the Gillette case are not complicated. Gillette and Grace Brown had come to the Adirondack region of central Herkimer County and had registered as man and wife at a hotel before arriving at Big Moose Lake. There Gillette had rented a boat, and the couple had rowed toward a part of the lake called South Bay. The next day the boat was found capsized; the woman's body was floating on the water, the face bruised, but an autopsy showed that she had drowned. It also revealed that she was three or four months pregnant. Among her possessions at the hotel was a card from Chester Gillette, and in his baggage were letters from Grace and

another, far wealthier young woman.

No one knows why Theodore Dreiser chose the case of Chester Gillette as the model for the story of how his fictional Clyde Griffiths murdered a woman who had become troublesome and then paid for his crime. Dreiser had written the first chapters of the book from 1920 to 1922, and they had no relation to Chester Gillette. The Gillette case was only one of several that the novelist had gathered over the years, but none of the other cases of hapless young women murdered to permit their lovers to move into higher society appealed to Dreiser as much as this unhappy drama that began on Big Moose Lake in July of 1905.

Once he had decided on the Gillette case, Dreiser's insatiable appetite for details forced him to move from California to New York to begin intensive research. After learning all he could from press accounts of Gillette's life and trial, he drove to the Adirondacks with Helen Parks, his future wife, to view the scene of the murder and trial. Late in June 1923, the couple arrived at Big Moose Lake, rented a boat, and rowed to South Bay. After rounding a point they were in the bay, shut off from view, and in the lonely spot where Grace Brown had died. The quiet and the solitude of the pine- and spruce-bordered bay bore down on them, and Helen Parks later wrote that "we found our-

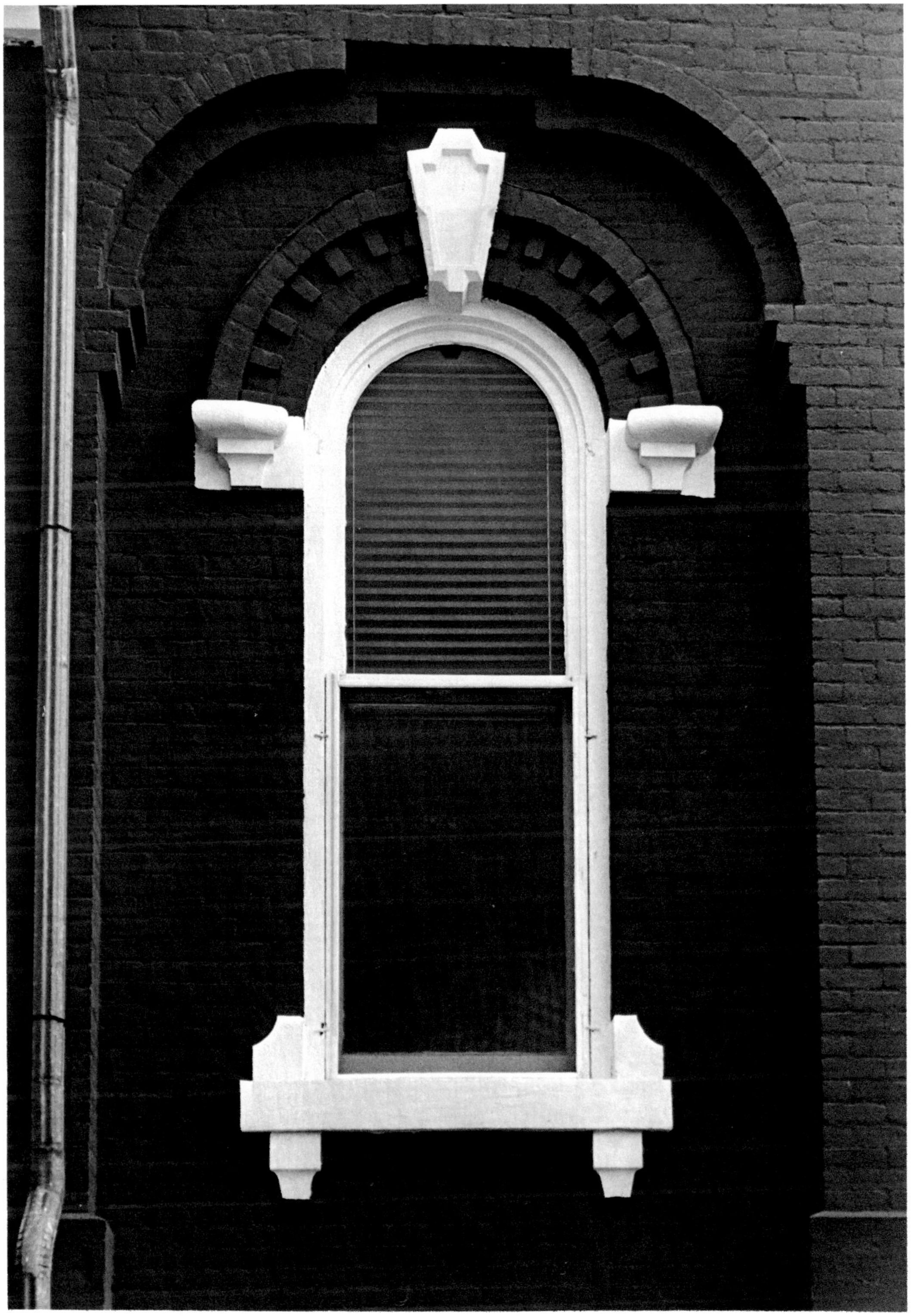

selves drifting into a quiet, deathlike stillness [and] . . . the mood of the most dramatic note of the tragedy seized us both. The emotion and the mood of this moment never left me and never will. A death moment . . . or as near as one can come to it, perhaps." After returning, the couple went on to research less emotionally disturbing.

We do not have an itinerary for Dreiser as he went about making the Gillette tragedy come alive to himself, but in all probability, after leaving the lake, he drove to the village of Inlet some eight or ten miles to the southeast, where Gillette had been apprehended as he fled. From Inlet, Gillette had been taken back into Herkimer County to Old Forge (Inlet lies just across the line, in Hamilton County), where he was arraigned before a local justice of the peace, who held his court in the rambling hotel Forge House, overlooking Old Forge Lake. The ar-

raignment was recorded on the stationery of the hotel, and the documents were given to the sheriff and district attorney, who escorted the young man to Herkimer, the county seat.

At Herkimer, Dreiser found the lengthy record of Chester Gillette's arraignment, trial, and conviction. There were, however, elements of the story that he would not find in the public records. He had to depend mainly on newspaper accounts for indications of the public interest the trial aroused and—more pertinent—to learn how local politicians used the trial to further the election of District Attorney George W. Ward to the office of county judge. Gillette had been given a trial before the election day of 1906 through a special term of the Supreme Court; had the normal calendar been followed, the trial would have been delayed until the following January, 1907, too late to help Ward in his election campaign. Also, once Ward had been elected county judge, he refused to extend the time allotted for Gillette's attorneys to prepare their extracts for the appeal from the five volumes of trial testimony.

In his fictional trial Dreiser did not make a point of the difficulty of impaneling the jury, although in the Gillette case two hundred forty potential jurors were examined. Even after this careful sifting, most of the men who were seated admitted that they held a strong opinion of the accused's guilt, but unlike those who were rejected, they said that they could be convinced of the contrary by evidence the defense might submit.

Nor did Dreiser, in his novel, present such a lengthy parade of witnesses—ninety-seven—as testified against Gillette before the Herkimer County grand jury. The novelist, however, did incorporate into his book the three-part indictment returned by the grand jury. It charged Gillette with the three possible ways constituting felony that Grace Brown could have met her death. First, it charged that Gillette had beaten her into unconsciousness and then thrown her into the lake. Second, it claimed that he had smothered and strangled her while she was in the water. And third, it proposed that he had inflicted deadly wounds before throwing her into the water. Later, at his trial, Chester Gillette was to assert that the woman had lost her balance and had upset the boat as she fell into the lake. When he had come to the surface, he said, he was several yards away from her, and he swam for the shore to save himself. But Gillette was not able to explain why he did not report the incident to the authorities as soon as possible, nor why he struck out through the woods for Inlet.

The trial was long and provided more than enough material for Dreiser in the shaping of his novel. The prosecution amassed a large body of circumstantial evidence. No expense was spared in gathering this evidence, and a sizeable bill was presented to the Herkimer County Board of Supervisors for expenditures. For instance, two days' wages were given to the man whose single contribution was to search for and find the tennis racquet dropped by Chester Gillette near the scene of the "drowning." And the boat involved in the crime was brought to Herkimer by railway express and used to recreate the scene for the edification of the jurors. Gillette's court-assigned counsel traveled to Albany and to Cortland (Gillette's home) to obtain medical experts and character witnesses for their client; their bills are also listed in the court records.

Dreiser ignored Gillette's testimony that he was working as a stock clerk and had spent two years at Oberlin College before coming to New York State to seek his fortune. He had provided his Clyde Griffiths with a different background well before he decided to use the Gillette case as the basis for the murder and trial episodes in his book. And while Dreiser supplied his fictional murderer with rich relatives who paid for his defense, the real Chester Gillette was forced to plead his poverty and was assigned counsel for his trial and for the subsequent appeal of his conviction.

After Chester Gillette was convicted, he was sentenced to die in the electric chair in Auburn State Prison. A stay postponed the execution until after his appeal to the Court of Appeals had been decided and the sentence of the trial court affirmed. Then, on March 30, 1908, Chester Gillette paid the penalty for his crime, and was pronounced dead at 6:18 A.M. A post mortem examination showed no brain damage or malfunction, and except for a slight case of pleurisy, no physical illness.

Dreiser was never able to get permission to visit Auburn State Prison as part of the research for his novel, but as a substitute he did manage a visit to Sing Sing's death house on the pretense of writing the confession of a condemned man for a New York City newspaper. The author felt that he had gained little from the Sing Sing visit and could have reconstructed Gillette's experiences at Auburn just as well from his imagination.

In spite of the minor discrepancies between Dreiser's account and the actual events in Herkimer County, one can get a fairly accurate description of the trial of Chester Gillette by reading *An American Tragedy,* for Dreiser's eye for detail and his ability as a chronicler of events are outstanding. In one small detail he was misled by the passage of time into committing an anachronism. He referred to the Herkimer County Courthouse as an "old" building. When Dreiser saw the courthouse in 1923, it was fifty years old, not especially ancient as such structures go, but perhaps with enough years to excuse Dreiser's use of the adjective. What he forgot was that when Gillette was tried in 1906 the courthouse was only thirty-three years old; moreover, it had been remodeled a few months before the trial began, and to spectators at Gillette's trial, it would have appeared an up-to-date building.

The courthouse had been built in 1873 according to the plans of architect A. J. Lathrop and had cost $46,471.12. The 1906 changes consisted of interior alterations and redecorations; at that time several door openings were closed to provide the courtroom floor with a more utilitarian plan. The exterior has not been changed since the courthouse was built, while across from it still stands the jail that held Gillette in 1906; the jail is being replaced by a new building and will become the probate department. The courthouse—for which plans to refurbish are now underway—is a unique and charming building, and it has aged gracefully; today, more than fifty years after Dreiser called it old, the building still appears to have a great many good years left in it.

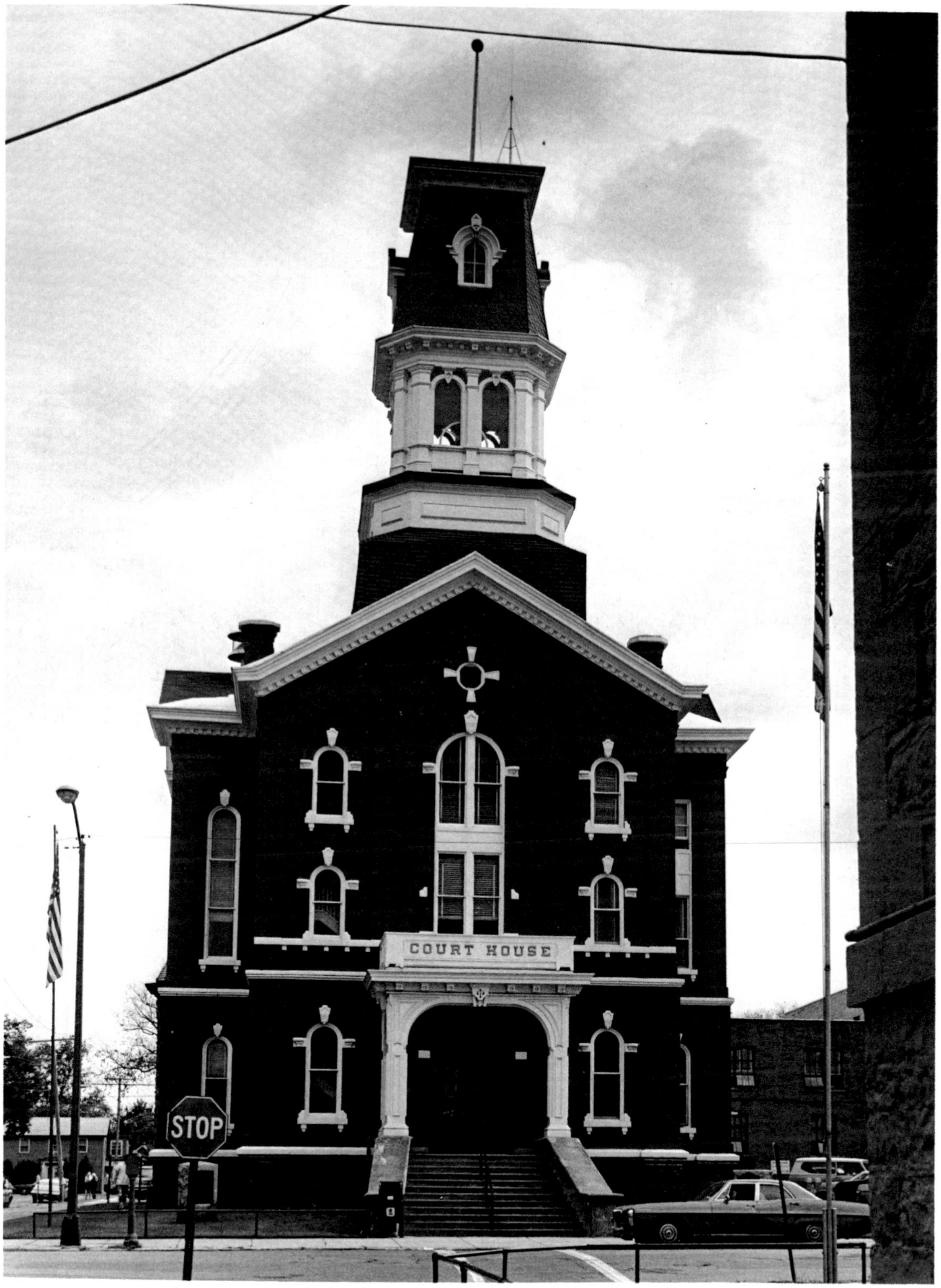
COURT HOUSE
STOP

JEFFERSON COUNTY

The courthouse serving Jefferson County at Watertown is one of Horatio Nelson White's several surviving edifices, and the remarks about White and his architectural style made in describing the Chemung County Courthouse are just as pertinent here. A comparison of the photographs of the two structures will reveal that they came from the same head and hand. The Watertown building, however, has an ornate circular staircase rising from both sides of the entryway to the second-floor courtroom; this is characteristic of White's interior design but was omitted from the Elmira courthouse, probably for reasons of economy.

When Jefferson County was established in 1805, Watertown was chosen county seat more or less as a compromise, but after some initial grumbling, it proved to be a generally satisfactory choice. The first courthouse, erected in 1807–1808, was partially destroyed by fire in 1817 but was patched up and continued in use until 1821, when it burned to the ground. A new courthouse was built, but increasing county business soon overtaxed its accommodations, and in 1858 a grand jury declared the building a nuisance. It was replaced by Horatio White's Anglo-Norman building, a red-brick structure with trim of locally quarried limestone, which was dedicated and ready for use in the fall of 1862.

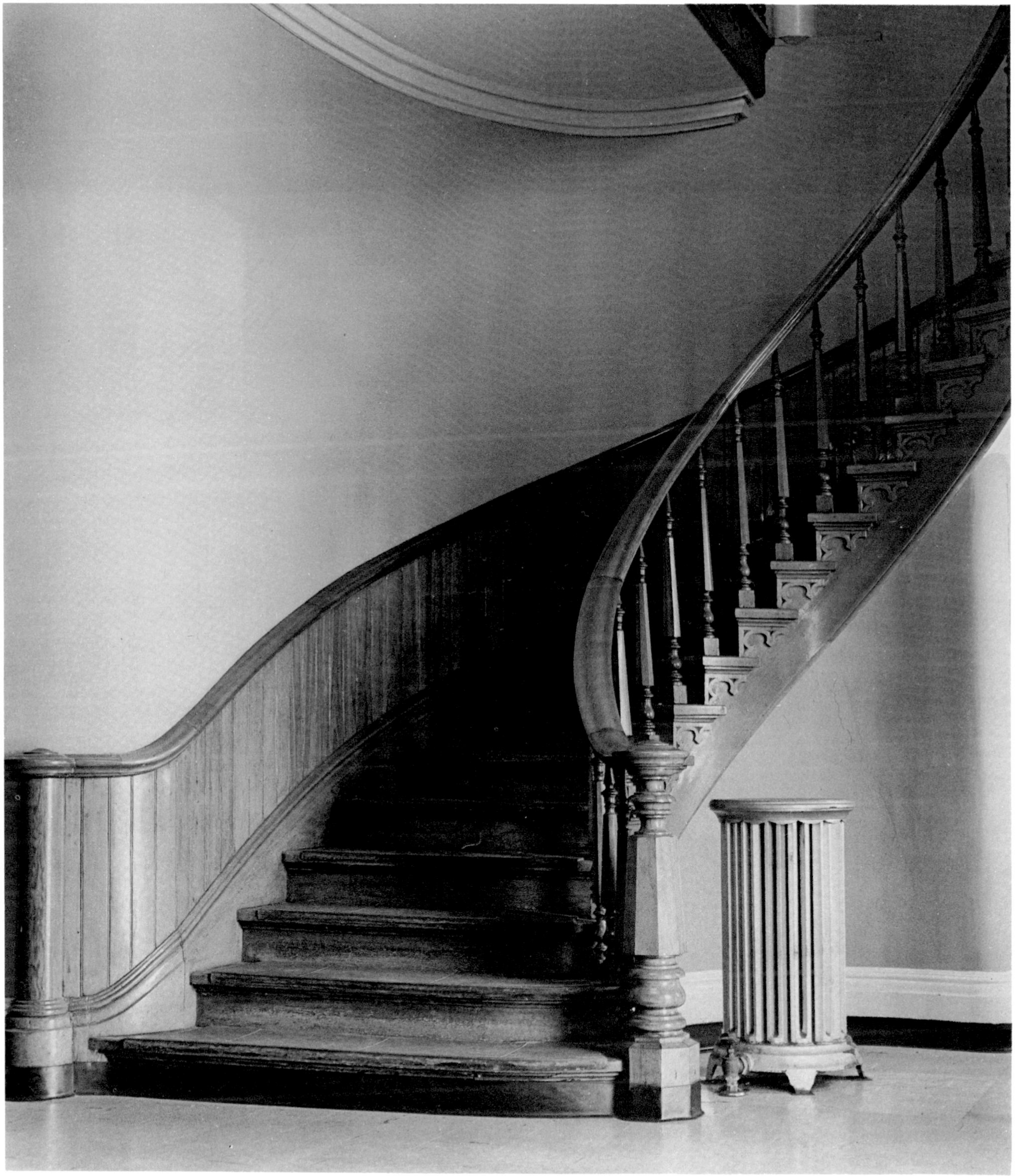

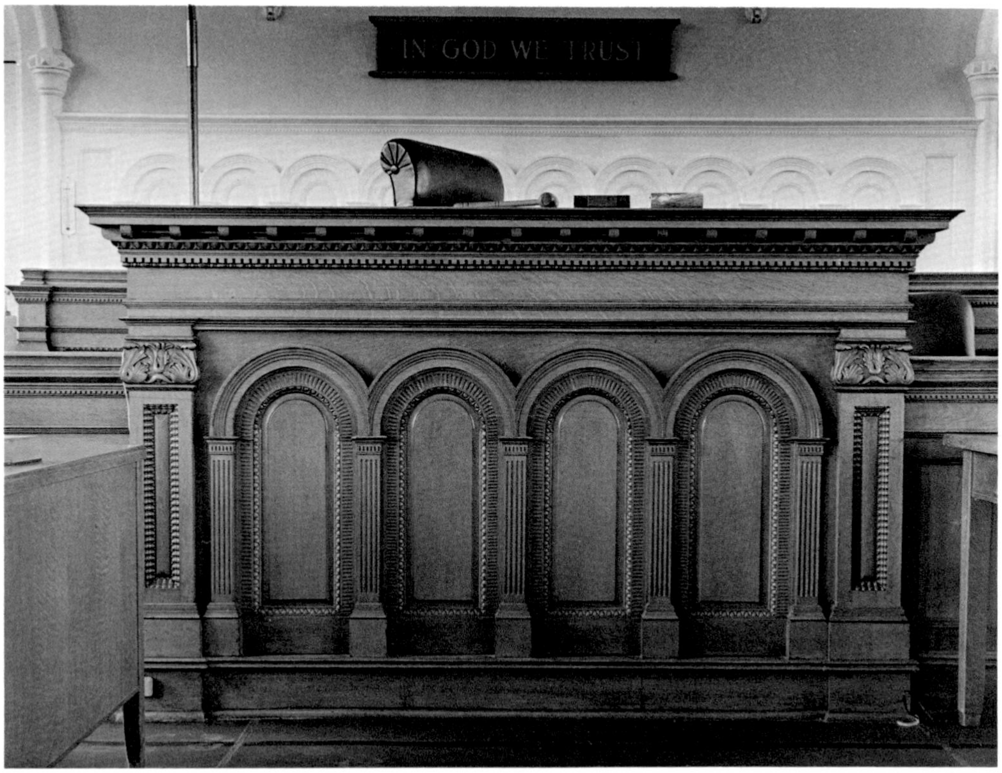
IN GOD WE TRUST

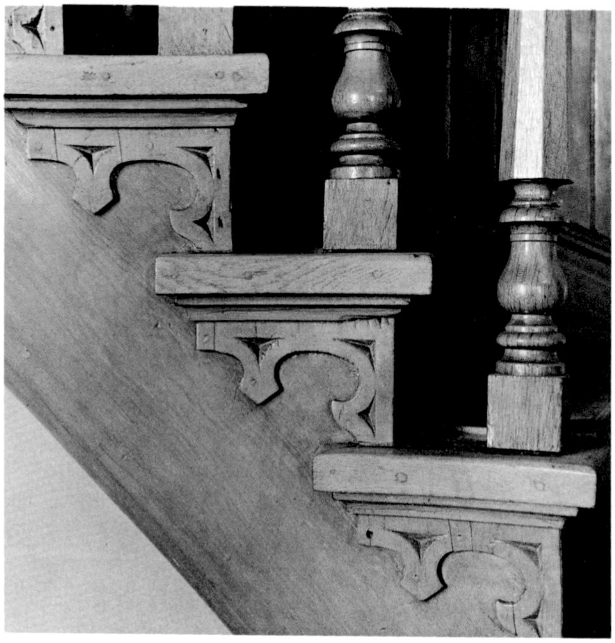

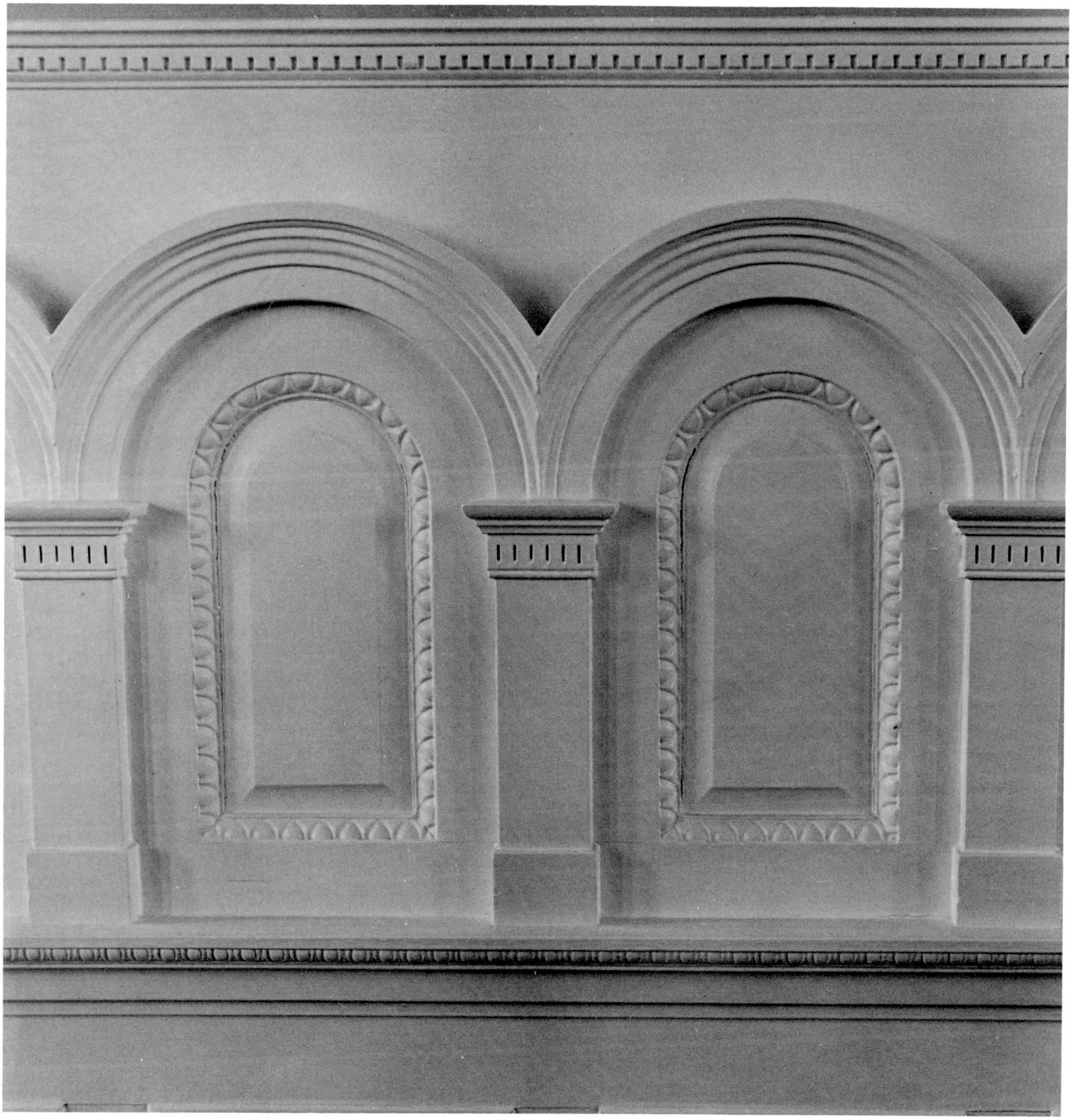

LEWIS COUNTY

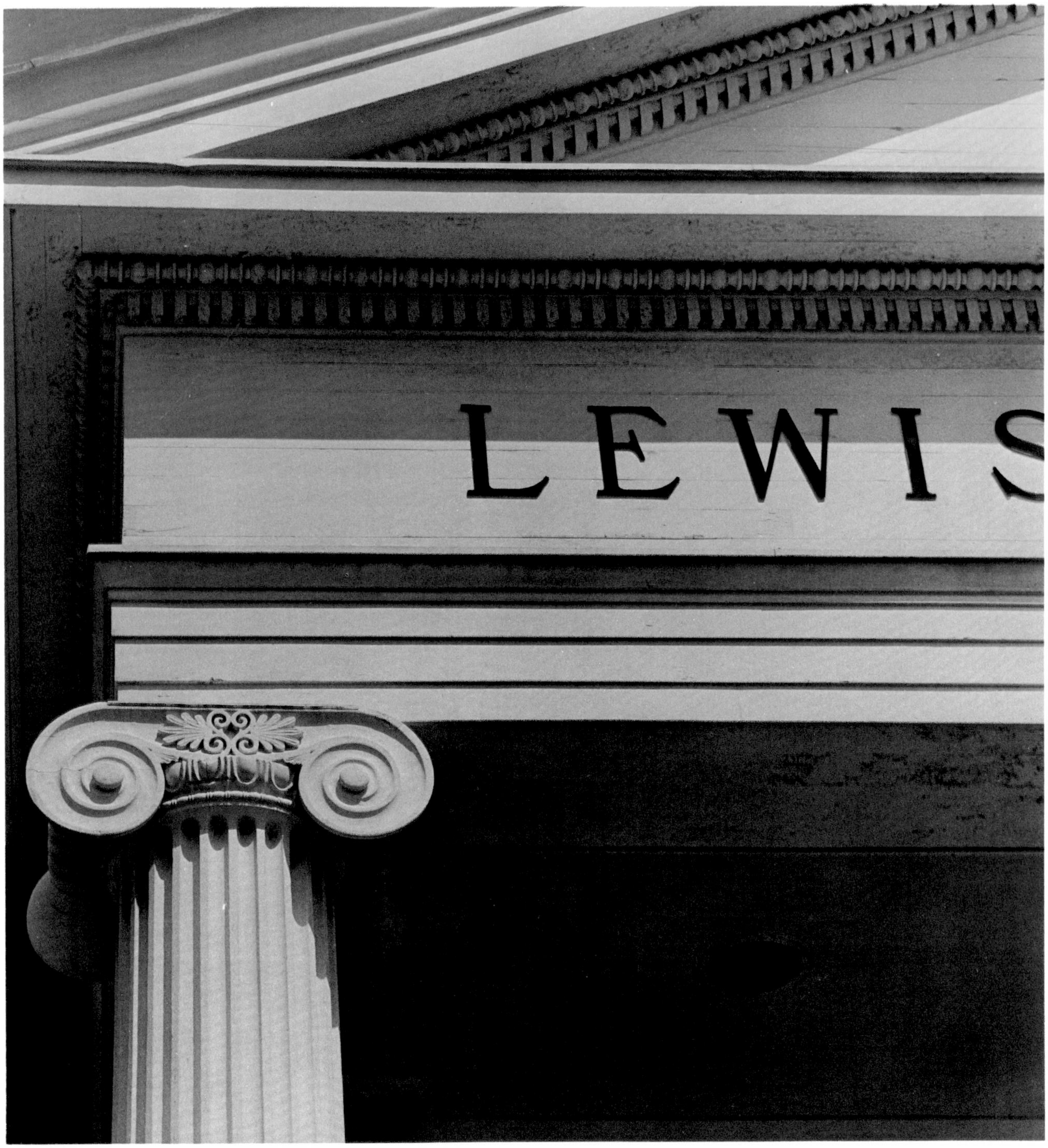
LEWIS

Lewis County has had only two courthouses since 1812, and both are still in use. The courthouse at Lowville, the one pictured here, was begun in 1852, after it was decided to move the county seat from Martinsburg to Lowville because the latter town was more centrally located and more industrially active.

Construction was begun by popular subscription, and the town of Lowville contributed $500 to the fund on condition that the building be free for town purposes. Thus, it served as the Lowville Town Hall from its completion in 1855 until the county occupied it in 1864.

The brick building cost less than $6,000 when it was built, but when fire swept through it shortly after midnight in late November of 1947, the damage to the structure alone was estimated at $300,000, entirely apart from loss of records, part of the law library, and furnishings. In repairing the damage, every effort was made to restore the original appearance of the building, with its handsome Ionic-columned portico. The principal alteration was the addition of a third floor, which, however, made little noticeable change in the outward appearance of the old building.

As for the first courthouse—the one built at Martinsburg in 1812— it became private property when the courts moved to Lowville, and for a time housed an academy, which failed in 1888. In 1891 it became the property of the town of Martinsburg, whose town hall it has been ever since. It is one of the oldest surviving buildings in Lewis County.

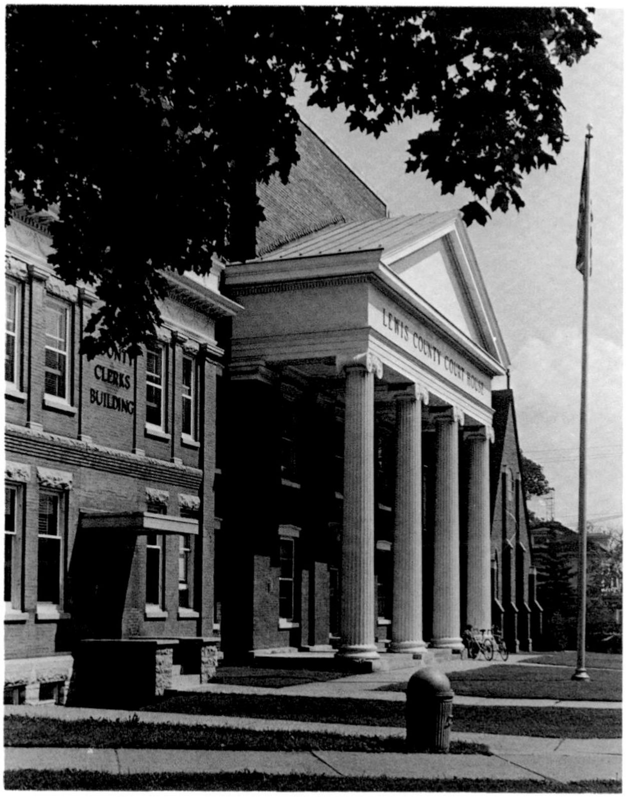
LEWIS COUNTY COURT HOUSE
CLERKS
BUILDING

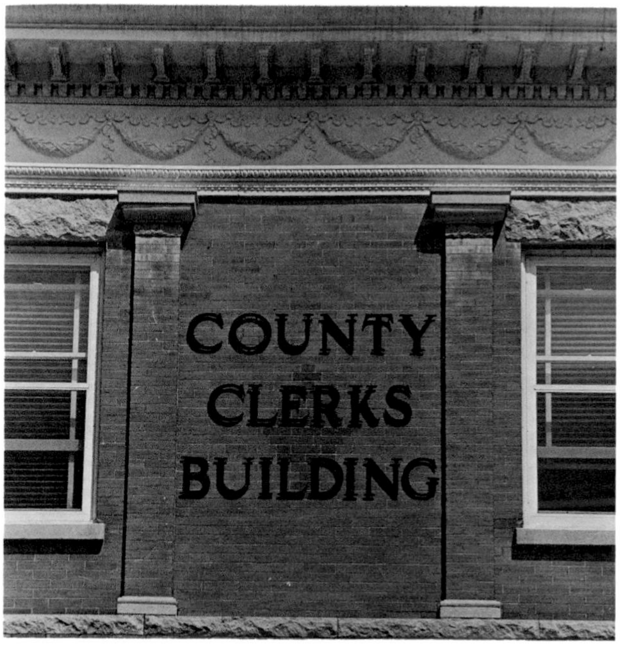
COUNTY
CLERKS
BUILDING

LIVINGSTON
COUNTY

In 1821 the New York state legislature created Livingston County, taking eight townships from Ontario County and four from Genesee County (others were later added to make the present seventeen). That same year four acres in Geneseo village, including the present site of the Livingston County Courthouse, were deeded to the county by William and James Wadsworth, two pioneer settlers, for one dollar.

The new county established itself with few

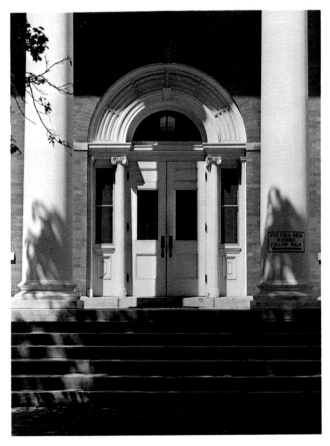

Bradgon and Hillman of Rochester. The date of completion is uncertain, but could have been the same year, 1898.

The new building, a graceful structure with a portico of Ionic columns, was described in *The Brick Builder*, an architectural publication, as "another most excellent example of brickwork. . . . The building is . . . a colonial combination of Flemish bonded brick, with stone quoins and a center treatment consisting of a high two-storied colonnade with pediment presumably of wood, a design which, handled with less nicety of proportion and sense of fitness, might easily become commonplace, but which is a charming bit of composition."

growing pains; by 1823 the first courthouse was completed and occupied, and the building continued to serve until 1897. By that time, however, it was showing its age to such an extent that there was concern about its safety; an investigating committee confirmed those fears, and the old structure was condemned.

An abortive attempt to steal the county seat was made by Mount Morris, whose citizens offered to build a new courthouse at their own expense, but their efforts failed. The old building was razed in the early spring of 1898 and construction started at once on the present courthouse, designed by the architectural firm of

MADISON
COUNTY

New York's discarded courthouses—if they escape the wrecking ball—end up in many new guises: a museum, an office building, the home of a fraternal lodge. The building at Morrisville in Madison County found survival in becoming part of a college campus.

Madison County was created in 1806, with the villages of Sullivan and Hamilton as its two county seats; neither ever had a proper courthouse, and courts were held alternately in the two villages' schoolhouses. In 1810 Cazenovia was named county seat and a brick courthouse was built there, a structure that later became part of Cazenovia Academy. Once again, in 1817, the county seat was moved, this time to Morrisville because of its more central location.

The first Morrisville courthouse was built in 1817 and served the county for more than thirty years, although it was a shoddily built structure, condemned year after year as unsafe. It was replaced in 1849 by a building that burned in 1864 during the trial of a member of a notorious gang of horse thieves operating in the region. The fire was probably started by other members of the gang to destroy damaging evidence; certainly the blaze was not accidental, for the fire company answering the alarm found all its hoses slashed and useless.

A third courthouse on the same site was built in 1865; an addition was made in 1872, but no other major changes occurred while the building served as a courthouse. Madison County could not, however, shake off its habit of changing county seats from time to time, and in the fall of 1907 the seat was shifted to Wampsville, and the Morrisville building stood empty.

Morrisville, faced with the prospect of becoming a ghost town with the loss of its main industry, began a campaign to have the state found an agricultural college there. They were successful; the abandoned courthouse and other county buildings were ceded for use as a school; and in the autumn of 1910 the first class of students met in the old courthouse, renamed Madison Hall.

The interior of the building was, of necessity,

much altered. The county supervisors' chambers, for instance, became a soils laboratory, the cloakroom was turned into the veterinarian's office, and the courtroom was remodeled into a meeting hall (and for a time served as a gymnasium). The exterior, however, remains basically as it was when the building was a courthouse. The original college is now the Morrisville branch of the State University of New York, and at the moment Madison Hall stands empty on the campus while ways are sought to give it still another lease on life.

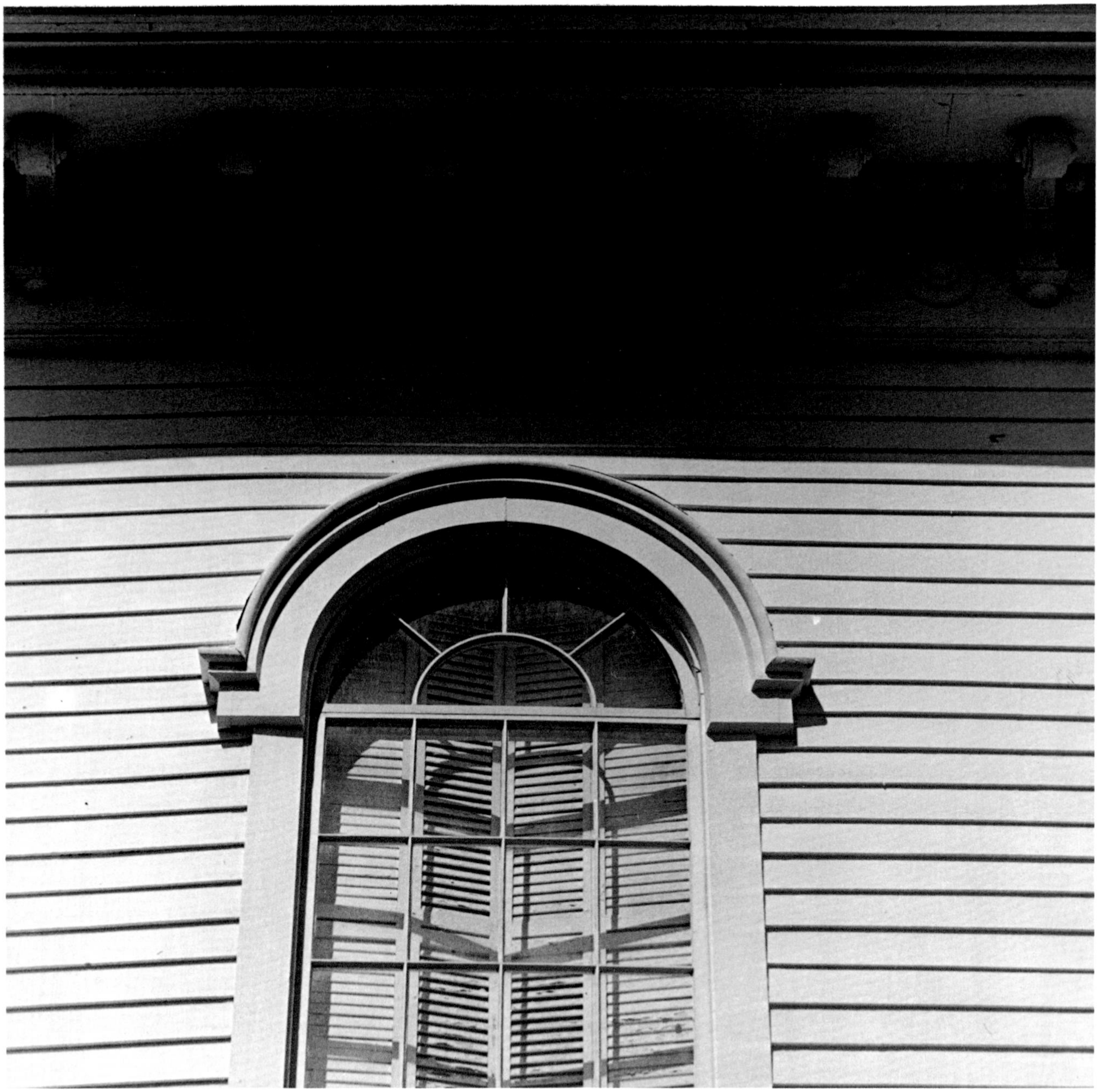

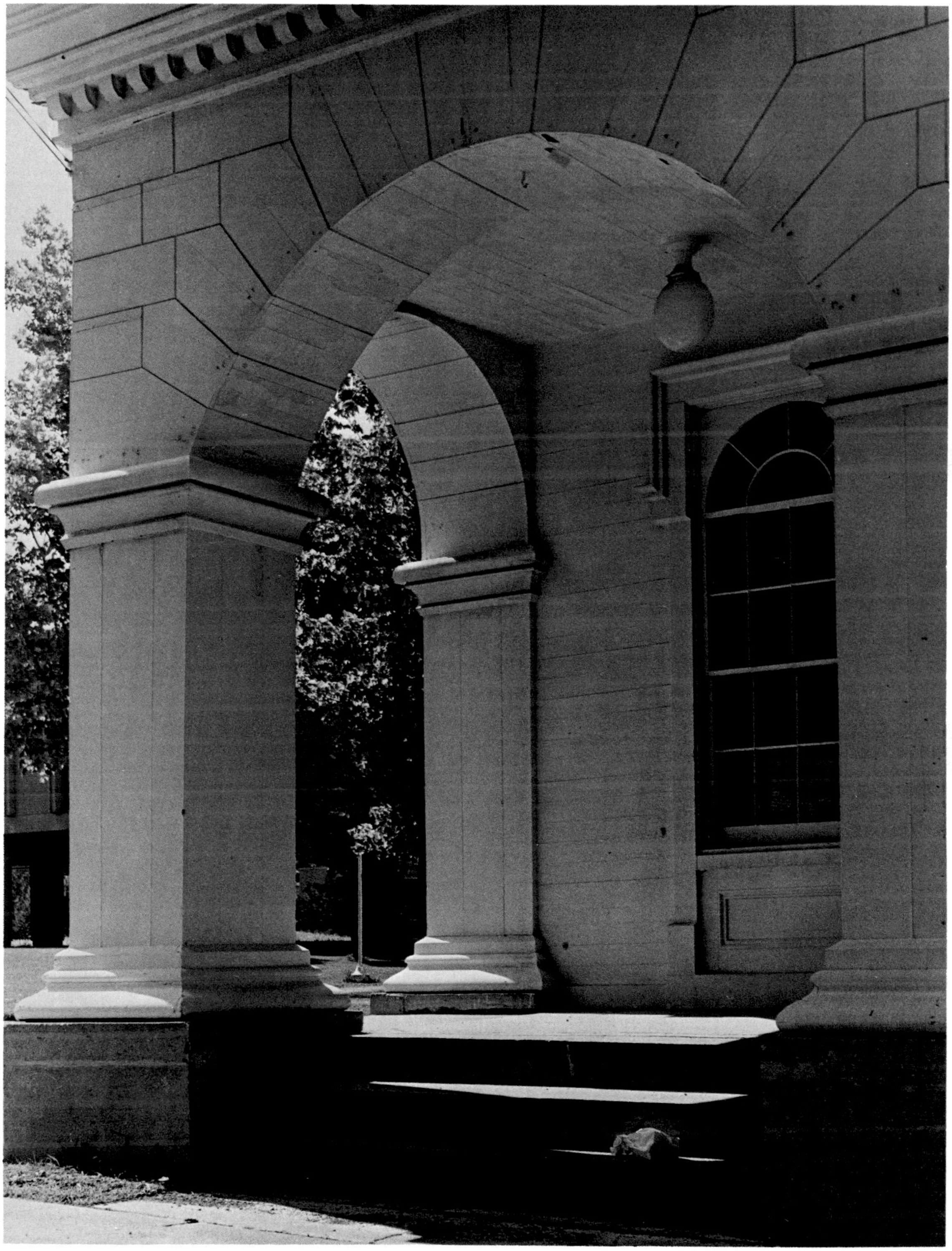

MONROE COUNTY

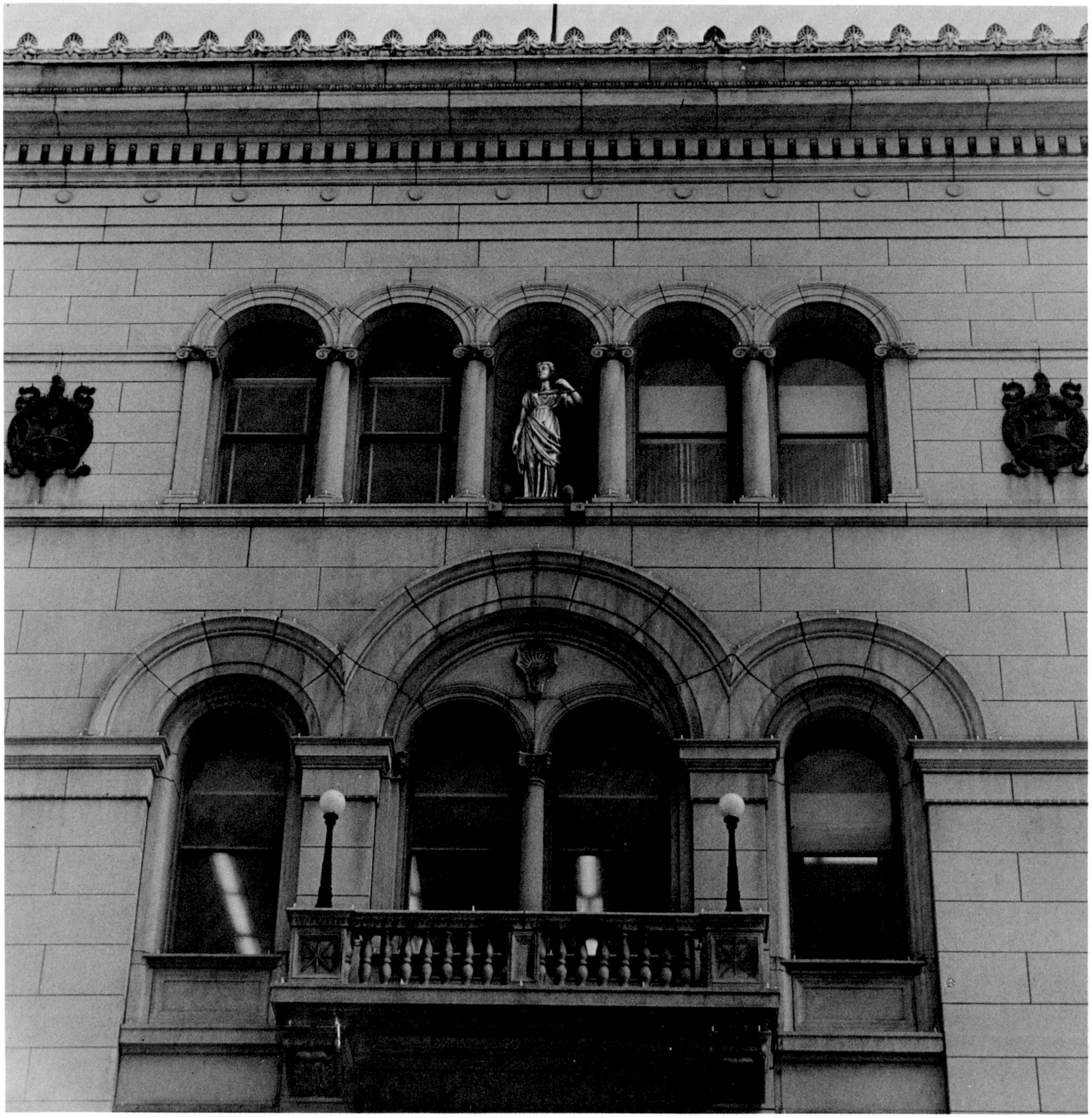

The New York legislature created Monroe County in 1821 from parts of Ontario and Genesee counties. There were fourteen towns in the new county; the principal one was Rochester, and it became the county seat. An extra inducement to locate there may have been a gift from three pioneer townsmen of a site for the courthouse and other county offices.

The first courthouse was completed in 1822, a much more substantial structure than the first courthouses of most counties, for it was built mainly of bluestone with red sandstone trimmings and was described as having been constructed "in two parts"; each part had a portico supported by Ionic columns.

By 1850 the first courthouse had become inadequate, and it was replaced by a larger structure. The latter was designed to be used by both the county and the city of Rochester, and served this dual purpose until 1875, when the city erected a municipal building. Eventually the courthouse became too antiquated and too small even for county purposes alone, and in July 1894 the cornerstone of the third—and present—courthouse was laid.

The 1894 building is a four-story structure, one hundred sixty feet by one hundred forty. It is built of smooth-dressed New Hampshire granite, and is generally Italianate in style, with four polished columns on its north, or main, front. The courthouse has aged gracefully, and still serves Monroe County with a dignity it has had for more than eighty years.

MONTGOMERY COUNTY

The old Montgomery County Courthouse at Fonda has not been used for court purposes for more than eighty years now. When it was replaced by a newer structure, it was converted to use for county offices, and the inside has been so completely altered that the old-time courtroom fixtures, and even the size of the courtroom, can only be guessed at. The alterations have had some effect on the exterior, but by and large the outside of the old building, with its massive Ionic columns and silver cupola, looks much as it did in July 1837, when Barney Hare, the court bell-ringer, announced the first term of court.

It was hardly two years after that opening that the man who would probably be the best-known litigant in the history of the old building was standing before the bench and acting as his own lawyer in a libel suit in which he was the plaintiff. The man was James Fenimore Cooper, famous as an author, but with some personality traits that made him far from universally liked and respected.

Cooper was raised with the prejudices and notions of the landed gentry on his family's estate at Cooperstown, but he had his share of the rough-and-ready life: five years as a sailor before the mast and three as a midshipman in the navy. On his return he married and resumed country life. In 1820 he published his first novel, *Precaution,* on a challenge from his wife after

he said, while reading an English novel to her, that he could write a better one. His book was possibly one of the worst ever written, but instead of being discouraged, he rose to the challenge, and next year *The Spy,* a big success, appeared. Two years later *The Pioneers* introduced Natty Bumppo (Leatherstocking), the noble, competent scout who was to appear again in *The Last of the Mohicans* and other books. Cooper was a literary success, but he wrote of a never-never land: his forest was a symbol of space and goodness in life; his Indians were noble figures of romance, chivalrous beings uncorrupted by civilization.

In 1826 Cooper went abroad for seven years, and while there wrote books full of patriotism for his own country and praise for democracy, but at the same time his basic aristocratic principles were being strengthened by his European sojourn. When he returned to America he suffered a great shock on finding that the natural patriotism, the simple demeanor, the private and public virtue of Americans that he had been writing about in Europe existed largely in his imagination. So did the ideal forest that he had fantasized.

One of his first reactions was against his immediate neighbors at Cooperstown, who had been accustomed to use a place on Lake Otsego called Three Mile Point as a picnic place. The site was Cooper land, but James Fenimore's

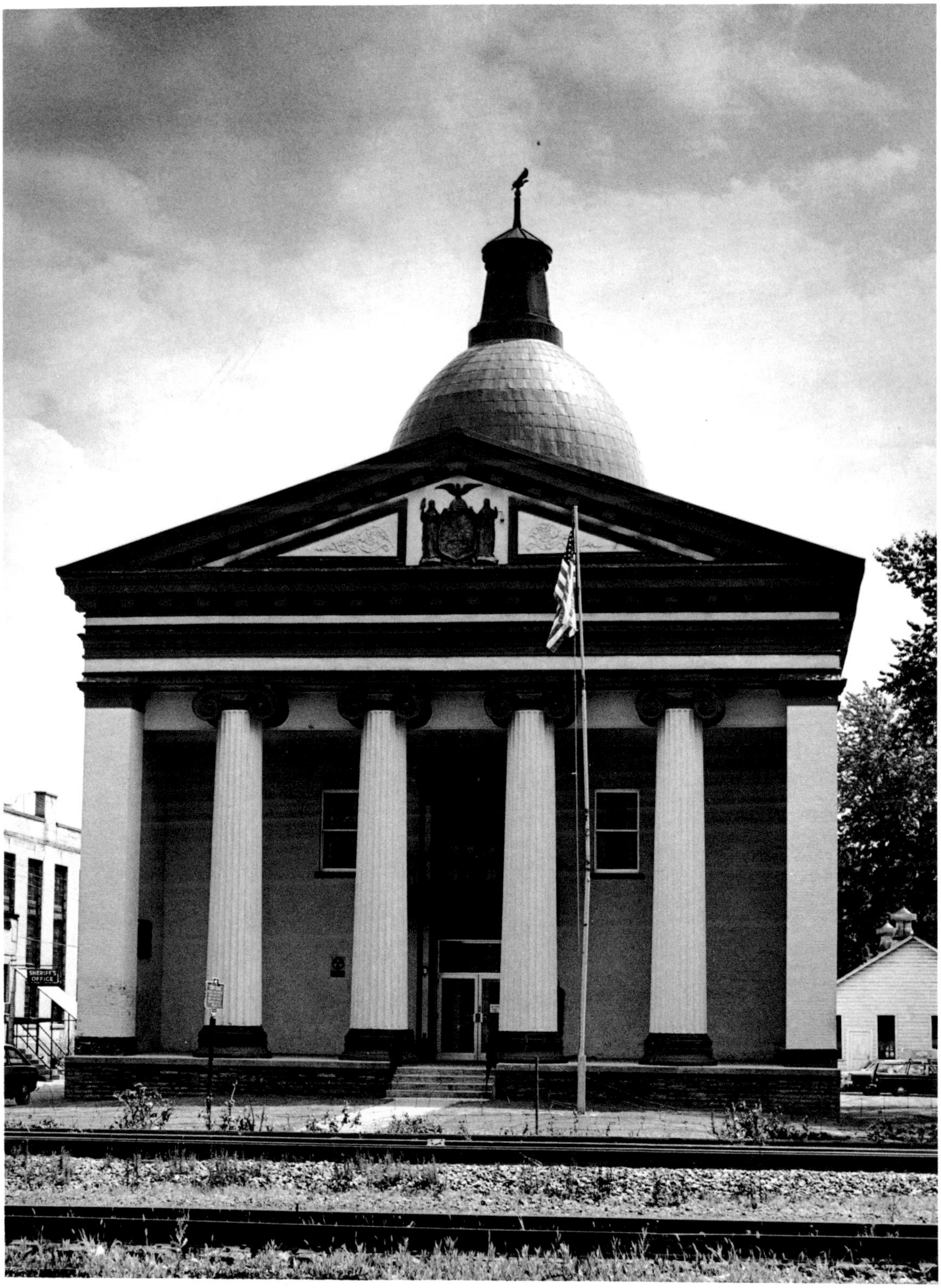
SHERIFF'S OFFICE

father had never objected to its use by the public. Not so his son, who now closed it to trespassing, and when the public ignored his ban, went to court. His action earned him the enmity of his neighbors, and he was strongly criticized in newspaper editorials throughout the state.

The Three Mile Point episode would have been forgotten in time if Cooper had not set out to remedy what he considered the defects in the American character. He did this in a number of writings, especially two novels, *Homeward Bound* and *Home as Found,* in which the noble, magnanimous, aristocratic landowner-hero and his English friends are contrasted with the mass of degraded, buffoon-like Americans. Even by the free-wheeling standards of that day, the reviews that greeted the two novels were extremely vitriolic and unrestrained.

Cooper responded with a flurry of libel suits, which he prosecuted himself, and so skillfully that he won most of them. The first of those suits to be argued in the Fonda courtroom was against Andrew Barber of the *Otsego Republican,* in which the judge directed a verdict of four hundred dollars in favor of Cooper. The judgment was appealed by Barber but upheld by the Supreme Court. Cooper was not satisfied with having his honor vindicated; he directed the sheriff to seize Barber's property, bankrupting the unfortunate editor, then gloated, "Barber is annihilated, and my letter [to the sheriff] has brushed off that mosquitoe."

Cooper's appearances in the courthouses of New York were to take him twice more into the one at Fonda. James Watson Webb, editor of the *Morning Chronicle and New York Inquirer,* wrote in his review of the two offending novels that the author was "a base-minded caitiff, who has traduced his country for filthy lucre . . . a traitor to national pride and national character." According to Webb, Cooper's noble landowner-hero was only a thinly disguised attempt by the author to pass himself off to the reader as a person of aristocratic descent, when in fact he was the son of a New Jersey laborer who had migrated to Cooperstown after he had failed in his trade as a wheelwright. The father at least was an honest man, conceded Webb, but the novelist was a viper, and all true Americans should pray that he would soon leave America once more, "never again to disgrace with his presence a land to which he has proved an ingrate. . . ." Cooper, of course, sued Webb for libel.

Although the offending review had appeared in 1838, within a week after the second of the two books was published, the libel case did not come up for trial until the November 1841 term of the circuit court for Montgomery County. By that time Cooper had two more suits pending before the same court, both against the noted editor and politician Thurlow Weed. Weed had first roused Cooper's spleen when he took the side of the author's neighbors in the Three Mile Point controversy. Later, when Cooper began his barrage of libel suits against editors, Weed printed an editorial claiming that Cooper's intention was to support himself by judgments against newspapers throughout the state. "There was a period in the springtime of his popularity," wrote Weed, "when Mr. Cooper, strong in the deserved favor of the public, bore with equal equanimity their praise and reproof. Now on the slightest occasion, he breaks forth into all the irritability and petty peevishness which ever attended the consciousness of a waning reputation." Cooper commenced an action for civil damages, and persuaded the authorities to secure an indictment against Weed for criminal libel as well.

Webb, like Weed, had also been charged with criminal libel. His case on the criminal libel charge was heard first, and Cooper was so confident by now of his ability as a prosecutor that he offered his services to the court in trying Webb, but Judge John Willard refused to permit such an unorthodox procedure. The prosecution quickly established the text of the libel, its publication, and rested its case. Judge Willard then ruled that the defense might submit in evidence those parts of the novels that it claimed justified the passages in the reviews that Cooper complained were libelous. This judicial ruling resulted in the defense's reading to the jury, not selected passages, but the entire text of both novels, a numbing monologue that required eleven hours and was followed by ten hours of summation by the prosecuting attorney, who commented at length on the text of the books. One editor, who had already been sued by Cooper, commented, "Can the reader . . . imagine a more grievous torture than that to which the Court and Jury were subjected during the reading of Mr. Cooper's stupid and slanderous trash? . . . Oh, it was too much—five jurymen are supposed to have been carried out fainting."

When this grueling performance was over, Judge Willard charged the weary jury, stating that the important question was whether Webb had confined himself to criticism of the author, or whether he had gone beyond criticism of the work to assail the character of the man. If Webb's comments were directed only at the author, then there were no grounds to sustain the indictment. "It is the privilege of Editors and Reviewers, to use the strongest language, the severest invective and the most poignant satire and ridicule against an author when reviewing his Books. . . . There should be no restriction upon the Reviewer so long as he does not abuse this privilege. . . ."

The jury was unable to decide on a verdict, but it appeared that this was because of a single holdout, who shared a friend with Cooper, and who insisted that Webb not be acquitted. All the other jurors, it was said, were ready to bring in a verdict of not guilty within five minutes of leaving the courtroom.

A second and third trial prolonged the case for two years, until November 1843, when Judge Willard ordered a trial before defense counsel was prepared, barred the reading of the novels, and abruptly sent the jury out to deliberate. In ten minutes it returned with a verdict of not guilty.

In the interim, the cases against Thurlow Weed had come to trial, immediately after the deadlocked first trial of editor Webb. Weed was in Albany and not represented by counsel when his cases were reached. His daughter was critically ill, and he had been advised by her doctors not to leave her side. When this information was sent to the court, it won him a single day's delay in the trial for civil libel, but the following day Cooper insisted that the action proceed, and that he be permitted to enter a default judgment against Weed. Although he was technically completely within his rights, Cooper's spiteful insistence on vengeance against a man in a very vulnerable position was taking an extremely unfair advantage of an adversary. After being awarded four hundred dollars in damages, he tried to push his conquest even further by threatening to send the sheriff after Weed, who, however, promptly paid.

James Fenimore Cooper ultimately succeeded by his litigation in silencing his critics; they just stopped reviewing his books. Cooper, however, kept on writing. His novel *The Two Admirals* appeared in 1842 (Thurlow Weed read it during one of Cooper's cases against him for criminal libel) and was well received. But in typical Cooper fashion, the author was convinced that *The Two Admirals* was praised because he had taught the reviewers a lesson and not because it was a better book.

Work on the courthouse that witnessed Cooper's libel suits began in the summer of 1836, early in August. Just four months later, on December 3, two workmen completed the tinning of the dome, and the building was closed in for the winter with the exterior complete except for the Ionic columns for the front porch. Some trouble had developed over supplying both the lumber and specifications for the columns, and so they were not put in place until well after the rest of the building was completed.

There was apparently much pressure to get the county records transferred from the old courthouse at Johnstown to make the change of county seats official, and so work on the clerk's office was given some precedence. In May 1837 the old records, dating back to 1772, were loaded into the wagon of George Yancey, who hauled them to Fonda and was paid $1.25 for his services. (The abandoned courthouse at Johnstown again became a county-seat courthouse when Montgomery County was divided and the northern part became Fulton County.)

Although extensive records of the construction of the Fonda courthouse survive, they do not add much to our knowledge of what the courthouse was like when it was young. So many hundred pounds of plaster, so many feet of cornice, wood floors laid—it does not make a picture, except to give an impression that there was a considerable flurry of work going on to get things in order for the 1837 term of court. The old records do inform us that the old courtroom was a spacious one, sixty-two feet by fifty-three feet, with windows nearly ten feet tall. The courtroom took up most of the second floor; almost all the rest of the space seems to have been occupied by jury rooms and the judge's office. We have hardly a clue to what the courtroom looked like: an unexplained bill for Doric columns raises the strong likelihood that these were used in the courtroom, either behind the judge's bench or at the four corners of the courtroom.

The remodelings (the building was extensively remodeled in 1910 and 1911) that left the interior unrecognizable hardly affected the outside until 1966, when the tall windows on both the first and second floors were greatly shortened because of the changes inside. Otherwise the exterior is very much as it was a hundred and forty years ago, when the first session of court sat in the building. James Fenimore Cooper would have no trouble recognizing it today.

NEW YORK COUNTY

The old New York County Courthouse stands, in sharp contrast, behind New York City's delicate Federal-period city hall. The courthouse seems now a rather nondescript building, still being used for governmental purposes despite periodic threats to demolish and replace it. The overall impression one gets from it is one of grime and grubbiness—which is probably very fitting, because the building is a monument to William Marcy ("Boss") Tweed, whose name has become a synonym for political corruption.

Closer study of the courthouse reveals some occasionally attractive architectural details that excite admiration despite the grime around them. This legacy of Tweed's to the city of New York consists of four floors, each of which has its own points of interest and its incongruities. There is a temporary roof of sheet metal above the fourth floor, placed there more than ninety years ago as a substitute for the dome that was canceled when the "Tweed Ring" fell from power. The fourth floor is empty now. Its rooms are damp and cold in winter and blazing hot in summer, but a bathtub and plumbing fixtures remain from the time when the caretaker of the building had his apartment in this uncomfortable location.

On the second and third floors are the courtrooms, judges' chambers, and clerks' offices. One of the offices has tiled floors with intricate designs and an elegant fireplace. Many of the rooms have massive oak doors with frosted glass panes etched with the seal of the city of New York. Each of the courtrooms is graced by a handsome judge's bench with a shell-like canopy. The ceilings on these floors are almost fifteen

feet high and are decorated with geometric and floral designs. Tall, narrow windows add to the visual height of the courtrooms and give the occupants a generous view of City Hall Park or of City Hall.

Central to the design of the building is open space in the middle, a colonnaded well that extends from the ground floor to skylights that substitute for what would have been the dome had the building been completed. The columns around this well are trompe l'oeil and decrease in size on the upper floors. The lighting fixtures are quietly cursed by all who have to work by their poor illumination; they seem to have been installed soon after Tweed's time.

Although the courthouse is so closely tied with his name, it was not a product of Tweed's fertile imagination. It had been authorized by the state legislature in 1858 and begun in 1861; $150,000 was appropriated, and it was expected that that sum would almost take care of all costs. In justice to the genial boss, it should be noted that the courthouse was well on its way toward the million-dollar mark by 1866, when he gained absolute control of the county board of supervisors and the comptroller's office went to his colleague Richard H. Connolly, more familiarly known as Slippery Dick. Tweed found his opportunity for municipal graft vastly increased soon after, when another crony, Abraham Oakey ("The Elegant Oakey") Hall, became mayor. Most of the Tweed Ring's graft—variously estimated to have totaled between thirty and two hundred million dollars—came from the kiting and manipulation of building contracts, and the courthouse offered just one more opportunity for boodle.

A student of the Tweed Ring has commented

that though the boss was not honest, he was always level—in other words, he kept his word. And in his own way, Tweed did carry through on his promise to the people of New York: He had told them that he would build them a courthouse that was worthy of the city and a fitting monument to the law. Some funds appropriated for building the courthouse were used for that purpose, but vouchers were grossly inflated, and the Ring obtained its percentage through kickbacks from contractors or inflated profits from corporations controlled by the Ring. Some of the workers on the payrolls actually performed their duties, but a great many were paid only for their political canvassing for

Tweed and those who shared in the swindle.

A great many talented contractors worked on the courthouse during the Tweed regime. Plastering was contracted out to Andrew J. Gervey, one-time grand marshal of Tammany Hall, who became known during the Tweed reign as the Prince of Plasterers. Gervey did all the plastering in the courthouse—and it came to quite a good number of dollars, which was strange, since the courthouse was supposed to be an all-marble structure. Or perhaps not so strange, for the marble was to have been supplied by a Tweed company. In any event, Gervey's bills over three years added up to $2,870,464.06—and more than a million of those dollars were for repairs to plastering he had done a couple of years, or a couple of months, before. An 1871 pamphlet, *The House That Tweed Built,* had a jingle about Gervey:

> This is the Plasterer, Gervey by name,
> The Gervey who made it his little game
> To lay on the plaster, and plaster it thick
> On the roof
>   And the walls
>   And the wood
>   And the brick
> Of the wonderful House that TWEED built.

The plumbing contract went to John Keyser & Co., a man who had failed in business several times before he made a happy arrangement with Tweed. Keyser's bills amounted to something around $1,500,000; then there was an additional voucher for $50,000 for repairs to the plumbing already installed.

The expense of furnishing the courthouse compared favorably with the costs of construction. Carpets were an important part of the decor of a courtroom in the Victorian era, and

Robert Gregg, submitting his bill of $47,010.52 for replacement in 1869 of carpets only a year or two old, felt his conscience impelled him to explain why new carpets were needed so soon. It must be understood, he said, "that carpets in public offices wear out quickly, and that the New York Bench has a very capricious taste on the subject of carpets—the judges requiring frequent changes of patterns of which their eyes become weary."

Awnings for the courthouse windows were provided by James W. Smith, who charged $150.00 for each awning—and insisted they were worth it—although competitors estimated their value at $12.50. But even at $150.00 each, Smith could not explain why he was paid $41,746.00 on his contract for awnings, since the courthouse had nowhere near two hundred seventy-eight windows.

At the same time Smith was installing his deluxe awnings, Matthew Kane was putting in window sash at a monthly cost of $11,155.00. Thermometers for the courthouse cost $7,500.00, and the city paid $179,729.60 for three tables and forty chairs. In time even the imagination of the members of the Tweed Ring failed, and on one of the vouchers—all of which were printed by a Tweed company for a mere $186,000.00 for the lot—some Tammany clerk noted this courthouse expense: "Brooms, etc. . . . $41,190.95."

When the Tweed gravy train came to a halt in 1871, an investigating committee claimed that $13,416,932.00 had been spent on the courthouse to that time, as best it could determine. The Democratic Tammany machine in New York denied that the figure was anywhere near that amount; they admitted expenditures of only $8,223,979.89, and pointed out that most of that —$6,052,045.96—had been spent for furniture, those carpets and thermometers, and other miscellaneous items.

Tweed had begun his political career as a New York alderman at the age of twenty-eight, and at once showed a remarkable genius for grafting. He organized a faction in Tammany Hall to oppose Fernando Wood, a notoriously corrupt mayor, and so covered himself with a patina of virtue when Wood was defeated. He had himself made a member of various key boards and commissions, and from these posts was able to get his crony Peter Sweeny made district attorney, and other henchmen named to influential positions. After he was made Democratic central committee chairman for the county in 1860, he got A. Oakey Hall into the district attorney's office, and thereafter his position as boss in New York City politics was supreme.

Tweed rose even higher. Elected a state senator in 1867, he dictated the nomination of the Democratic candidate for governor the next year, and so gained political control of the state. In his hotel suite in Albany, the Tweed Ring decided that all bills against New York City or New York County should be 50 percent fraudulent; that is, they should be kited so that half would go to the contractor, half to the Ring. Later, as the Ring became impatient at the slow rate at which the millions were coming in, the proportion was raised to 85 percent fraud on the bills.

The Tweed Ring was able to nominate governors, to control mayors, to buy judges and aldermen, state legislators and judges. It is not surprising if Tweed felt secure in his power, but in the spring of 1871 two disgruntled county officials turned over to the *New York Times*

courtroom spectators. When the case was retried in November of 1873, the jury had been carefully screened for undesirables and Tweed supporters, and this time Tweed was convicted on fifty-one of the fifty-four charges and sentenced to twelve years in prison and a fine, though this was reduced on appeal to one year.

On his release from prison, he was immediately arrested again, this time to await disposition of the civil suits against him. After six months Tweed's confidence cracked at last, and he fled. It was not a very difficult jailbreak; he had been accustomed to go for a carriage ride every afternoon with the warden, after which they would drive to Tweed's own home for dinner with Mrs. Tweed. One December day in 1875 he simply walked out of the house while his custodians were enjoying themselves, and made his way to New Jersey, where he lived in disguise while awaiting the outcome of his case.

The verdict in the case came in March 1876; $6,537,117.38 was assessed against the once-powerful boss; this was two-thirds of the amount demanded in the complaint plus interest. Tweed fled to Spain, was identified and extradited, and by November was back in jail, under much closer and less sympathetic guard.

There had been a time when he had been a millionaire; now he was unable to pay the large judgment against him. Since the beginning of his troubles his health had declined rapidly; in prison he suffered from heart trouble, diabetes, and bronchitis. He gave extensive testimony about many of his crooked operations, hoping that thereby he could gain a measure of leniency, but this gesture did not help him. He died, broken and bitter about being betrayed and abandoned by his old supporters, on April 12,

proofs of the Ring's swindles. The material was published, a Committee of Seventy was formed to take action, and in December, Tweed was indicted for misfeasance; this was soon followed by two cases for civil damages, asking recovery of more than seven million dollars. By this time the Ring had collapsed; some of its leaders had fled the country, but Tweed stood his ground, draped in a cloak of injured innocence, prepared to withstand legal attack.

Tweed's lawyers did not offer any evidence in rebuttal when the first case came to trial in January 1873, but only contended that the statute creating the board of audit—whose functions were involved in the trial—was unconstitutional. When the jury returned after seventeen hours to report that it could not reach an agreement, there were cries of bribery from

1878, not long before his fifty-fifth birthday.

The old courthouse was only one money-making project among many undertaken during the high-flying days when the Tweed Ring was sucking money out of every municipal and county contract in New York, but it is one of the very few that have survived. How long it will remain is problematic. Not long ago the municipal government talked again of razing the building and replacing it with a modern structure, more suitable to the needs of today. Preservationists responded by arguing that it is cheaper to remodel an existing sound structure than to wreck it and start from scratch, that the Tweed courthouse is basically sound, and that a city's architecture—especially in its administrative and judicial center—should be a harmonious mix of the old and the new. The recent financial straits of New York City may mean that the courthouse has a reprieve and will not be replaced soon. For the more distant future the signs are less clear, but it seems likely that one day the old building will go the way of William Marcy Tweed.

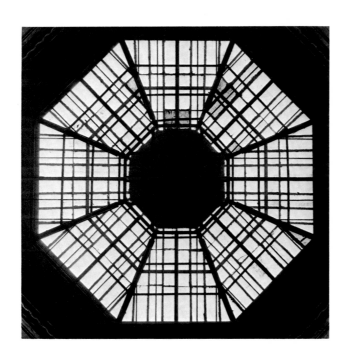

NIAGARA COUNTY

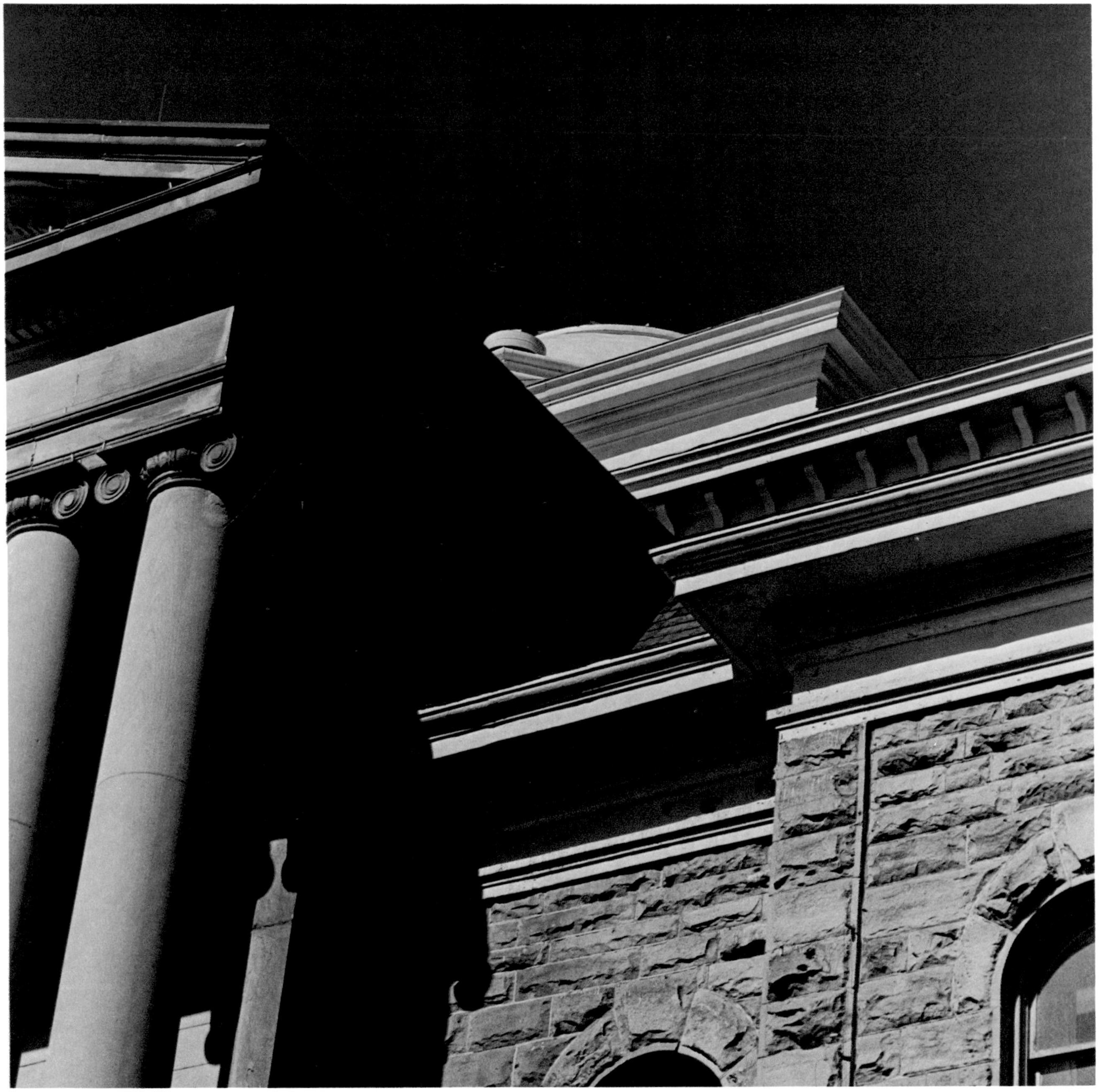

Niagara County lies on the far western border of New York State; only the Niagara River separates it from Canada, and Niagara Falls (the American half) is within the county. Buffalo was by far the most important city of the new county when it was created in 1808, and it became the county seat.

Court sessions were held in a tavern in Buffalo until a wooden courthouse was far enough along toward completion to be occupied in 1809. This building was damaged when the British burned Buffalo in 1813, but it was repaired and continued in use for twenty-odd years more.

In 1821 Erie County, which included Buffalo, was formed from the southern part of Niagara County, and Lewiston became the

temporary seat of the diminished Niagara County. A year later a site selection commission settled on Lockport as the permanent county seat, and the first courthouse there was occupied in 1825.

The choice of Lockport was not a capricious one. The Erie Canal was being dug at the time, and Lockport not only was on its route but was the site of the canal's highest set of locks. No prophet was needed to predict that Lockport was destined to boom—and boom it did, prospering for years from the canal traffic.

The 1825 courthouse continued in use for sixty years, but old age and increasing county business eventually required its replacement. The old courthouse was torn down in 1885, and the courthouse that still serves Niagara County was completed a year later.

ONEIDA
COUNTY

When Oneida County was created in 1798 the legislature stipulated that a courthouse and jail should be built within a mile of Fort Stanwix. Courts were held in a schoolhouse until 1802, but by then the need for a real courthouse was becoming urgent. In order to secure the county seat permanently for his town, a landowner donated a site in Whitesboro village in Whitestown to be used solely for a courthouse and jail. Another prosperous landowner made a similar gift of land in the village of Rome, near Fort Stanwix.

The legislature prevented any conflict between the two towns by providing that Oneida be a half-shired county, with seats in both Rome and Whitestown. Courthouses were built in both places in 1807.

Whitestown, however, remained a county seat

Whitesboro

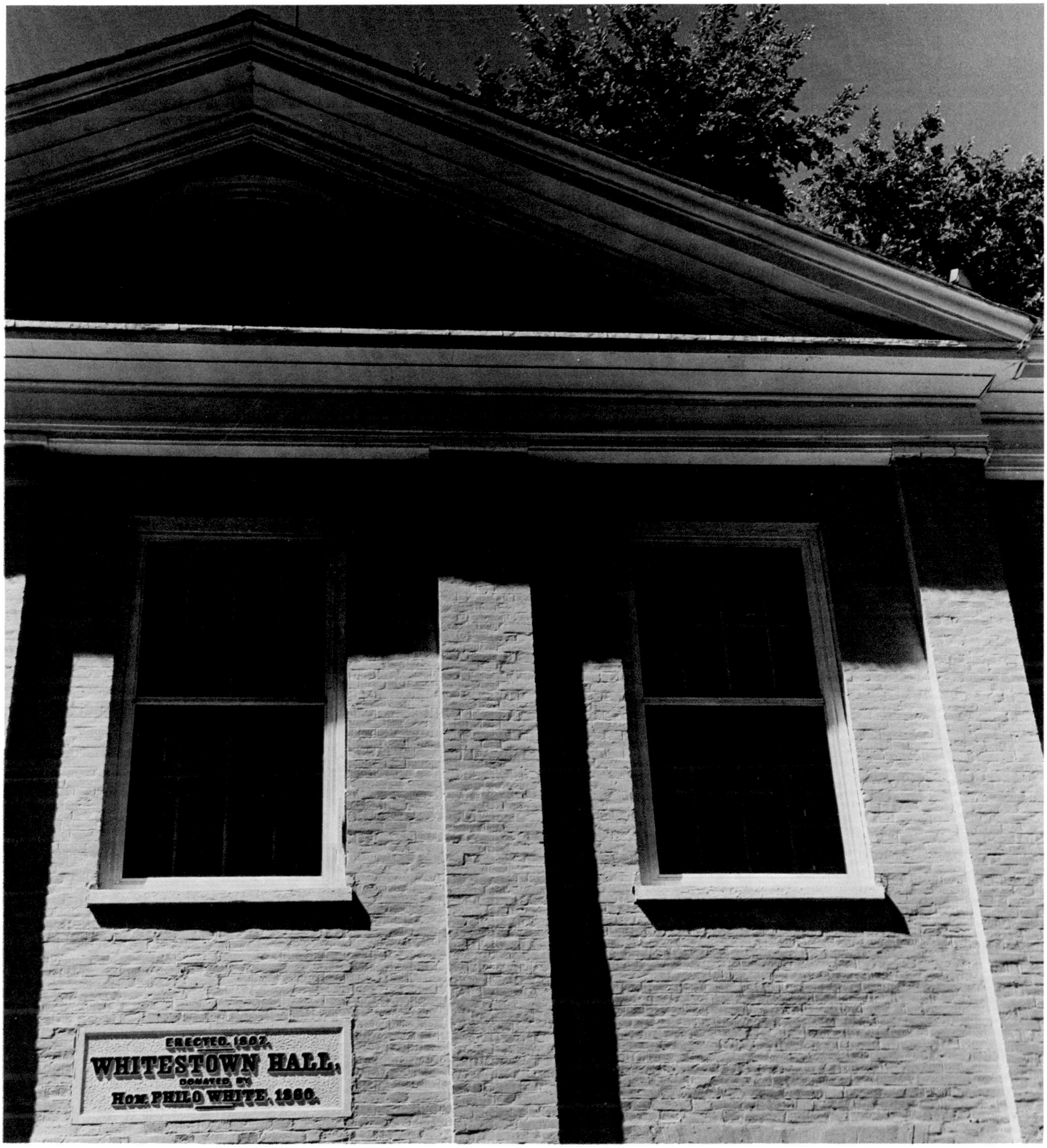
ERECTED. 1807,
WHITESTOWN HALL,
DONATED BY
HON. PHILO WHITE, 1860.

Whitesboro

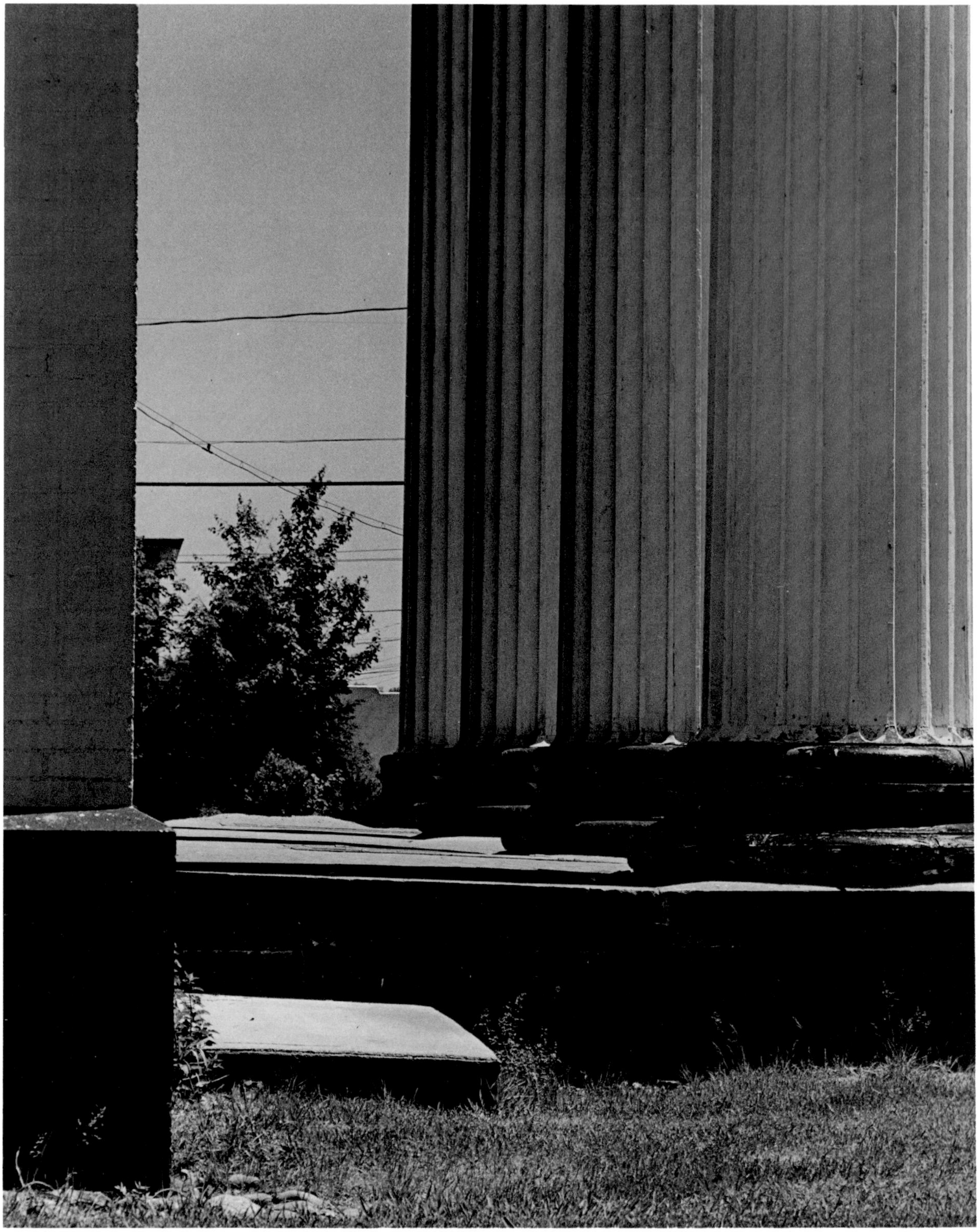

Rome

for only a short time. Even as early as 1802, sessions of the United States district court were being held in Utica, and soon the Whitestown county seat was transferred there. Nevertheless, the old courthouse in Whitesboro remains in use, the oldest public building in the county. When it ceased to be a county courthouse, its site and the building reverted to the donor's estate, and in 1860 were conveyed to Whitestown; the old courthouse is still serving as the town hall.

The 1807 courthouse in Rome was not quite so long lived. It burned down in 1848 and was replaced in 1851 by a Classical-Revival structure on the same site. This building, a century and a quarter later, is still an active county courthouse.

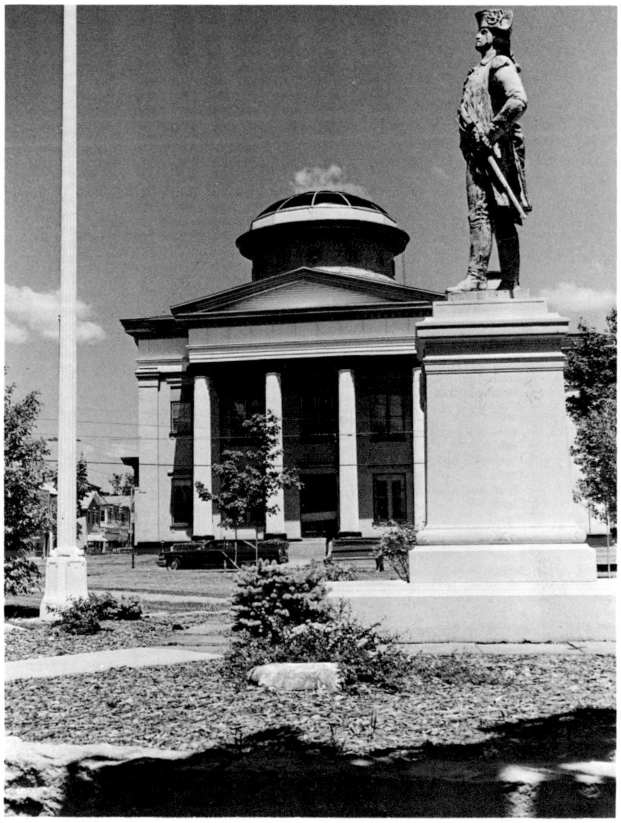

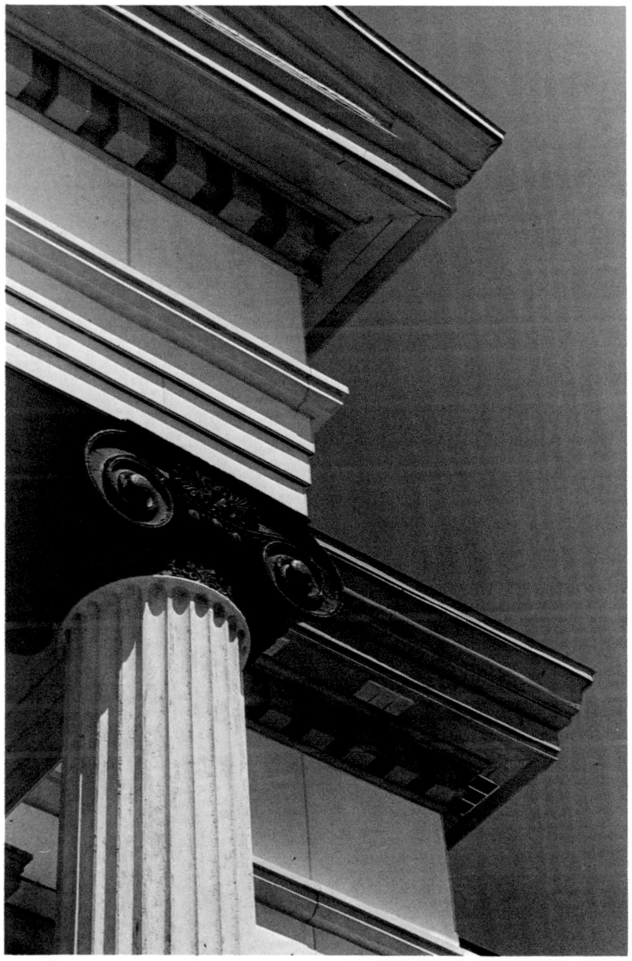

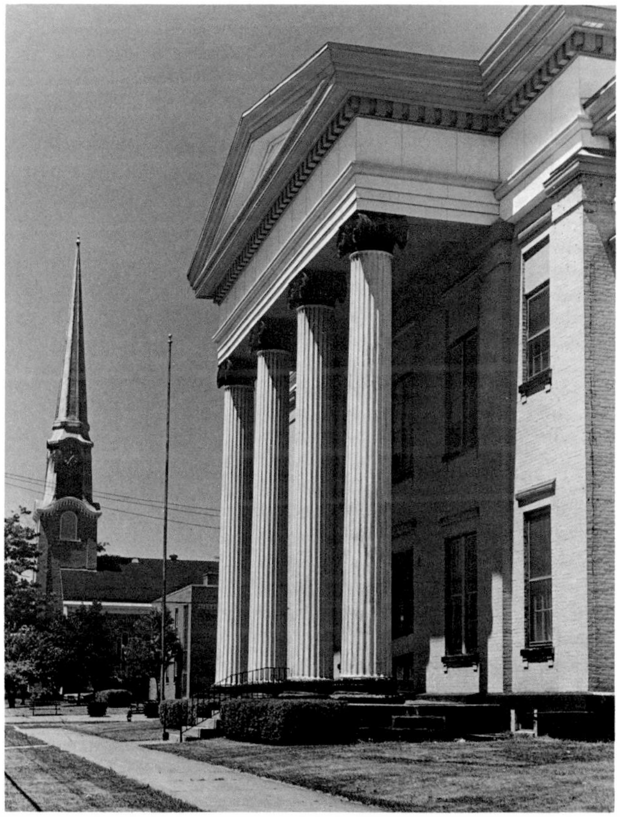

Rome

ONTARIO COUNTY

1824

Canandaigua, the county seat of Ontario County, possesses not just one historic courthouse but two: the old one, built in 1824 and long since retired as a judicial seat but still in active use as the Canandaigua Town Hall, and the new building that replaced it in 1858 and is still the Ontario County Courthouse. The two buildings are diagonally across the street from one another, and each has seen its share of New York courtroom drama. For contrast, a modern federal courthouse stands directly across the street from the "new" courthouse.

The new courthouse was just fifteen years old when, in 1873, it was the scene of its most publicized trial, that of Susan B. Anthony, the great woman-suffrage pioneer. Anthony had already given twenty years of her life to the cause of votes for women when she decided in 1870 to test how far the Fourteenth and Fifteenth Amendments applied to her sex. Till then her travels had kept her from meeting residence requirements, but by the time the 1872 presidential election neared she had been at home caring for an ailing sister long enough to meet the requirements for voting at Rochester. She was further encouraged by the Republican platform, which declared that the party was "mindful of its obligation to the women of America."

This pledge had led Anthony and several other suffragettes to campaign vigorously for the reelection of Ulysses S. Grant, and they planned to climax their efforts by testing both the constitutional amendments and the sincerity of the Republican party assurance. So, on November 1, 1872, fifty women of Rochester marched to the registration offices to enroll as voters. All were turned away except sixteen who went with Anthony to the Eighth Ward office. Even there they were enrolled only over the strong objections of a Democratic inspector of elections, but Anthony's reading of the Fourteenth and Fifteenth Amendments and the New York state election law to the election board persuaded the majority of the inspectors, and the women's names were duly entered. Two days later a Democratic newspaper demanded that the Eighth Ward's inspectors of election be prosecuted for misfeasance in office.

Very shortly that newspaper and other opponents of female suffrage had something more upsetting to get exercised about. On election day, November 5, all sixteen women appeared at Rochester's Eighth Ward polling-place and voted. Nothing happened until the twenty-eighth, but then, on Thanksgiving Day, arrest warrants were issued against Susan Anthony and her associates. The chief marshal offered to let Anthony go unattended to the offices of the United States court commissioner, but she insisted on being escorted, probably to attract attention to her case as well as to embarrass the marshal by making him be seen escorting a middle-aged woman through the streets of Rochester.

After several hours of waiting in the commissioner's anteroom, Anthony was called in, and after long questioning she and the other fifteen women were released on bail of five hundred dollars each. Only Anthony was brought to trial, the government declining to prosecute the others.

In January of 1873 the federal grand jury returned an indictment of two counts, charging Anthony with "knowingly, wrongfully and un-

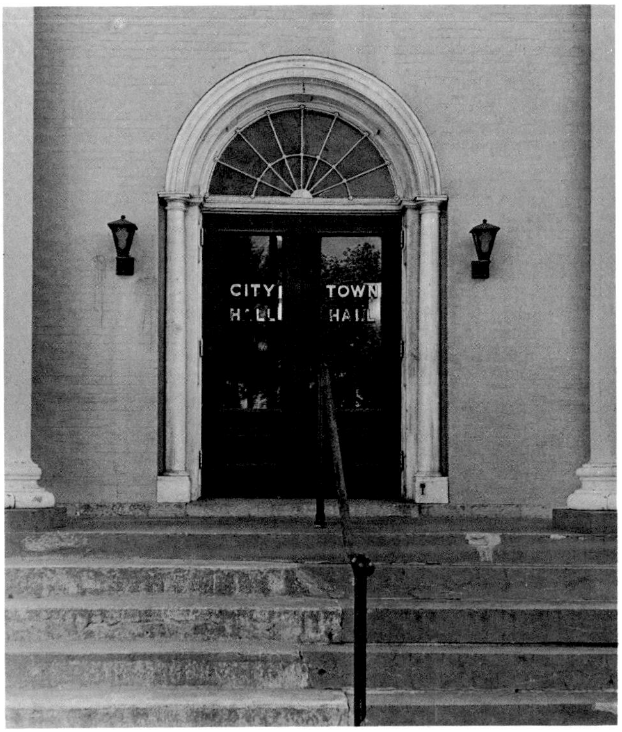
CITY
TOWN

1824

lawfully voting for a Representative in the Congress of the United States . . . without having a lawful right to vote in said election district (the said Susan B. Anthony being then and there a person of the female sex). . . ." She pleaded not guilty to the indictment, and the case was set for trial at the next sitting of the circuit court.

Before the court met, Anthony had a heavy schedule of speaking engagements to keep, and at Fort Wayne, Indiana, the strain of her work, together with anxiety over the health of her sister, caused her to collapse while she was delivering a speech. But she recovered rapidly, went on to continue her tour, and then returned to Rochester to begin a campaign in Monroe County that would have put most politicians to shame. In less than two months she had, single-handedly, made a suffragette assault on all

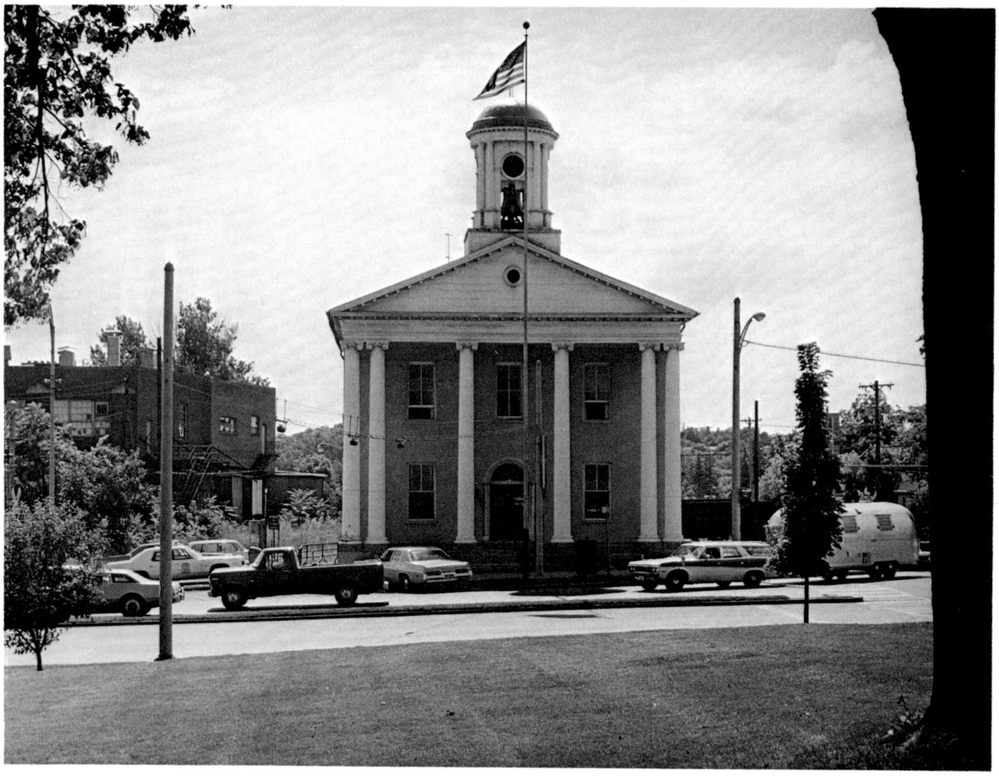

1824

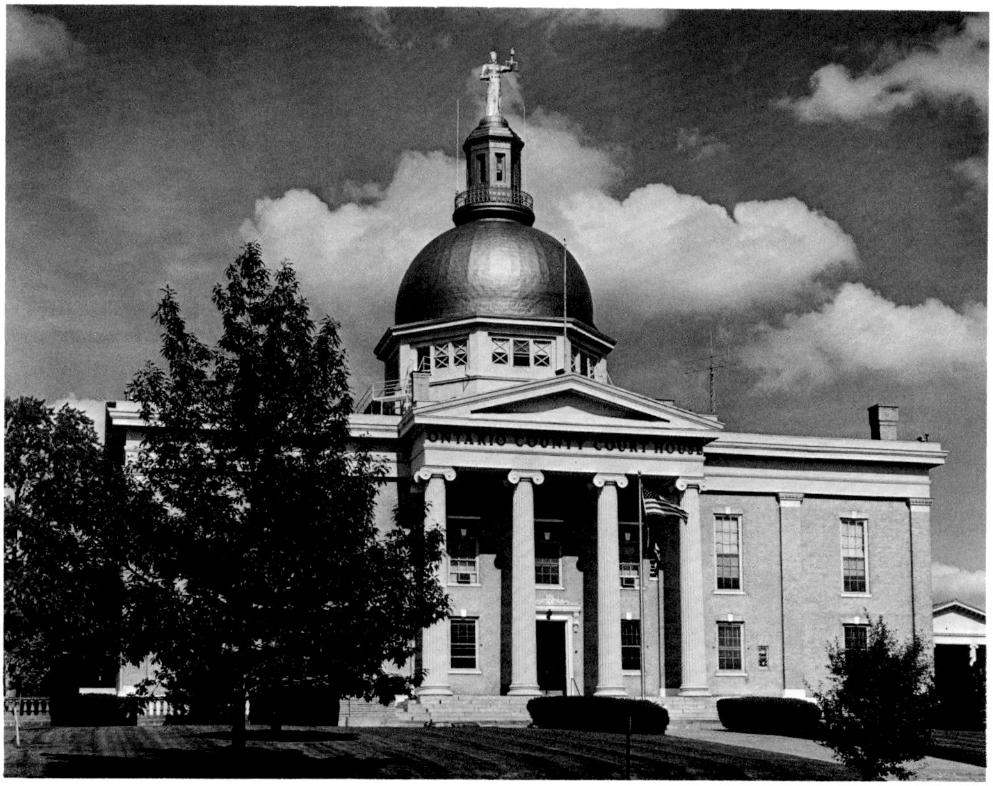
ONTARIO COUNTY COURT HOUS

1858

twenty-nine post office districts of the county. So effective were her speeches that the United States attorney asked for a change of venue to another county. And so it was that the trial of Susan B. Anthony came to the courthouse at Canandaigua; the circuit court granted a change of venue to Ontario County, and at the same time granted a postponement of the trial till June 17, 1873.

The change of venue did not help the prosecution any as far as avoiding an informed public was concerned. Anthony set out on another whirlwind speaking tour, this time in Ontario County, and spoke in twenty-one of the county's post offices, while another suffragette, Matilda Gage, was speaking in another sixteen. When the trial date arrived, not only did most of the people of Ontario County, including most of the jury panel, know of Susan B. Anthony and her message, but people far away had heard of the case. The suffragette leader had a national reputation even before her arrest, and the case had drawn considerable newspaper comment. One of those who had been watching developments with great interest was former President Millard Fillmore, who came from Buffalo to be present on the first day of the trial, a considerable trip for a seventy-three-year-old man.

Unfortunately, the record of the trial does not give the number of challenges used by the government in an attempt to secure an unbiased jury. Certainly almost all residents of the county were at least familiar with the case, for most had seen or heard of Susan Anthony. Nevertheless, United States Attorney Richard Crowley obtained a jury, and after reading the indictment to them, eliminated the question of her sex at the time of voting with heavy humor: "At

that time she was a woman. I suppose there will be no question about that." He then went on to inform the jury that the government based its case upon the premise that the defendant had acted unlawfully regardless of whether she knew her voting was prohibited by law. In other words, she need not have had criminal intent in casting her ballot; the mere fact of having cast her ballot subjected her to penalty by law.

Susan Anthony's counsel, on the other hand, said the defense held that she was entitled to vote, and that even if she were not so entitled, she could not be convicted unless she had acted in bad faith. Anthony had an excellent defender, Henry R. Selden, a former judge of the New York Court of Appeals, whom she had retained immediately after she had registered to vote. To support his contention that Anthony had acted in good faith in voting, Selden testified under oath that she had consulted him concerning her rights under the Fourteenth and Fifteenth Amendments before she voted, and that he had given his opinion that the two amendments secured to women the right to vote. However, when Selden tried to call Anthony to testify, the court ruled that she was not competent to testify in her own behalf. The court, however, apparently considered Anthony competent to testify against herself, for it permitted the prosecution to read her statement made before the United States commissioner at the time of her arrest, in which she had denied that Selden had advised her to vote.

The constitutional position on which the defense rested was a powerful one, though contrary to contemporary understanding of the Fourteenth Amendment. Selden argued that "all citizens of a State, who are bound by its laws, are entitled to an equal voice in the making and execution of such laws." Women, like all other citizens, should have an equal voice in creating the rules they are required to obey. Selden pointed out that to deny political rights to women was to reduce them to political servitude —and political servitude was inconsistent with their status as citizens, for "the citizens of America are equal as fellow citizens and as joint tenants in the sovereignty." And, he said, since the Fourteenth Amendment declared in its first section that all persons born or naturalized in the United States of America were citizens, it included women; and therefore the Fifteenth Amendment, conferring on all citizens the right to vote, necessarily gave the vote to women.

1858

A weakness of Selden's position was that the second clause of the Fourteenth Amendment, which outlined the sanctions to be brought against a state refusing to grant the rights guaranteed by the amendment, stated those sanctions in terms of the male inhabitants of the state. Selden argued this away as an oversight on the part of the drafters of the amendment, who had been influenced by the wording of the original Constitution. It was only the broad scope of the first section that was positive law, said Selden (the second, he claimed, was only to compel compliance). And finally, Selden asserted, even if the writers of the Fourteenth Amendment had not specifically meant to include women, the amendment was broad enough to do so. After all, he asked, was not Magna Carta a much more potent body of liberties than the barons who prepared it dreamed it could be?

Selden's efforts went for nothing. Associate Justice Ward Hunt entirely rejected Selden's argument and held that state law governed who might vote in both state and national elections. The Fourteenth Amendment, he ruled, had not changed this principle in regard to woman suffrage. Hunt then directed the jury to return a verdict of guilty, which they had no choice but to do. Selden's request that the jury be polled was denied. The next day, June 18, was set for sentencing.

The government had prevented Susan Anthony from testifying in her own behalf, and it had not taken the chance that a jury might rule in her favor, but she at last got her opportunity to speak when Justice Hunt asked whether she had anything to say before sentence was imposed. She did.

"Yes, your Honor, I have many things to say;

for in your ordered verdict of guilty, you have trampled underfoot every vital principle of our government. My natural rights, my civil rights, my political rights are all alike ignored. Robbed of the fundamental privileges of citizenship, I am degraded from the status of a citizen to that of a subject; not only myself individually but all of my sex are, by your Honor's verdict, doomed to political subjection under this so-called Republican government."

Continuing, she remarked on the court's refusing to let the jury consider the case: " . . . had your Honor submitted my case to the jury, as was clearly your duty, even then I should have had just cause to protest, for not one of those men was my peer, but each and every man of them was my political superior, hence in no way my peer." (Six years later just that sort of reasoning would be used by the Supreme Court of the United States in declaring invalid a West Virginia conviction of a black defendant by a jury from which blacks were excluded by state statute.)

Anthony continued with her statement of grievances, and after several attempts to stop her, Justice Hunt lapsed into silence and heard her out. He then sentenced her to pay a fine of a hundred dollars, but he did not order her jailed pending payment of the fine, probably because he well knew that Anthony's Quaker conscience would not permit her to pay it, and neither he nor the government wanted to have such a popular political prisoner on their hands.

Even so, the press was outraged by the trial and sentence, and the *New York Sun* proposed that Justice Hunt be impeached. Gifts of money from everywhere came to Anthony, and she used these to pay her attorney, to pay the fines of the

1858

inspectors of election who had been prosecuted for enrolling her as a voter, and to print a pamphlet of the proceedings of her trial, which was sent to newspapers across the nation. Local tradition says that the arm holding the scales on the statue of Justice on the courthouse dome fell to the ground the day Hunt passed sentence on Susan B. Anthony.

If Justice lost her arm that day, it was not because of age, for the statue was only fifteen years old at the time. The building had been begun in February 1857, after nearly a year during which the board of supervisors had been unable to make up their minds to build. They were moved to action, however, when they learned that the federal government would contribute $30,000 of the $40,000 estimated as needed for construction; their decision was made even easier when they discovered that the town of Canandaigua would buy the old courthouse for use as a town hall. The offer by the federal government to contribute so much toward a new building was obtained by an ingenious argument of proponents of a new courthouse. Canandaigua needed larger post office facilities, and the county also needed better federal court facilities. Both these needs, the argument continued, could be taken care of in a new and enlarged courthouse. The federal government rose to the bait and paid most of the cost of the new courthouse.

The board of supervisors accepted the courthouse on December 6, 1858, although some minor work remained to be done, and the building remained unchanged until 1908, when two wings were added at a cost of almost $126,000, an amount nearly three times the original cost of the building. Unhappily, the addition of the wings brought about remodeling inside the old building that destroyed the courtroom in which Susan Anthony was tried.

Today the Ontario County Courthouse no longer houses the federal courts or the post office; the new federal post office and courthouse stands directly across the street. Diagonally across the street is a smaller, less pretentious Greek-Revival building, with graceful columns supporting its pediment and an attractive cupola on its roof. This is Canandaigua's town hall—once the county courthouse—the building that was sold to the town in 1858, and in its day the scene of the trial of a rather notorious case.

William Morgan had joined the Masonic order but after a time had decided to withdraw and publicize the "secrets" of freemasonry. His intentions were well known, and so when he suddenly disappeared without explanation, suspicion soon centered on several members of his former lodge. In January of 1827, indictments were returned in the Ontario County Court of Oyer and Terminer against five men, charging them with kidnapping Morgan and with conspiring to kidnap him. The charge of kidnapping was later dropped, and because of guilty pleas, only one of the five came to trial on the conspiracy charge. The longest sentence given was two years in the county jail; the shortest was one month.

As for poor William Morgan, the suspicion is that someone got off very easily, for he was never heard from again and his body was never found. But the suspicious circumstances surrounding his disappearance and the failure of the trial at Canandaigua to clear up the mystery cast a cloud over the Masonic order. This eventually had an impact on national politics in the form of the Anti-Masonic party, which elected a couple of governors and had some small effect on a presidential election or two.

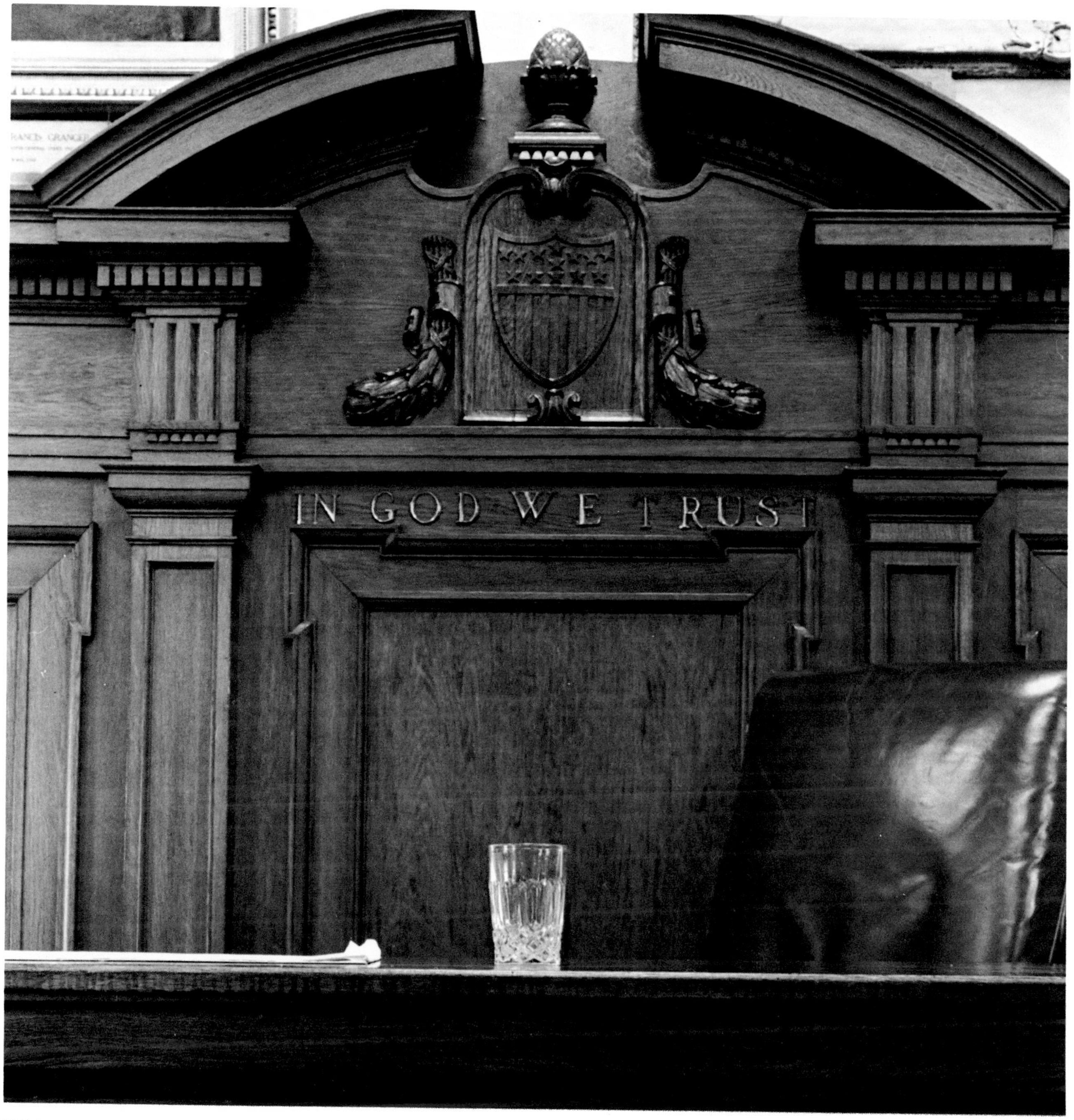
IN GOD WE TRUST
1858

ORANGE COUNTY

Orange County is half-shired, with its seats at Goshen and Newburgh. The courthouse in each town is well-mellowed by time and use; what is unique about the two is that they are twins, designed by the same architect, built on almost the same plan, and constructed at the same time (in 1841–42).

Orange is a very old county, established in 1683 (though no practical organizing work was done until 1703, when a first court session was held). The first and second courthouses were at Orangetown, but that village's reign as the county seat ended in 1737, when the assembly voted to build a courthouse and jail at Goshen and move the county seat to that town.

Goshen

But in time—and as so often happened in pre-automobile days, when travel was slower and access to the county seat more important—secessionist sentiment arose. The people of Newburgh and other northeastern towns demanded that a new county be created, until, after years of such agitation, the county board of supervisors agreed in November 1840 to have two county seats and to build two courthouses, one at Newburgh and a replacement for the one at Goshen. A local architect, Thornton M. Niven of Goshen, was paid $162 for his designs and specifications for both buildings, but as the photographs indicate, there was little difference between the two. One distinction: the jail at Goshen was in a separate building; the Newburgh courthouse had cells in the basement.

One unusual incident occurred during construction; work appeared to be going along well on the Goshen building in the fall of 1841 when it simply collapsed. It was put up again, but after the courthouse was finished and in use, there were ominous predictions that it would fall down again, most likely during a court session. The building, however, has stood ever since without a quiver.

More legend and folklore have collected around these two courthouses, it seems, than around most New York courthouses of the same vintage. For instance, there is a story that excavations during construction of the Goshen courthouse unearthed the remains of Claudius Smith, a Tory marauder during the Revolution who had been hanged by patriots in 1779 and whose body had been buried near an earlier courthouse. The tale has it that workmen filled Smith's skull with cement and sealed it in the wall above the entrance of the new (the present) courthouse. The reason for this macabre business is unexplained. Another bit of folklore is that an iron step leading to the men's room in the Goshen building once served as a weight on the hangman's rope. The legend can date from no earlier than the 1890s, when hanging ceased to be the manner of execution and the Goshen courthouse privies gave way to indoor plumbing. There is no iron step today, and the story is highly suspect.

When the two courthouses were built, each stood in villages in basically rural areas. Today they are within the New York urban-suburban complex. Fortunately, both of the old Greek-Revival buildings still have appropriate backdrops. Mid-nineteenth-century law and business offices surround the Goshen courthouse. The Newburgh courthouse is in a rectangular park with a handsome, though rather faded, residential section shaded by tall trees around it. Both are still serving their basic purposes well, while at the same time standing as monuments to an era gone by.

Newburgh

117

ORLEANS COUNTY

It was built rapidly and cheaply, and yet it is considered one of the most beautiful courthouse buildings in New York State. The Orleans County Courthouse at Albion is the epitome of Greek-Revival courthouse architecture; the building, with its pillared portico and rounded cupola, or dome, has from some positions the appearance of a temple rather than a workaday county court building.

When Orleans County was established in 1824, Albion became county seat, according to tradition, through a bit of trickery by some of the townsmen. The commissioners sent to consider claims of various villages to become the county seat arrived in the middle of a dry season. Albion men, forewarned, had dammed the creek above town and collected a good supply of water; when the commissioners arrived, the water was let go, and the commissioners were impressed by a busy village with water mills operating on a good head of water. Albion got the county seat.

When in 1856 it became necessary to replace the county's first courthouse, a building committee visited neighboring courthouses for ideas, but in the end turned to an Albion townsman, William V. N. Barlow, an architect of long experience, whose persistent use of cupolas had earned him the nickname Hickety-Rickety Barlow (though the connection now seems to be lost). But Barlow, whatever his idiosyncrasies, planned so well that near the end of 1857, as construction proceeded, the building committee was able to report that the $20,000 appropriated for the building would be more than adequate. To complete a courthouse for less than the original appropriation was unusual; so were the speed with which it had risen and the beauty of the completed structure. Add to these three one more noteworthy fact: Barlow was just short of ninety years old when his little gem was finished in 1858.

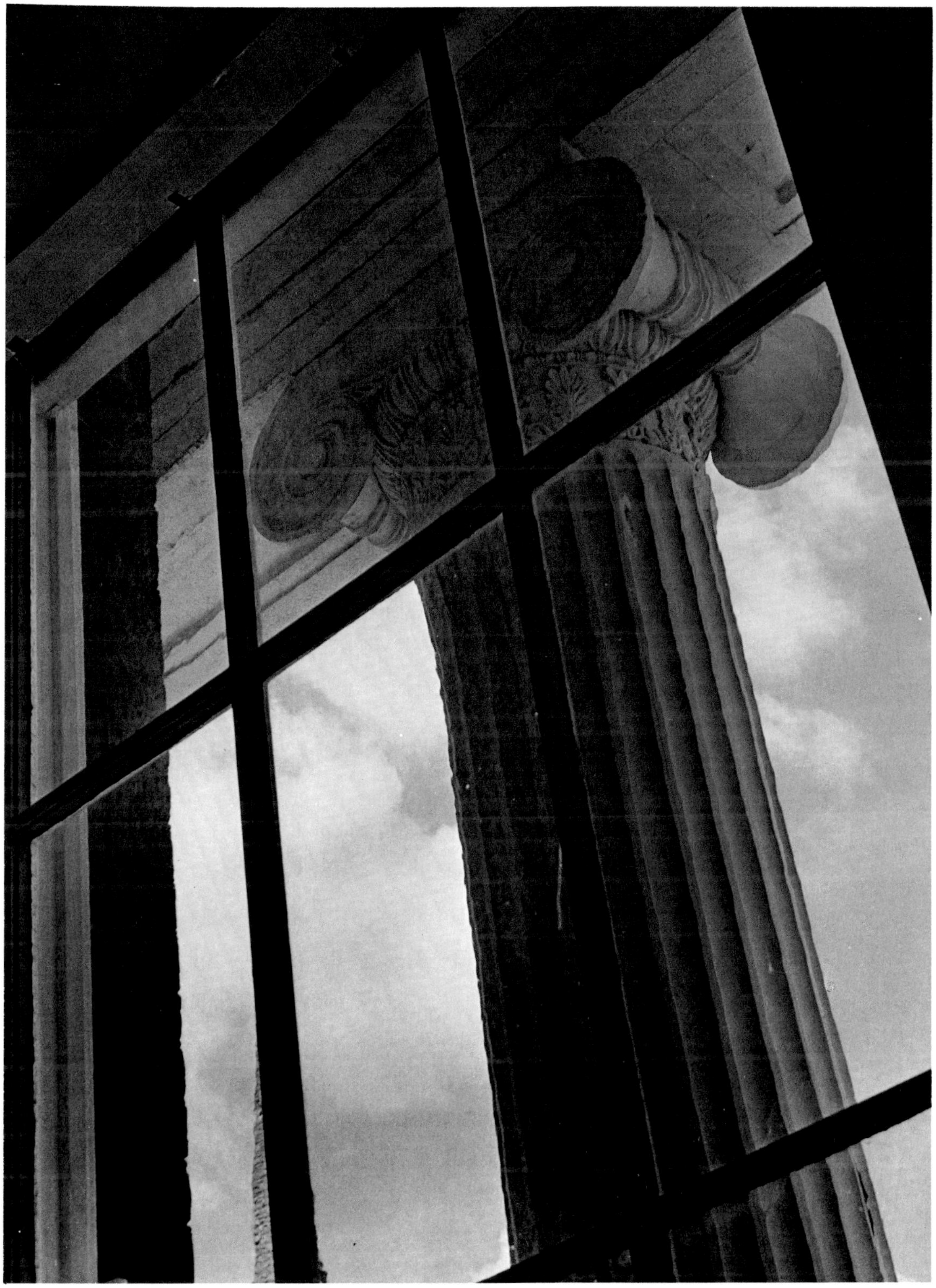

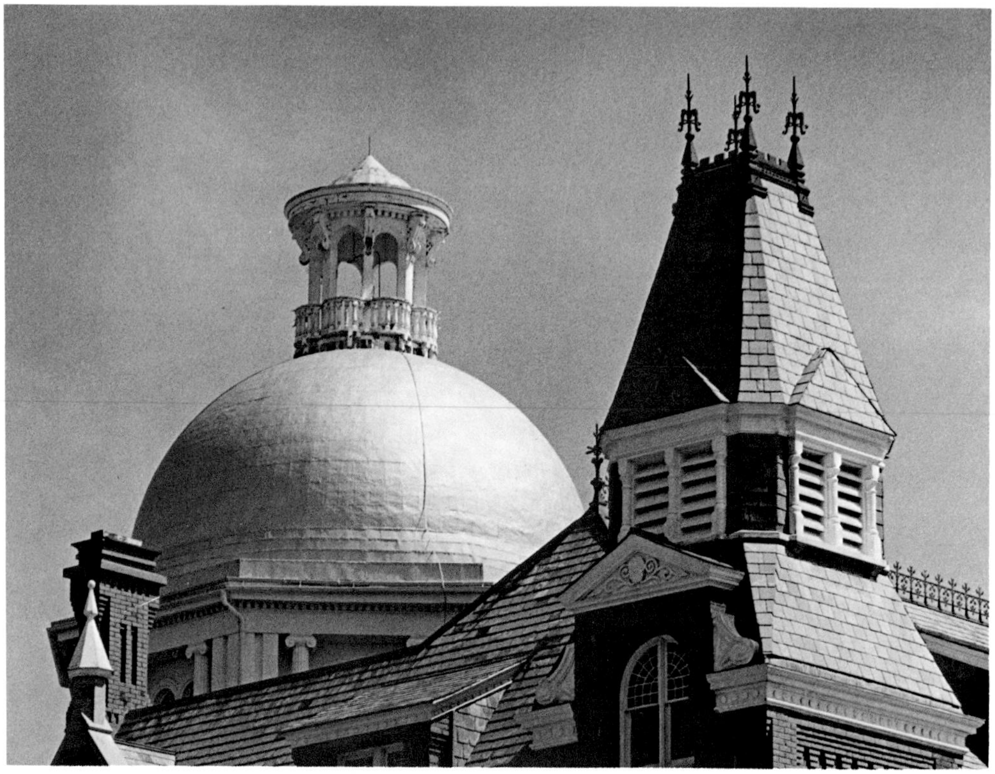

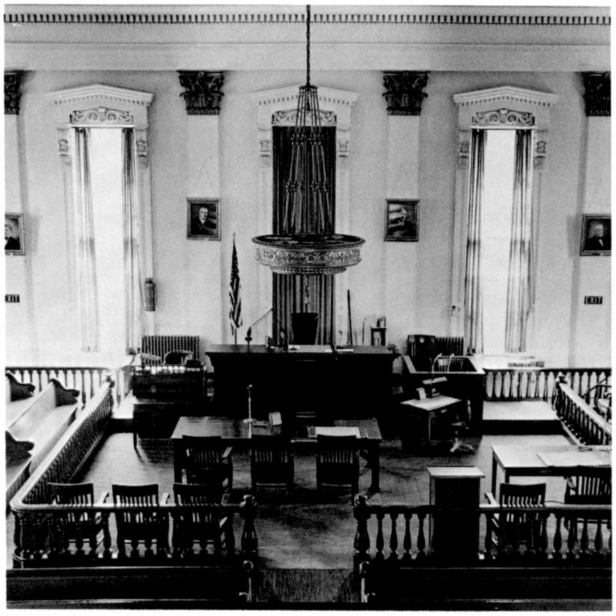
EXIT
EXIT

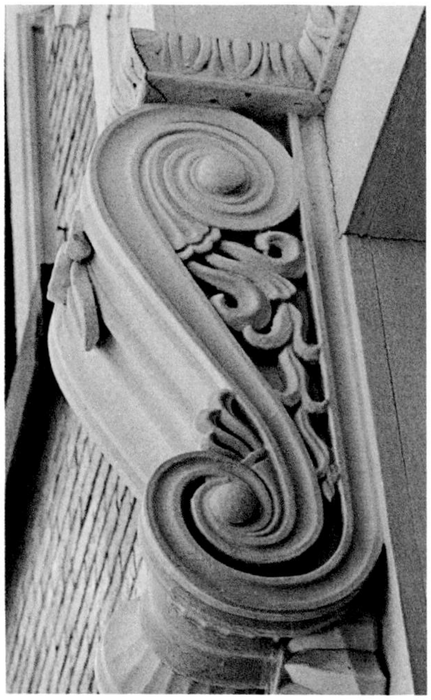

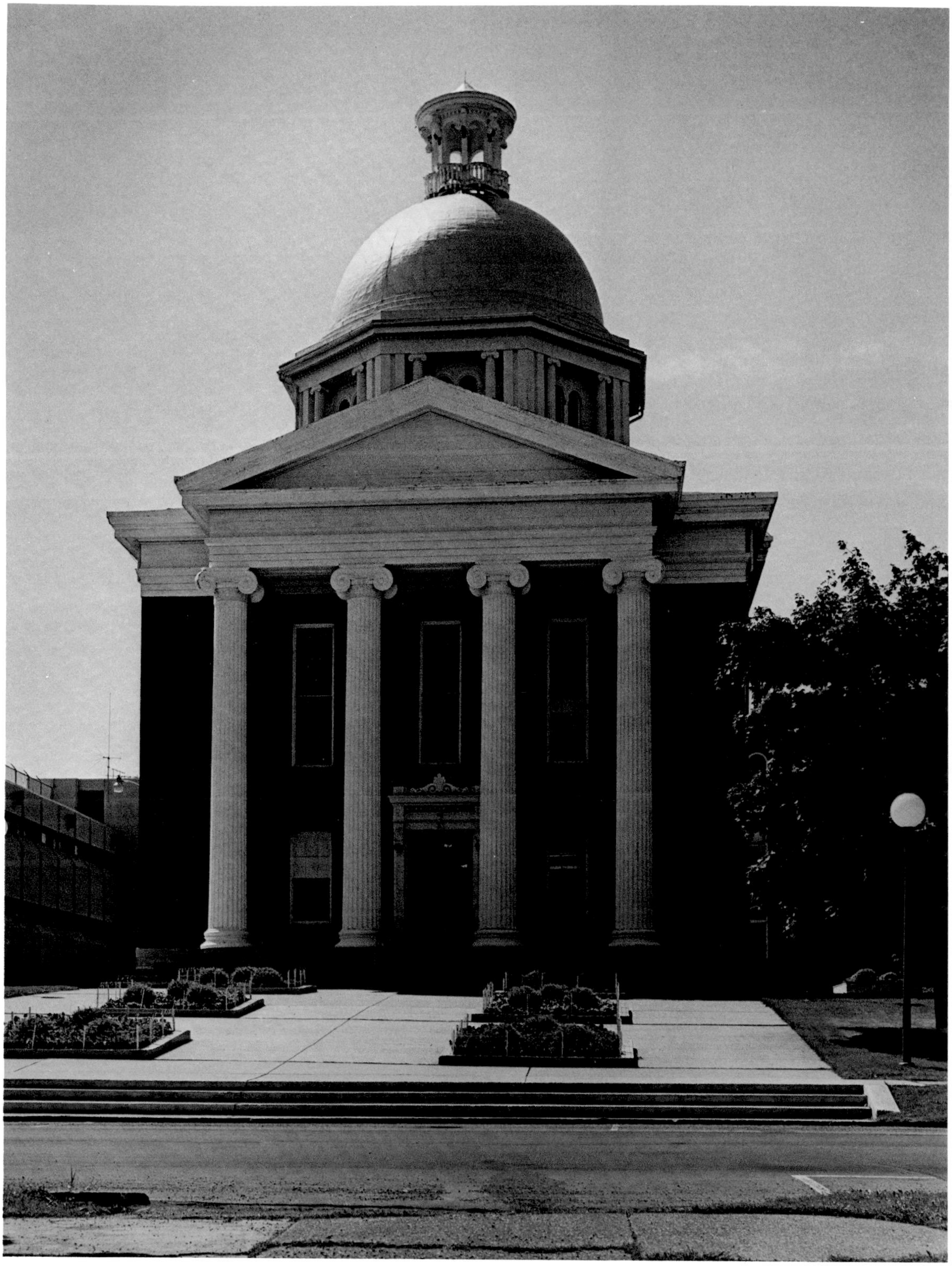

OSWEGO COUNTY

Oswego

Most of the records of the Oswego County Courthouse at Pulaski have been lost—an unfortunate happenstance, for the building ranks high among the state's courthouses in charm of both architecture and location. It is not, however, the county's only venerable courthouse, for Oswego County is half-shired, and Oswego, the other county seat, has a building that, though not as old as Pulaski's, is deserving of great respect.

According to local historians, the Pulaski courthouse was authorized by the legislature in

Oswego

1818, shortly after the creation of Oswego County, and was completed in 1822. As for the town of Oswego, its early courthouse was abandoned in 1848, and rented quarters were used for court purposes until a Supreme Court mandate forced the county to authorize a new courthouse in 1858. At the same time the Pulaski building was remodeled and enlarged; it seems to have remained essentially unchanged since that 1858–59 enlargement except for a bell tower attached in the 1870s and later removed.

The Oswego courthouse was completed in 1860. It was designed by Horatio Nelson White but is not one of his characteristic Anglo-Norman buildings. It lacks the towers and pseudo-battlements of his Chemung and Jefferson county courthouses, but it does have the graceful interior staircases he was noted for, and which also survive in the Jefferson County structure.

The Oswego courthouse has Greek-Revival features, and the Pulaski building, designed by Zina Stephens of Oswego, is definitely Greek-Revival, though with Egyptian-Revival motifs on its columns. Its charm is complemented by its setting on the Pulaski village square, with its tall shade trees. The square is the center of Pulaski, as it was a century ago, for change has come slowly to this village near the shores of Lake Ontario.

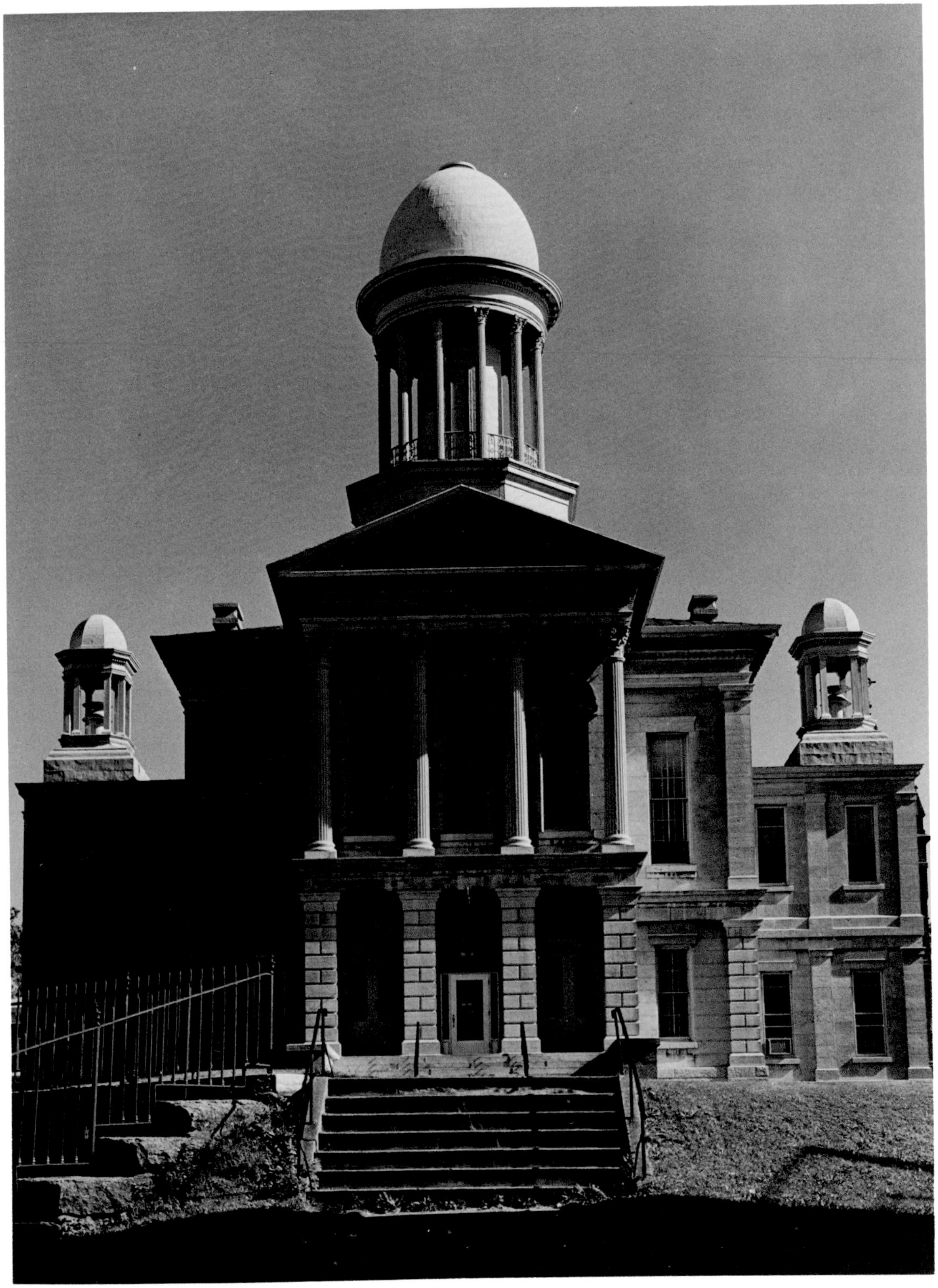

Oswego

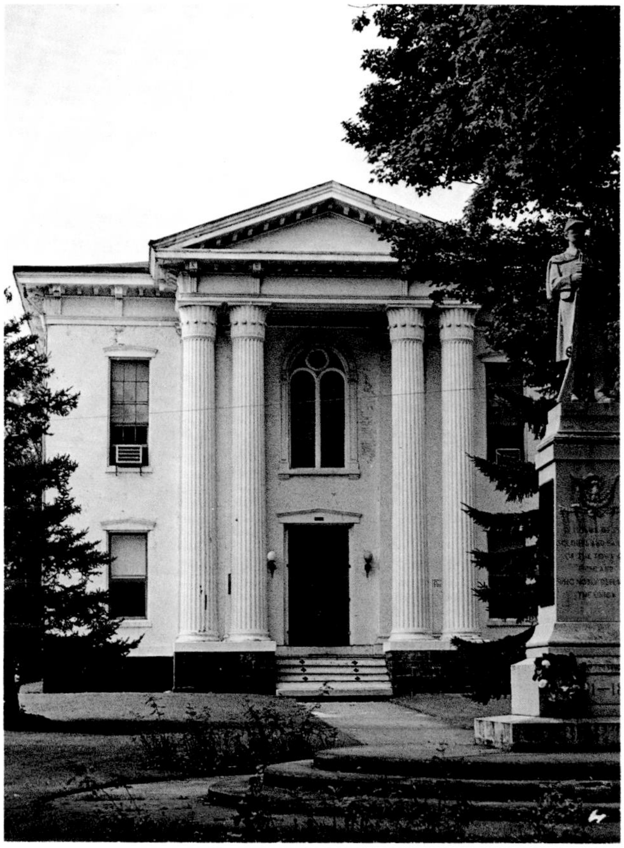

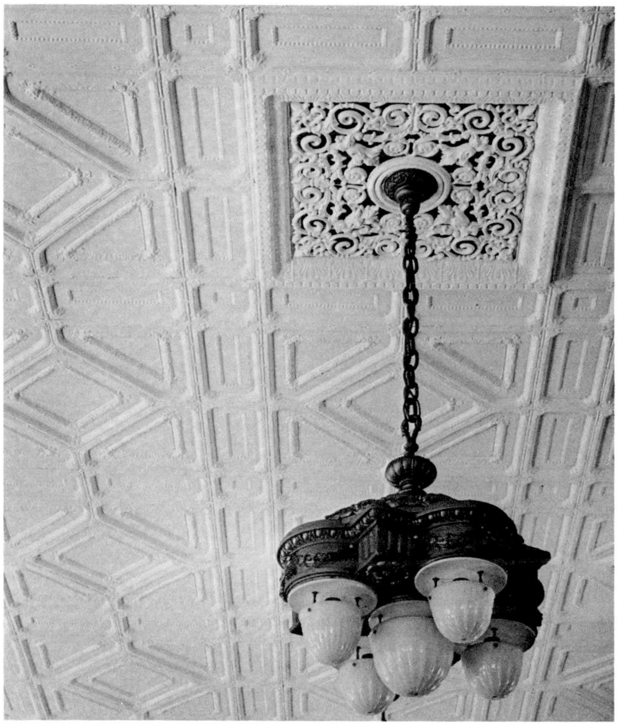

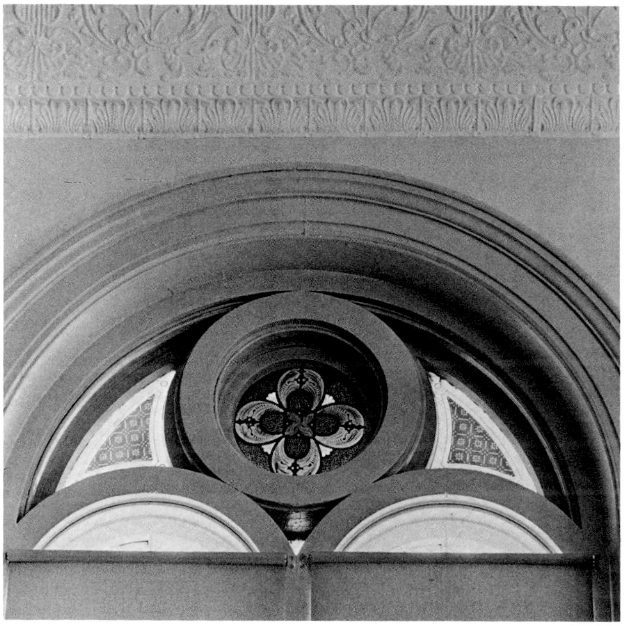

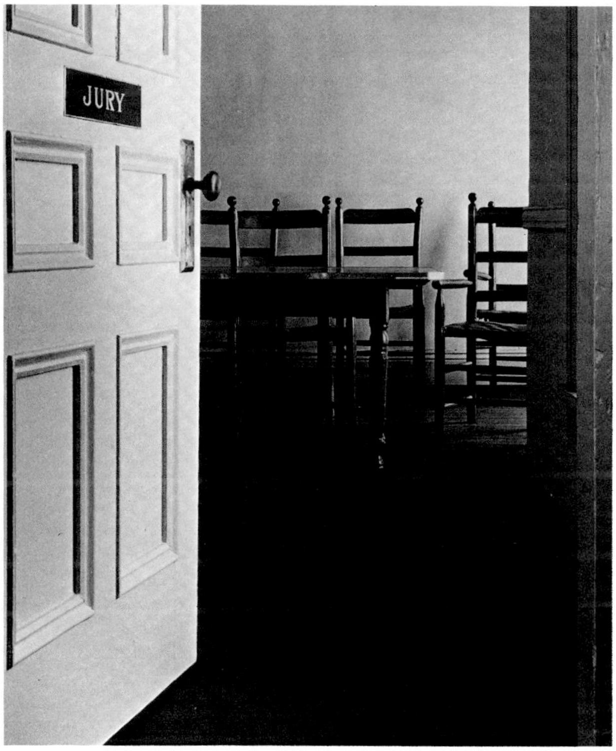
JURY

Pulaski

OTSEGO
COUNTY

New York's historic courthouses come in a wide variety of architectures; the edifice serving Otsego County at Cooperstown has an ecclesiastical appearance that makes it resemble nothing so much as one of the better-endowed churches of the city.

This unique courthouse, an 1881 structure, is the fourth to be built in Cooperstown. The first, a thirty-foot-square building whose lower story was made of logs and its second of framed lumber, was erected shortly after Otsego County was created in 1791. It was followed by a brick courthouse, built in 1806–1807, which was destroyed by fire in 1840 and replaced the next year by another put up on the same site.

By 1880 the last courthouse had outgrown its usefulness, and the cornerstone for the present structure was laid in June of that year. The first session of court was held in the new building less than a year later, in March 1881. The courthouse was designed by Archimedes Russell, a disciple of the innovative Horatio Nelson White. The central feature of its exterior design is a large Gothic window, and elaborate brickwork and an intricate floor plan add to its interest and charm. The result is one of the most unusual and striking courthouses in the state.

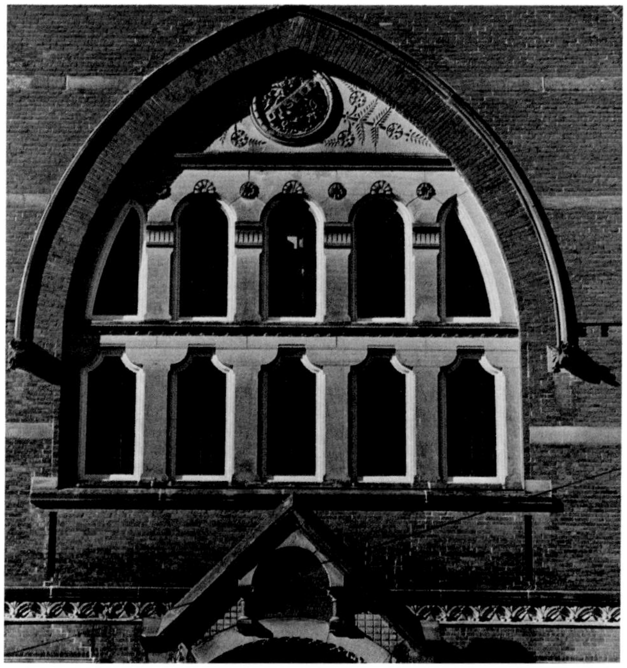

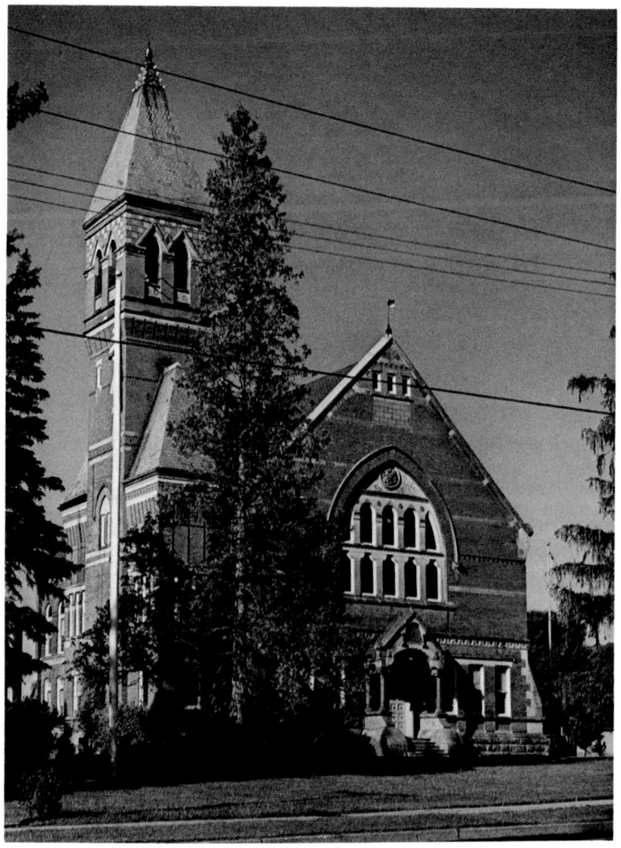

PUTNAM
COUNTY

The old Putnam County Courthouse at Carmel is a rather modest and chaste building, but it has been well maintained over its more than a century and a half of existence, and in its setting on the crest of a hill that slopes down to Lake Gleneida, it is one of the most attractively sited in the state. And surprisingly, though Carmel is not a large town nor Putnam an especially populous county, the trial dockets of its courts are among the largest in the Hudson River valley, with the exception of the metropolitan counties of New York.

And of all the individual records in the old files, perhaps the longest is that for the case of the contested will of Elijah Nelson. Not only was Elijah a frugal man but he was also known to be a wealthy one; after the will contest it was revealed that his estate was worth more than eleven thousand dollars, a substantial sum in 1851. Elijah Nelson made his will on September 17, 1844, when he was taken from his home in Putnam Valley to that of his son Peter Nelson at Somers in Westchester County, eight or nine miles away. It was an exhausting experience for a man in his early nineties who was suffering from erysipelas.

Elijah's wife, Susan, accompanied him on the trip, and at Peter's farm they were met by Dr. James Fountain, Elijah's physician, who wrote out the will according to instructions given him by Elijah and his wife. Son Peter discreetly withdrew during the drawing of the will, in which the old man's extensive real and personal property was apportioned among his children and grandchildren, with the exception of his daughter Mary Strang. To her and her husband he left nothing, commenting that the couple had "fooled away a thousand dollars of my hard-earned money, and they shall never fool away another dollar." However, he did make a small bequest to Mary Strang's children, to be held in trust for them until the death of both their parents.

After writing the will, Dr. Fountain read it aloud to Elijah, who nodded his head, presumably in approval of its terms, and then signed it with his X. The two witnesses then signed. One of these was Henry Hynard, a middle-aged farmer and a neighbor of Peter Nelson; he had also known Elijah for forty years, but had not seen him during the preceding twelve years because of the distance between their two farms. The other witness, Henry Travis, had never met Elijah before he was asked to come to Peter Nelson's house to witness the signing. Neither witness would see the old man again before his death more than four years later. The will remained in the possession of Dr. Fountain until it was surrendered to the surrogate after Elijah's death.

Elijah died in May 1849, and when his will was filed for probate with the surrogate of Putnam County, Mary and John Strang filed their objections on the grounds that Mary's father had been incapable of making a valid will. With the filing of those objections there began a parade of witnesses through the front door of the Putnam County Courthouse in a long and tedious hearing that would not be concluded for more than two years.

The Strang couple were undoubtedly correct in arguing that there was some question about Elijah Nelson's mental condition at the time the will was executed. But there are degrees of mental impairment, and a court is not eager to declare a will invalid on the grounds that the person who wrote it was wholly incompetent. County Surrogate Azer B. Crane heard and weighed the conflicting testimony.

Age and poor health had placed Elijah Nelson at a severe disadvantage in communicating with his family and friends at the time he made his will. Dr. Fountain and the witnesses admitted that when he signed the will he was very hard of hearing and it was nearly impossible to converse with him. After he had signed, he had asked the doctor to give him something to deaden his pain. The doctor told the surrogate that Elijah had suffered from an advanced stage of erysipelas, a debilitating disease that had bloated his face and eye cavities and made him appear expressionless. The disease had progressed to the point that it had affected the old man's brain, slowing his physical responses and greatly interfering with his speech. Yet despite this deterioration in Elijah's mind and body, Dr. Fountain and the witnesses were firmly convinced that the old man had been sufficiently aware of his surroundings and had understood well enough what his possessions and his family situation were to make a valid will.

However, on cross-examination Dr. Fountain admitted that in 1848 he had refused to help Elijah draw up a codicil to the will because, in the doctor's opinion, Elijah was no longer competent at that time. Although the incident had no direct bearing on the question of Elijah's capacity in 1844, the deterioration in the old man's mental capacity led to an inference that possibly even by 1844 it had reached a point where he was incapable of executing a valid will. The Strangs produced an expert witness to bolster this argument. Dr. John Collett of Yorktown had known Elijah Nelson for fourteen years prior to his death; he asserted that during

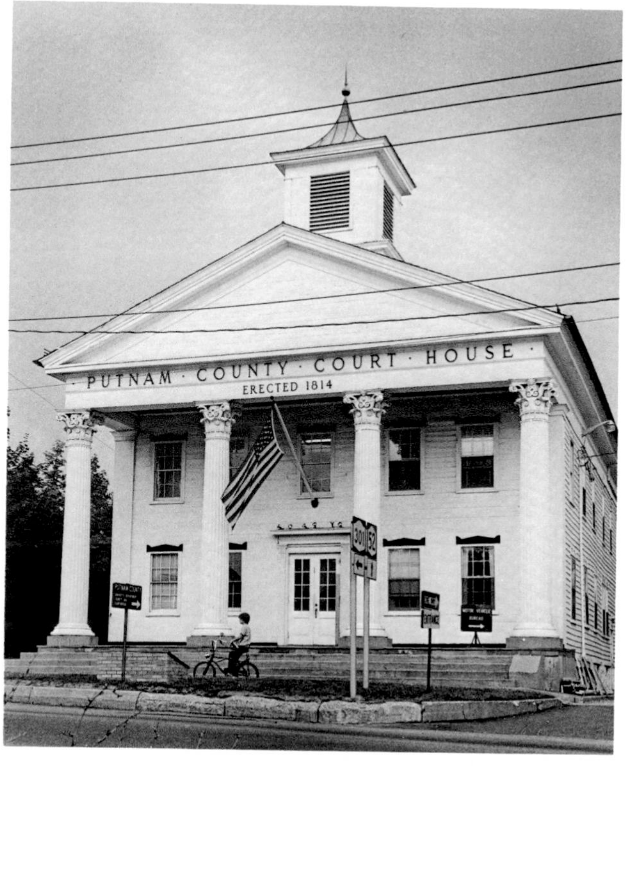
PUTNAM · COUNTY · COURT · HOUSE ·
ERECTED 1814

the years 1843–45 he had considered the old man's facial expressions to be "so vague as to indicate partial dementia." However, he was willing to call Elijah's disability only *partial* dementia—and the law held that even one suffering from an extreme mental illness may, in a lucid moment, execute a valid will. Furthermore, the law presumes that a testator has mental capacity and that mere senility or idosyncratic behavior is not sufficient to invalidate his will. For these reasons the Strangs had a difficult task ahead of them, and so they assembled a parade of witnesses to support their contention that Elijah Nelson was legally incompetent in 1843 and 1844.

The former Putnam County surrogate, Abraham Smith, testified that Elijah appeared before him in 1843 to get the judge's acknowledgment to Elijah's signature on a legal document releasing a mortgage on some land. The judge testified that he was not certain Elijah understood the effect of the document he was signing; it was only after considerable trouble that he was able to get from the old man a statement that the *X* on the instrument had been made by him, and even then the judge signed the acknowledgment with much misgiving. His testimony was corroborated by Abraham Requa, in whose favor the document had been drawn and who was present. Requa had mortgaged his farm to Elijah, and added that when he had discussed the last payment with Elijah, the old man had told him that he did not know how much property he owned, and that it would be best if Requa discussed the matter with "Sookey," Elijah's wife.

Peter Bancker, justice of the peace of Putnam Valley, told the court that he had known Elijah Nelson as far back as he could remember. Like Judge Smith, he had signed several legal documents for Elijah, but when asked whether he considered the old man of unsound mind at the time, he said he was unable to answer, for he believed that since no trustee or committee had been appointed to represent Elijah's interests, he could not consider him incompetent. Bancker did reveal that he had seen Elijah Nelson put wood in the fireplace on a hot summer day and told the court that at the time Mrs. Nelson had told him that her husband did not know what he was doing. The Methodist minister took his turn as witness, repeated the story of the summer fire-building, and stated that in his opinion Elijah's mind had been impaired from 1843 on.

Those closer to the family provided bits of colorful—though never quite convincing—information about Elijah Nelson's mental condition. Granddaughter Mary Hall, after first renouncing her contingent interests under the will, testified that in 1843 her grandfather had penned up a bull calf and announced that he intended to raise a fat milk cow by preventing the animal from exercising. Joseph Roake, present at prayer meetings in Elijah's house, testified that before 1843 the old man had been well mannered except that "he did not appear to be quite as particular to step aside from the view of his family in making water as I thought respectable." But after 1843 Roake found that Elijah never answered any of his questions except with a curt yes or no or with what Roake described as unintelligible mutterings. Solomon Survice, hired hand for one of Elijah's sons, testified that when the son visited his father in 1844, the old man asked who he was.

Testimony continued, month after month.

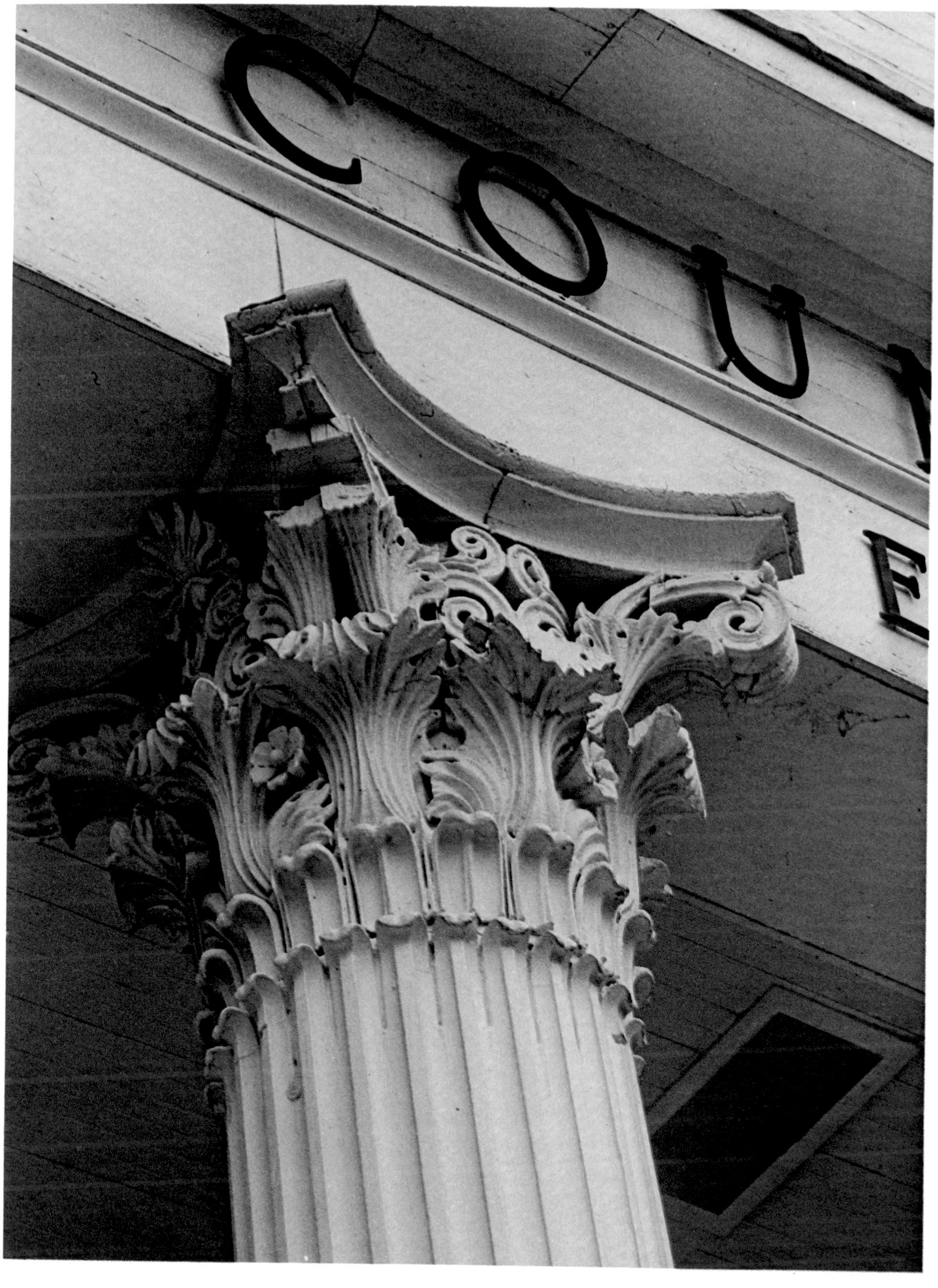
COU
E

Tempers grew short at times. When the Strangs' attorney questioned Dr. Fountain at one point about the standards he followed in keeping his records, the long-suffering physician retorted that he had done his best to anticipate "all manner of questions that I thought the fruitful imagination of a lawyer could invent." But after fourteen months and three hundred seventy-six pages of testimony, when neither party could think of any new evidence to offer, Surrogate Crane closed the case to further testimony on July 1, 1850, and from then until the middle of March 1851, he studied the testimony before coming to his decision.

That decision, when he reached it at last, was that Elijah Nelson had been competent to execute a valid will. So ended one of the longest and hardest-fought will contests up to that time —one that had been followed in the newspapers and about which most people in Putnam County had formed an opinion, one way or the other.

Ordinarily, the surrogate's decision to admit the will to probate would have ended his duties in the case. But Mr. Crane was faced with the thorny task of collecting from the county board of supervisors a fee that had some reasonable relation to the great amount of time he had spent hearing testimony on the Nelson case. The usual procedure for paying a surrogate was that he and the county treasury would divide the fee for probate between them. But the fee was a nominal one, and no provision was made for a probate proceeding that was contested and required a long trial. In the Nelson case, Surrogate Crane spent more than a hundred days in hearing witnesses, and he threatened that he would resign from office rather than accept the meager fee allowed him by statute.

When the board of supervisors ignored his request for adequate compensation, Crane refused to release to them their half of all the legal fees he had collected for the years 1850–53—until they would come to some settlement of his demand for payment on the Nelson will hearing. The board appointed a special committee to consider the matter, and in mid-December of 1854 they reported that Surrogate Crane clearly deserved a fair compensation for his labors on the Nelson case. As a result, Crane was paid the county's half of the fees for 1849 and 1850, the period of the hearings and Crane's deliberations, as well as his own statutory fees for the same period. Even so, it was small compensation long delayed and pointed up the need for a salaried county surrogate.

The need for a courthouse had arisen when Putnam County was created from the southern portion of Dutchess County in 1812. While awaiting better quarters, the county courts made do in the Baptist meetinghouse at Carmel. The courthouse was built in 1814 but was not used for court purposes until February 7, 1815, when the common pleas for Putnam County met there. The building has been in constant use ever since.

The details of the construction and the early years of the courthouse are lost, gone with the destruction of the early records of the board of supervisors. But early historians of the area say that the courthouse and jail cost $3,500. In 1842 a change of county seat was considered, but when an examination of titles indicated that the courthouse lots in Carmel would not be assets of the county but would revert to the original grantee, the thought of moving was forgotten. Instead the building was renovated, and it was

either at this time, 1842, or in 1852 that the Corinthian columns that make up its imposing facade were added. Whichever year it was seems unimportant today. Ten years one way or another—the courthouse remains today, looking down on the lake, much the same as it was when those columns were first put up some one hundred thirty, or is it only one hundred twenty, years ago.

QUEENS COUNTY

Queens County was created in 1683, during the reign of Charles II. The records of the early days are sparse, many of them having been lost through carelessness and the ravages of time, but we do know that by 1666, even before Queens County was formed and became a part of what was called the Yorkshire Riding, a sessions-house, or courthouse, and a jail had been built in Jamaica.

The people of Jamaica promised to keep the two buildings in good repair for twenty-one

years in return for the right to use the courthouse as a house of worship on Sundays. But by 1710 the buildings were no longer in good condition; they had become so dilapidated that the county supervisors were authorized to provide replacements. Nothing much was done, however, except perhaps the most basic repairs, and the decaying courthouse appears to have been still in use when British soldiers tore it down during the Revolution to use its lumber to build barracks.

When the Revolution ended the county had

neither jail nor courthouse; court sessions were held for a time in a church, where, incongruously, two men were sentenced to be hanged. Then in early 1785, the legislature moved the county seat to North Hempstead, a town it had determined was the geographical center of Queens County. A courthouse there was ready for business in 1787; the first case involving capital punishment was tried in 1790, when two women, black slaves, were convicted of arson and were sentenced to be hanged "at some public place in the neighborhood of the courthouse."

The county seat was again moved, to Long Island City, in 1874, and the courthouse was completed in 1876. This is the building that still stands in Long Island City. It is a four story edifice, brick with granite trim, and cost $276,000, a tremendous sum for that time.

RENSSELAER COUNTY

Rensselaer County, on the east side of the Hudson River, was named for Kiliaen Van Rensselaer, the Dutch patroon whose huge land grant included most of the region. The county was set off from Albany County by the New York state legislature in 1791.

The first court sessions in the new county began the year it was founded in a tavern, or public house, in Lansingburg, but after only three days the court adjourned, to meet again in a public house in Troy, where the remainder of the sessions were held. For the next couple of years the courts met alternately in the two taverns, and there was intense rivalry between the two villages for the county seat. Troy carried off the prize in 1793 by subscribing $5,000 to-

completed early in 1831 at a cost of $40,000, was made of marble, with Doric columns in front, and was said to have been modeled largely after the Temple of Theseus in Athens.

The second courthouse, in its turn, outlived its purpose and was replaced in 1898. That third courthouse—the one pictured here—is still the seat of justice for Rensselaer County.

ward the cost of a courthouse and jail. Construction began that year and produced what was described as "a handsome, substantial building for its day."

In time the courthouse became too small for the growing county, and in 1826 Troy petitioned the state legislature for permission to raise money for a new building; Troy agreed to raise two fifths of the total cost, which was not to exceed $25,000, the state to provide the remainder. When legislative approval was given, the old building was torn down, and court was held in the Methodist meetinghouse while the new courthouse was being built. The new structure,

RICHMOND
COUNTY

were satisfactory, and in 1729 the county seat was moved to Cocclestown, now renamed Richmondtown. There have been three courthouses in Richmondtown. The first—where the first court sessions appear to have been held in 1729 —was burned by the British during the Revolution. The next, first used in 1794, was a two-story building with a belfry and shingled sides; it lasted until 1839, when it was replaced by the present structure.

This third courthouse—the one that still stands in Richmondtown—is a handsome Greek-Revival building with front of local traprock and sides and rear of brick; four unfluted Doric columns support its pediment. Richmondtown was a busy place as the legal center of a growing county until 1898, when Richmond County was incorporated into New York City and the county offices were removed to St. George on the northern shore of Staten Island.

The old courthouse might well have decayed or been razed had not Richmondtown in recent years attracted the attention of preservationists, who set about saving this village that events had passed by. The village has become Richmondtown Historical District; its vintage buildings are being restored, and some historic buildings are being moved there from other parts of the island. And the 1839 courthouse, repaired and repainted inside and out, is a main feature of the historical district.

Richmond County, which coincides with Staten Island, is now a borough of New York City, but when its courthouse was built, it was a region of farms and villages, a long way from Manhattan and the big city. The county is an old one, established in 1683 with the village of Stony Brook as its county seat. The courthouse there was a small building of two rooms, one of them a crude jail of rough-hewn logs.

Though some improvements were made over the years, the facilities at Stony Brook never

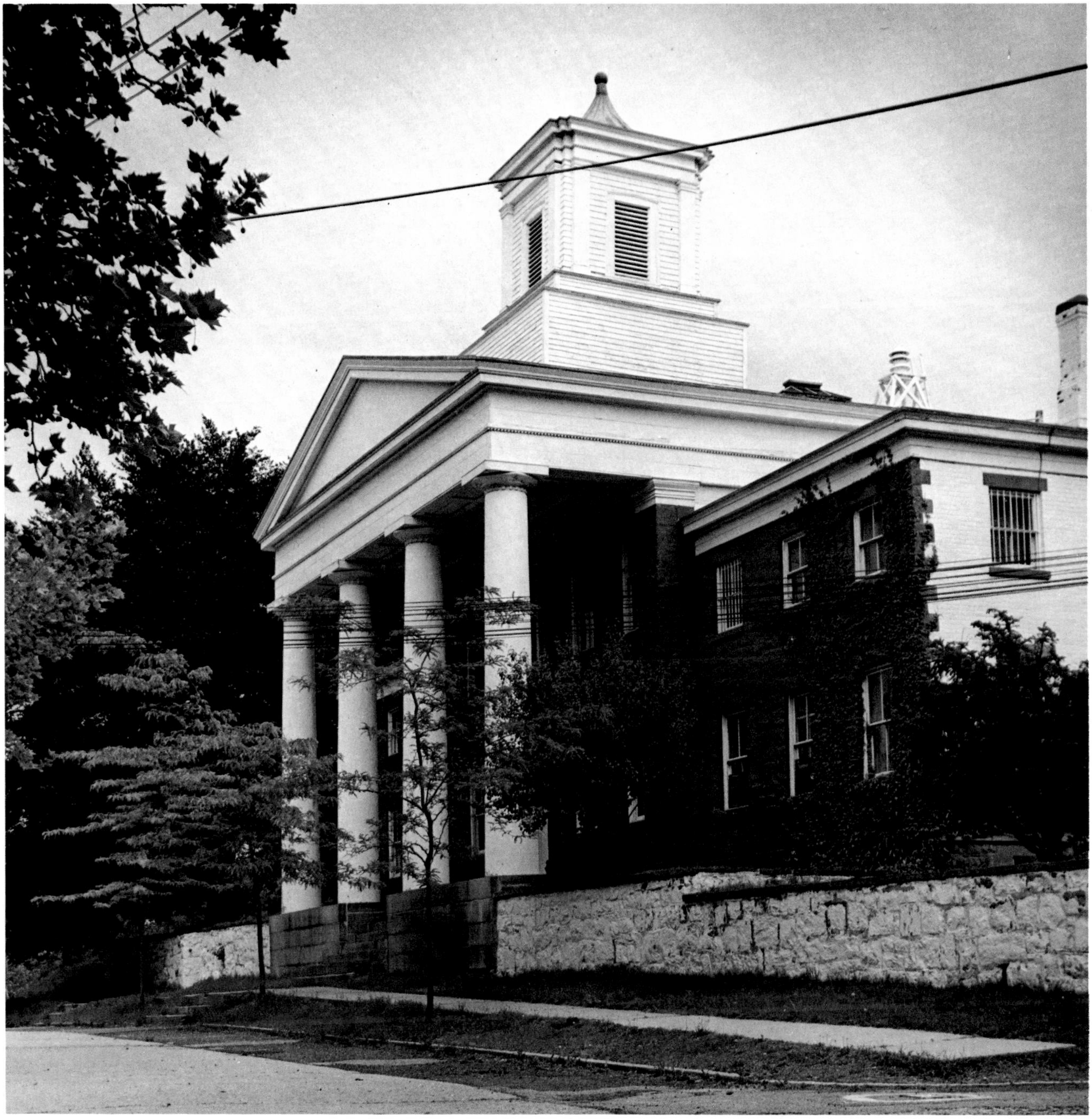

ST. LAWRENCE COUNTY

At the time St. Lawrence County was established in 1802, a leading landowner in the Ogdensburg area was so persuasive in arguing the case for old Fort Oswegatchie, at the junction of the St. Lawrence and Oswegatchie rivers, as a county seat—ready-made and available at very little cost—that a first term of court was held in one of the stone barracks in May of 1802. However, plans were made at once for a more conventional courthouse on the Ogdensburg side of the Oswegatchie, and it was built so speedily that it was occupied by November.

But objection to this hasty and somewhat high-handed choice of Ogdensburg as the county seat soon arose, especially as towns farther south were settled, and these objections developed into a move to take the county seat away from Ogdensburg after the British burned the courthouse in 1813. Eventually the legislature took heed and moved the county seat to Canton in 1828. A courthouse, built of local stone, was erected there soon after; in 1851 an addition was added, but even with this the courthouse had become so inadequate by 1893 that there was little mourning that year when a fire swept through the building, leaving only scorched walls.

There was talk then of moving the county seat again, but it remained in Canton, and a new courthouse, designed by architect James P. Johnson of Ogdensburg, was built, a two-story structure of Gouverneur ashlar with trim of Potsdam sandstone, topped by a tower. It was completed in 1895.

Once again fire struck, destroying everything but the walls in 1925. These, however, survived in almost perfect condition, and for that reason the rebuilt courthouse retains the appearance of the Romanesque 1895 building. Inside, however, there is not a piece of wood except in the handrails and courtroom seats; there will be no more fires.

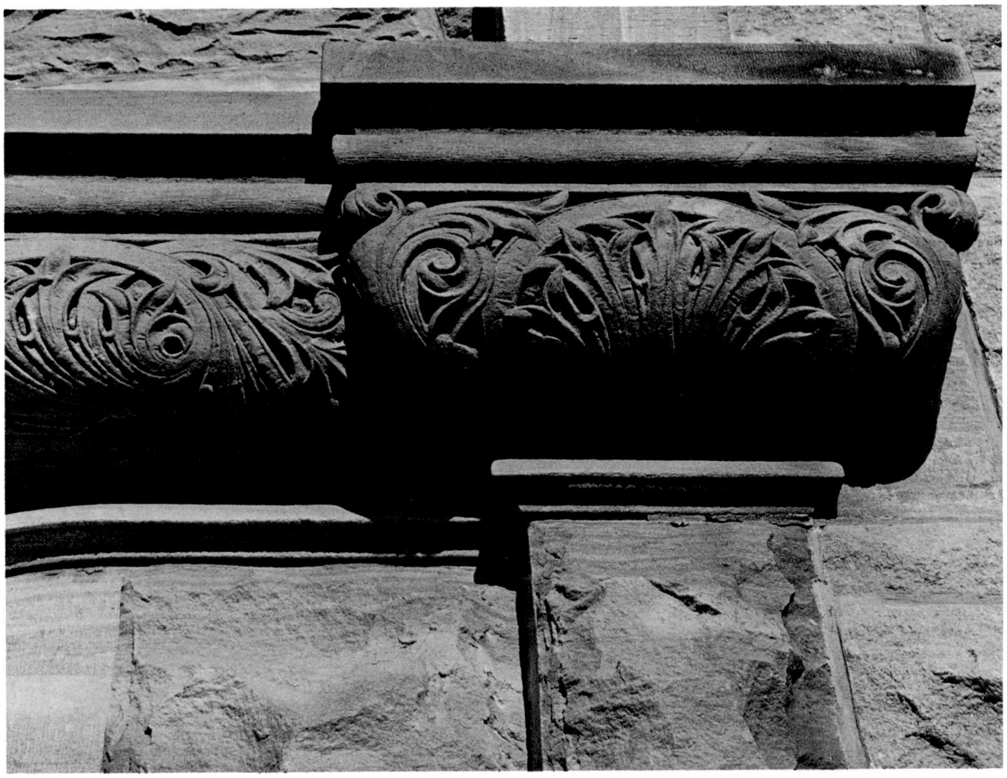

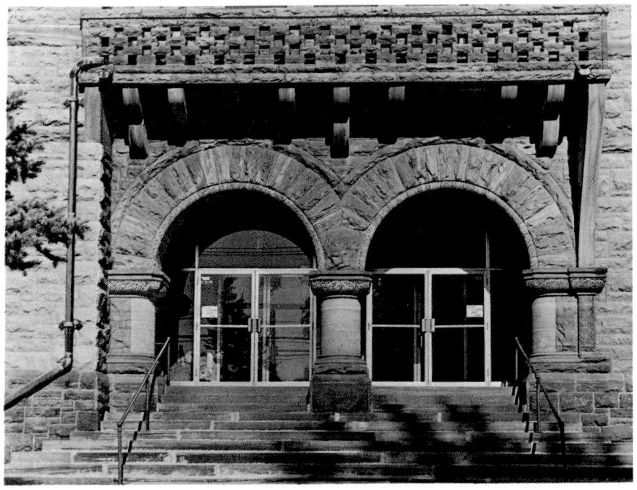

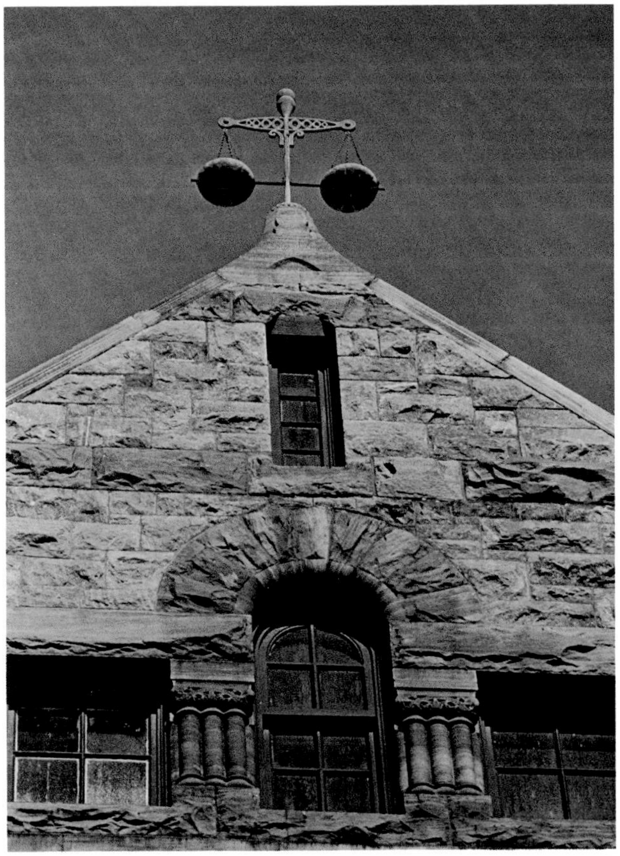

SCHENECTADY COUNTY

Schenectady County was part of Albany County for over one hundred and fifty years before it was detached to form a new governmental unit. At one time Albany covered a huge tract of land in the wilds of frontier New York State; then, from time to time, portions of it were organized into separate new counties, and it became the turn of Schenectady County in 1809.

Courts were established as soon as the new county came into being, and the town of Schenectady became the county seat. It was a historic site, for the town was built on ground that had once held an Indian village. The area had been settled by the Dutch in about 1662 and then had passed to the English in 1664, who ruled it until the Revolution.

Schenectady County has seen several court-

houses since its establishment in 1809, but only one has grown old enough to be called historic today. That one was built in 1831 and still stands at 108 Union Street in Schenectady. A long time has passed, however, since its days of distinction as the county courthouse, for it was remodeled and now houses private business offices.

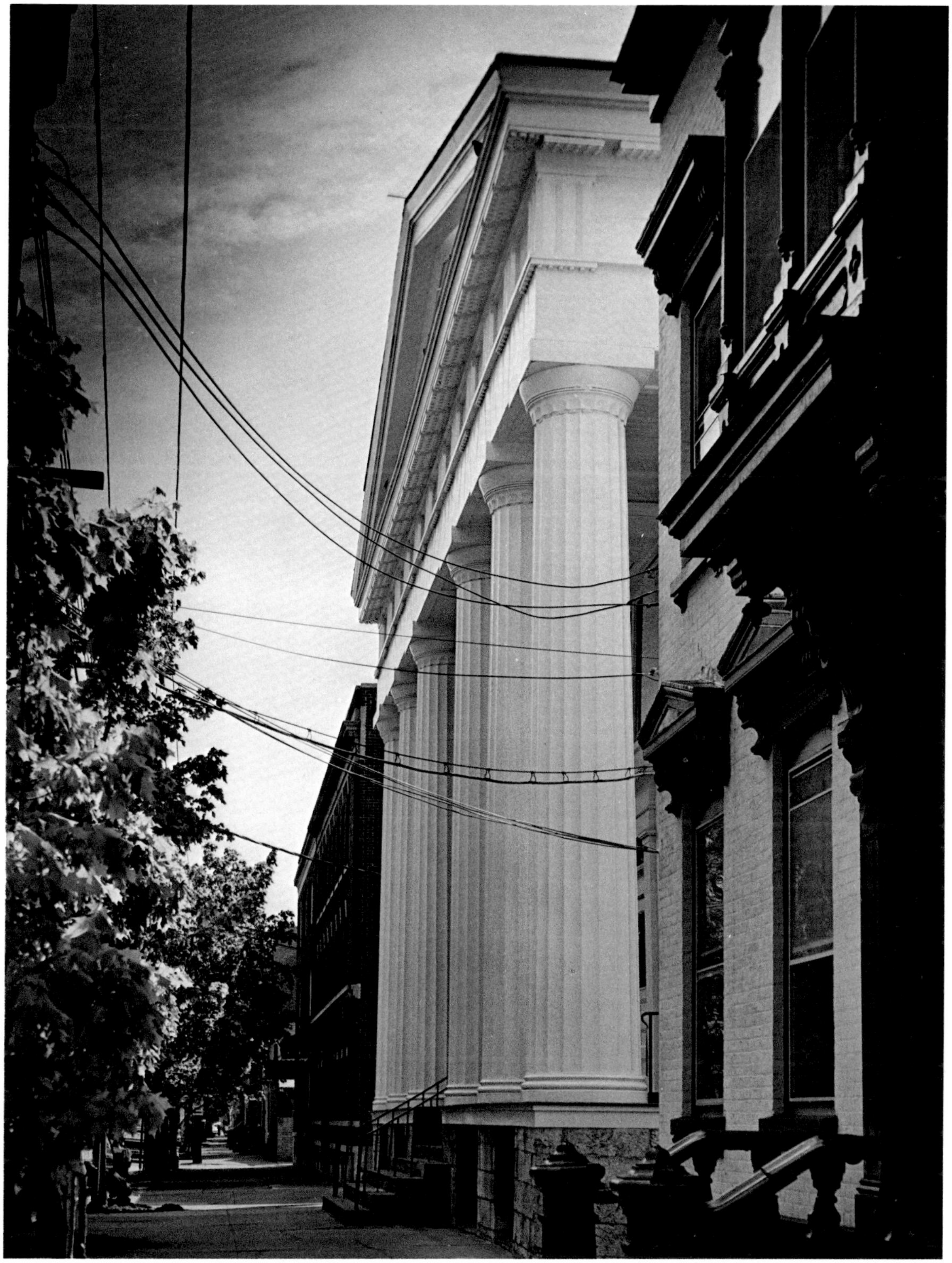

SCHOHARIE COUNTY

The histories of New York's former courthouses contain the phrase "destroyed by fire" again and again. Schoharie County has lost two of its courthouses to the flames; the present one has been saved from an equally ruthless enemy, the wrecking ball.

The first loss—at Schoharie, the county seat— came in 1845 when a prisoner in the county jail tried to burn his way through a cell door and set fire to the entire courthouse. Another courthouse was erected on almost the same site, and the builders made the structure as nearly fireproof as the knowledge of the times would let them. But in 1870 fire broke out in a hay-filled barn

near the courthouse, spread to adjacent buildings, and created such intense heat that even the stone courthouse could not withstand it.

The new courthouse was designed by architect John Cornelius, of Albany, and was finished in early spring of 1871. Of all the mansard-roofed courthouses in New York State, the one at Schoharie is the best preserved, and this is due in considerable part to the understandable efforts of the designer to make it as fireproof as possible; its dressed limestone and galvanized iron, meant to resist flames, have also resisted the elements.

A few years ago the old courthouse, though still hale and sound, was in danger of being razed because county offices had outgrown existing space in the building—its replacement to be a "modern" structure. Fortunately, a group of local citizens and the New York State Bar Association's Committee for the Preservation of Historic Courthouses were able to bring pressure; a separate county office building was put up to relieve the crowding, and the charming old courthouse was preserved.

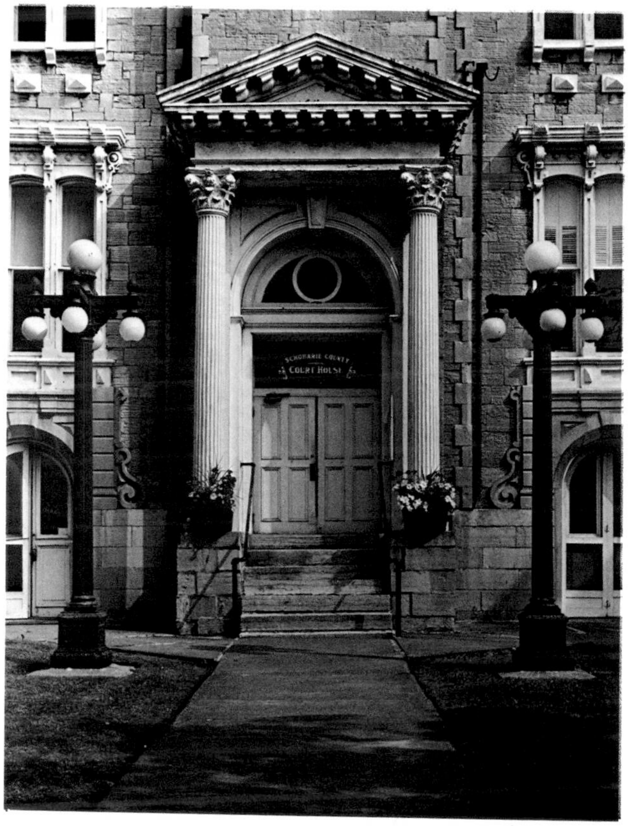

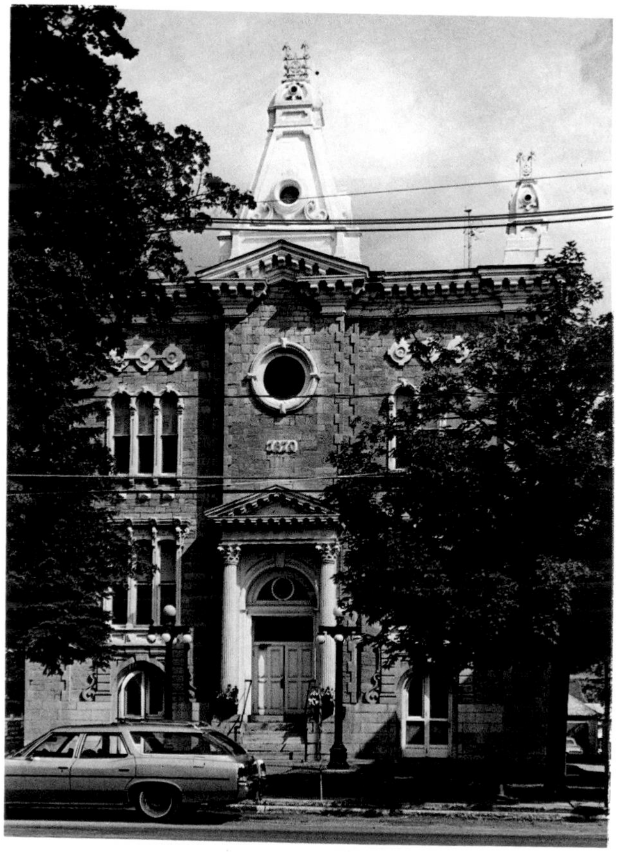

SCHUYLER COUNTY

Schuyler County claims two historic courthouses: one at Montour Falls and the other at Watkins Glen. However, though Montour Falls was the county seat for thirteen years, the building there was never legally a courthouse.

Soon after Schuyler County was established in 1854, a selection board of three men from three other counties was charged with choosing the county seat. After looking the situation over, they picked Havana (now Montour Falls). There was an immediate uproar; supporters of Watkins Glen as the county seat charged that there had been undue influence and a political fix. There may have been some merit in their claims, for one Charles Cook of Havana had been instrumental in the creation of Schuyler County, and he gave the land on which the courthouse and other county buildings were to be erected; it is not beyond possibility that he influenced the selection committee in its choice of Havana as county seat.

But Cook made one mistake; in donating the land for the courthouse site he attached a string: that if ever the county seat should be removed from Havana, the courthouse site would revert to the town. This restriction prevented the gift of land from being legally acceptable, and so the county had no right to build there. To further muddy the situation, the selection committee went beyond its authority, not only in accepting Cook's gift of the site but also in contracting for the erection of the courthouse and other buildings. Because of these legal flaws, the Havana courthouse (and jail and county building) were never acknowledged or accepted as county buildings, and the county clerk, the courts, and the sheriff usually rented other space.

With all this ammunition, the Watkins Glen advocates continued their fight for the county seat, and they won their battle in 1867, when the seat was moved to Watkins Glen. The courthouse there was completed the next year, and it stands today much as it did then, handsome, restrained, functional. Its facade is simple, and its most distinctive feature is a cupola that seems to have a hint of the Moorish about it.

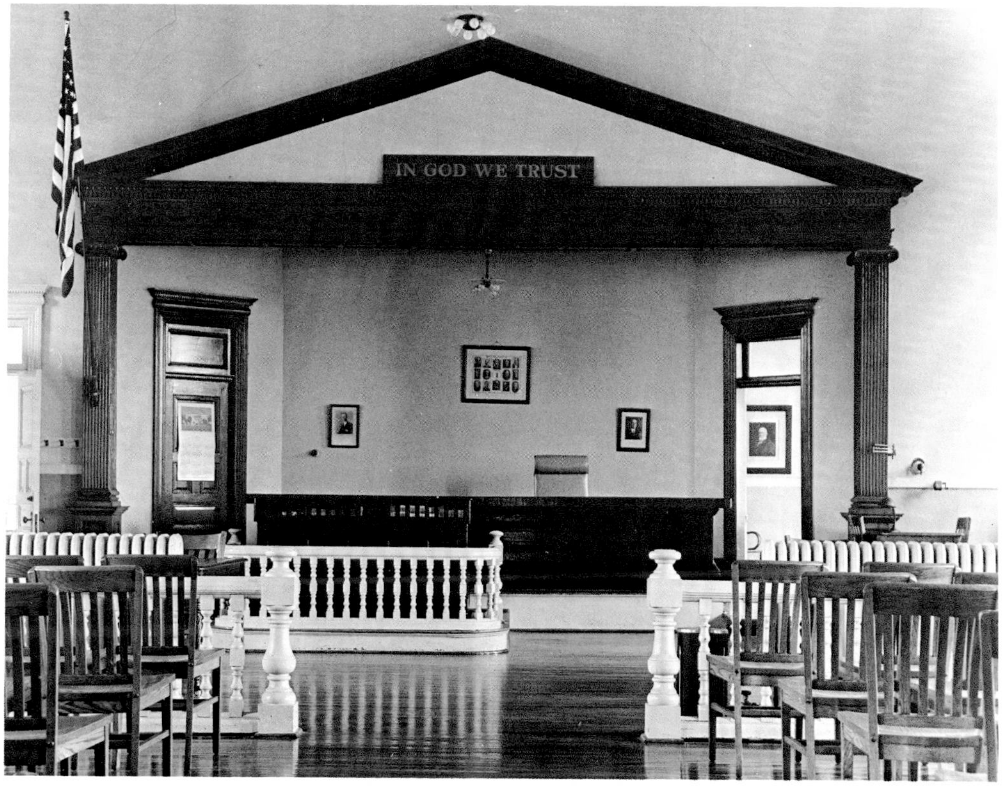
IN GOD WE TRUST

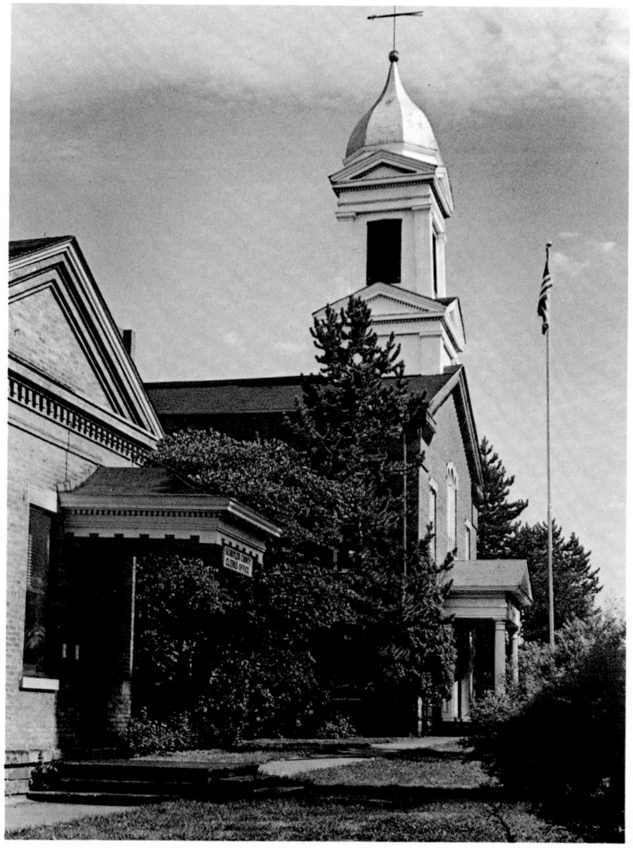

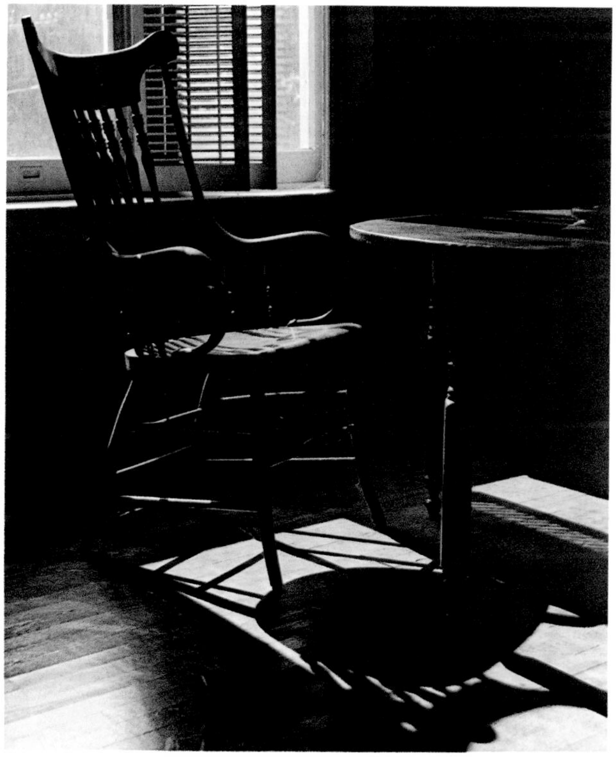

SENECA COUNTY

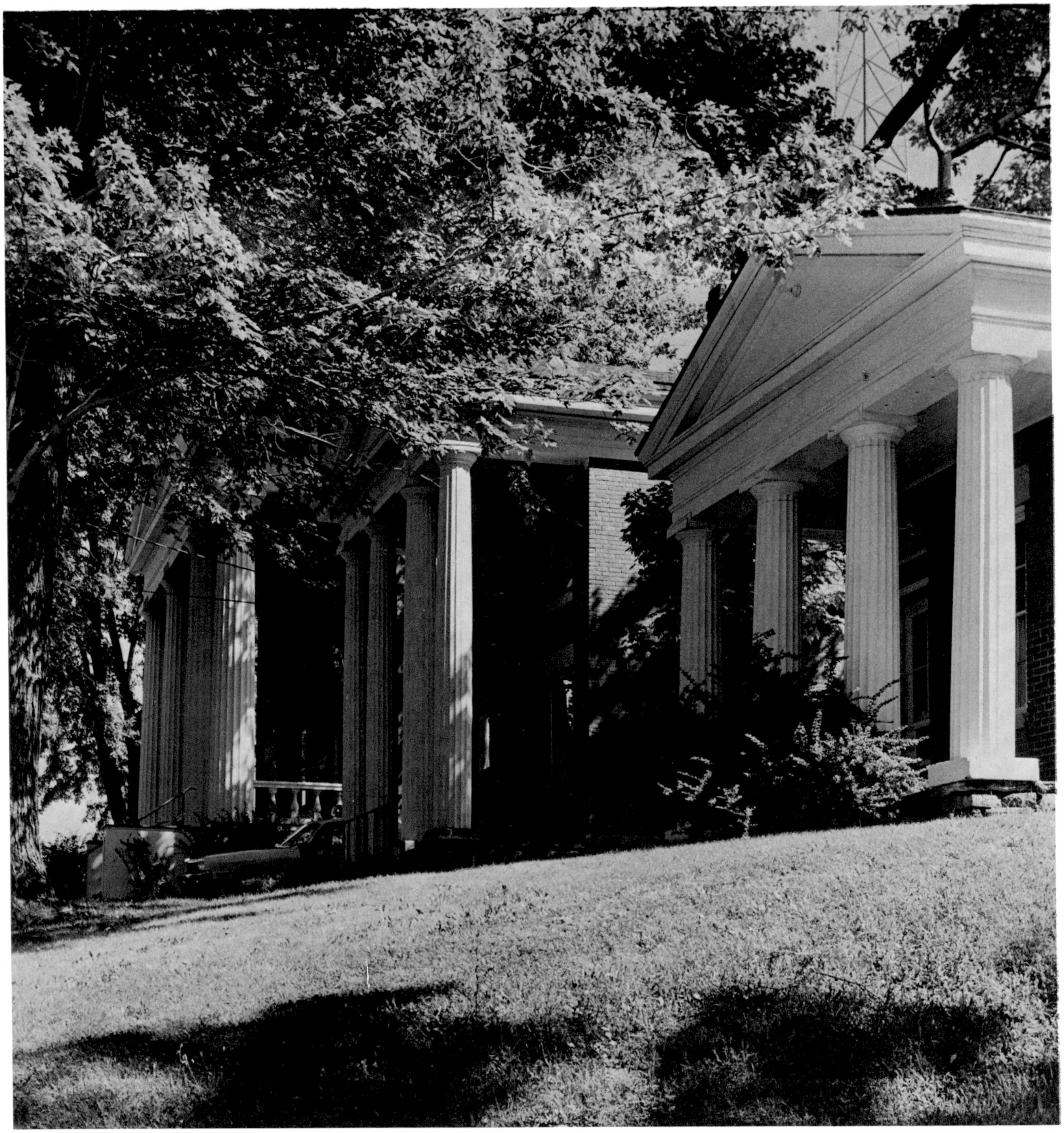

Ovid

Seneca County is one of New York's half-shired counties, with seats at Ovid and Waterloo. Each of the two towns boasts its own historic courthouse, and both of the old buildings are in active court service today.

Ovid was the original county seat, so designated when Seneca County was organized in 1804. At the time the county also included portions of today's Tompkins County to the south and Wayne County to the north. The town of Waterloo had also coveted the county seat, and in its own good time, after Tompkins County was detached, pressed its claim by arguing that it was then nearer the center of the diminished Seneca County than was Ovid. The state legislature listened and agreed; a courthouse was built in Waterloo and the stoves from the Ovid courthouse moved there in 1818 (apparently the definitive move signifying the end of court activity in Ovid). But only four years later the county was half-shired, and Ovid became the seat for the southern part. From that time—1822—until now, court sessions have been held in both towns.

In time the 1804 Ovid courthouse became too decrepit to bear further patching, and a new building was erected in 1845—although things went at such a leisurely pace, and furnishings were provided so slowly, that the court bell and bell ropes were not in place until 1862. The Ovid courthouse (known, with its two related structures, as "The Three Bears") has remained essentially unchanged since then, and the Waterloo building, except for minor refurbishings, remains much as it was when built in 1818. Both courthouses are modest structures, types to be expected in basically agricultural areas, whose forms were conceived by native architects working in basically native idioms.

An inspection of the old records reveals no dramatic cases as having been tried in the old courthouses. There is a man acquitted of horse stealing, a couple sentenced for keeping a disorderly house, the like. Perhaps the tenor of jurisprudence in these courts is typified by a breach-of-promise suit brought by Priscilla Hartranft against J. M. Chamberlain. Priscilla, at the age of forty-four, decided that a courtship of twenty-six years without a proposal of marriage was a bit long, and so sued Mr. Chamberlain. A jury in Ovid agreed with Priscilla and awarded her twelve hundred dollars damages, even though the reluctant suitor had been married twice during his long courtship.

Ovid

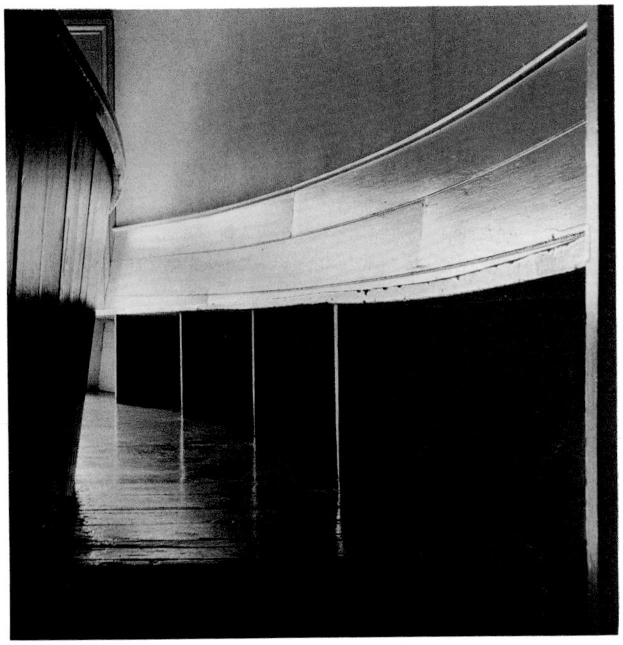

Ovid

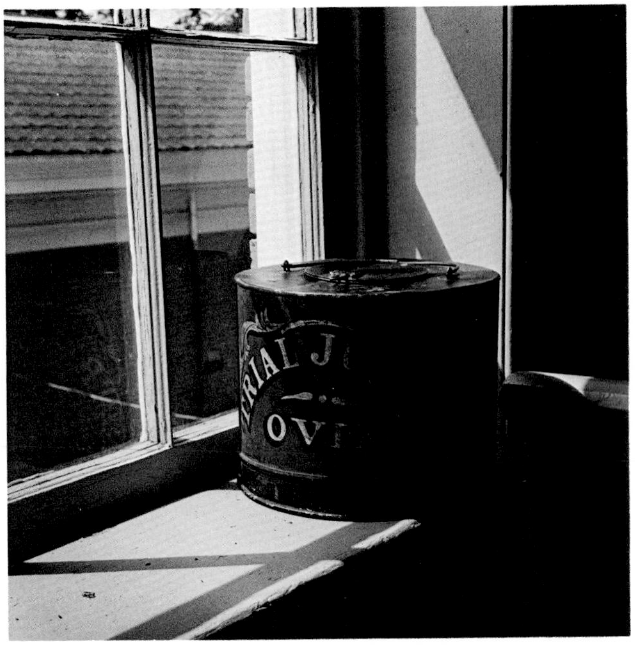

Ovid

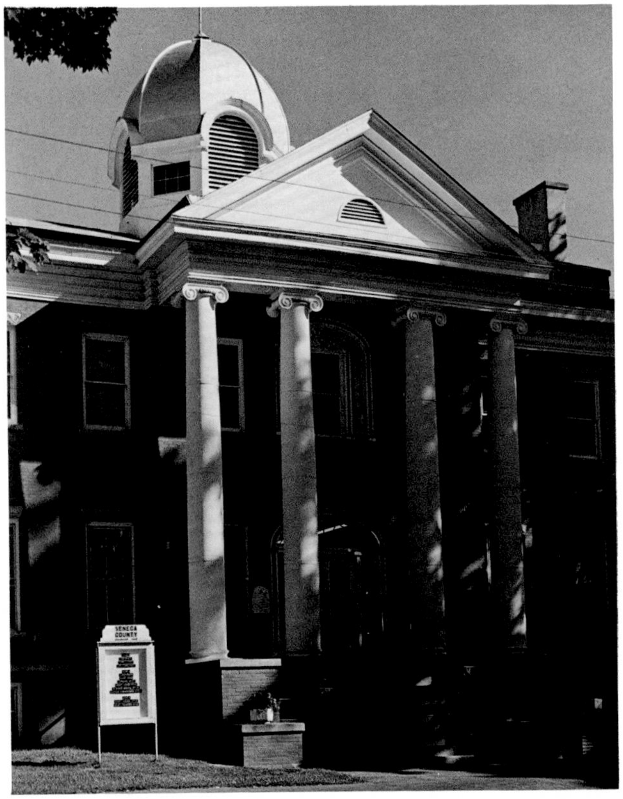
SENECA
COUNTY

Waterloo

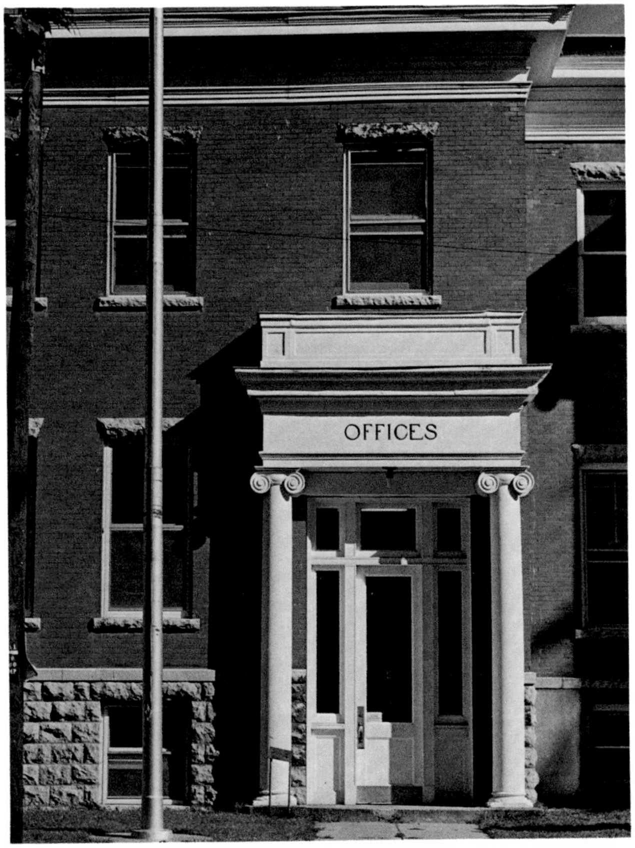
OFFICES

Waterloo

Waterloo

Waterloo

STEUBEN COUNTY

A few years ago the Steuben County Court-house at Bath was scheduled for the bulldozer, but local lawyers and the New York State Bar Association's Committee for the Preservation of Historic Courthouses helped to save the old building. It was a fortunate rescue, for the courthouse is one of the handsomest in New York, and its setting is reminiscent of a county seat of an era now gone.

The courthouse is the third in Bath since Steuben County was created in 1796; it was completed in January 1861 and replaced one that had burned two years earlier. The county supervisors specified that the courthouse must be adequate for the needs of the next fifty years, but they over-optimistically based their projections on a trebling of population in that period; growth was considerably slower, and so the courthouse still serves comfortably today.

The courthouse, with its twin white columns, is an interesting example of the last stages of Greek-Revival architecture in New York State; the use of stone to frame windows and the simple lines of the roof and the square cupola suggest that the architect was working in a style midway between Greek-Revival and the Victorian that would soon follow.

The passage of time has also been kind to the village green on which the courthouse faces. The surrogate's office and the county clerk's office—also facing the green—are in key with the courthouse, and the nineteenth-century houses are very much as they were when the courthouse was built.

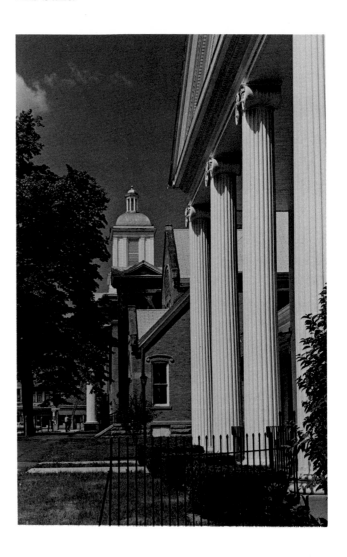

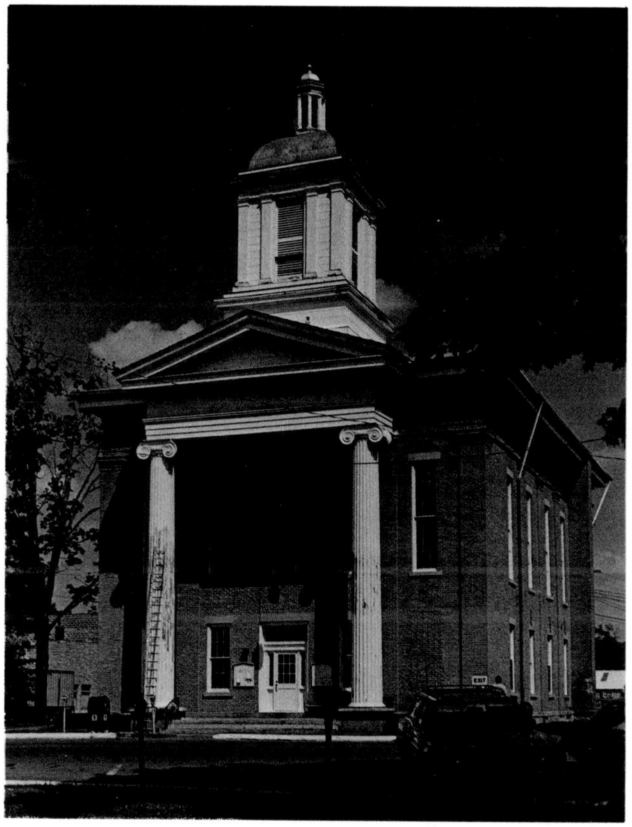

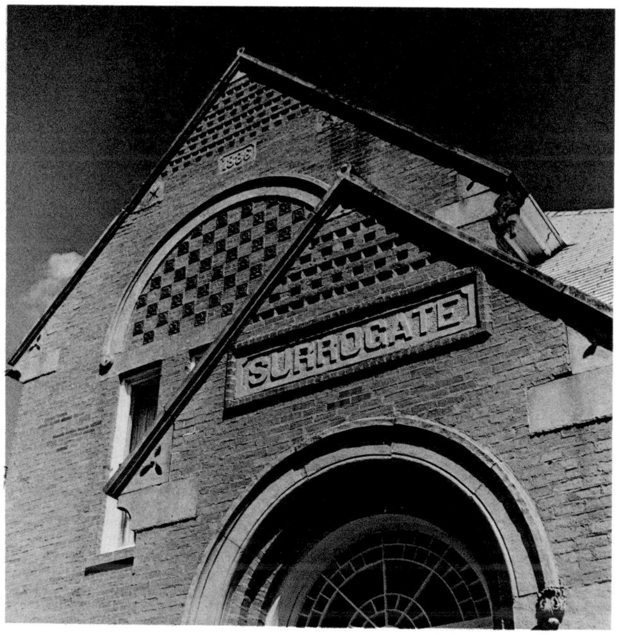
SURROGATE

Surrogate Building

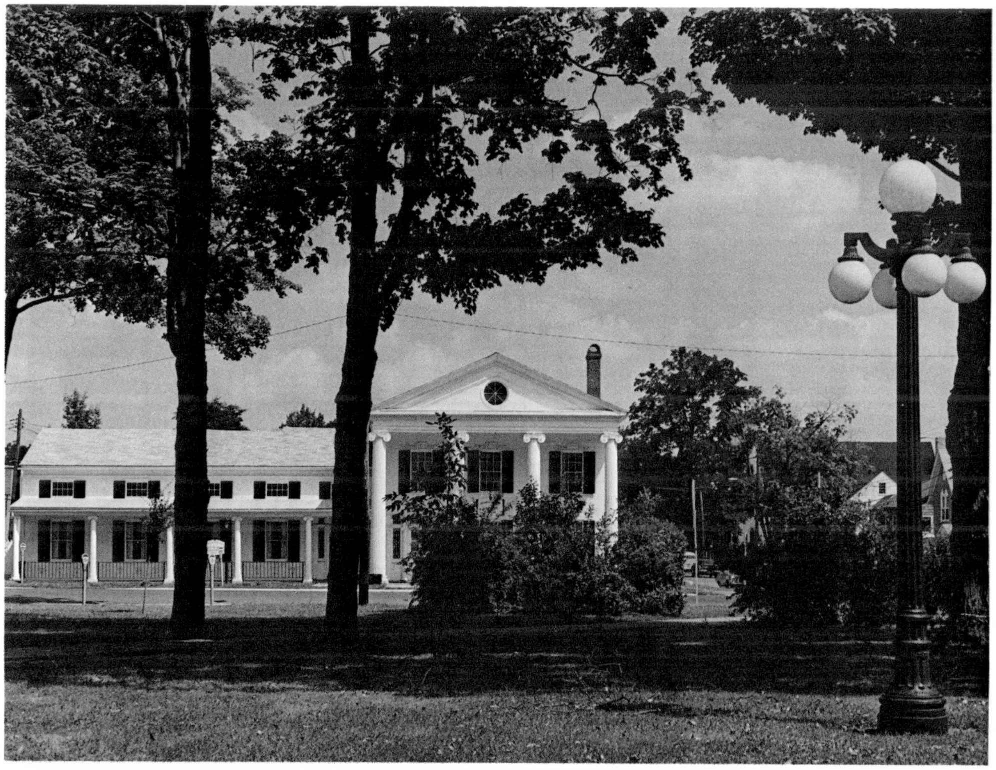

Judge's Chambers

TIOGA COUNTY

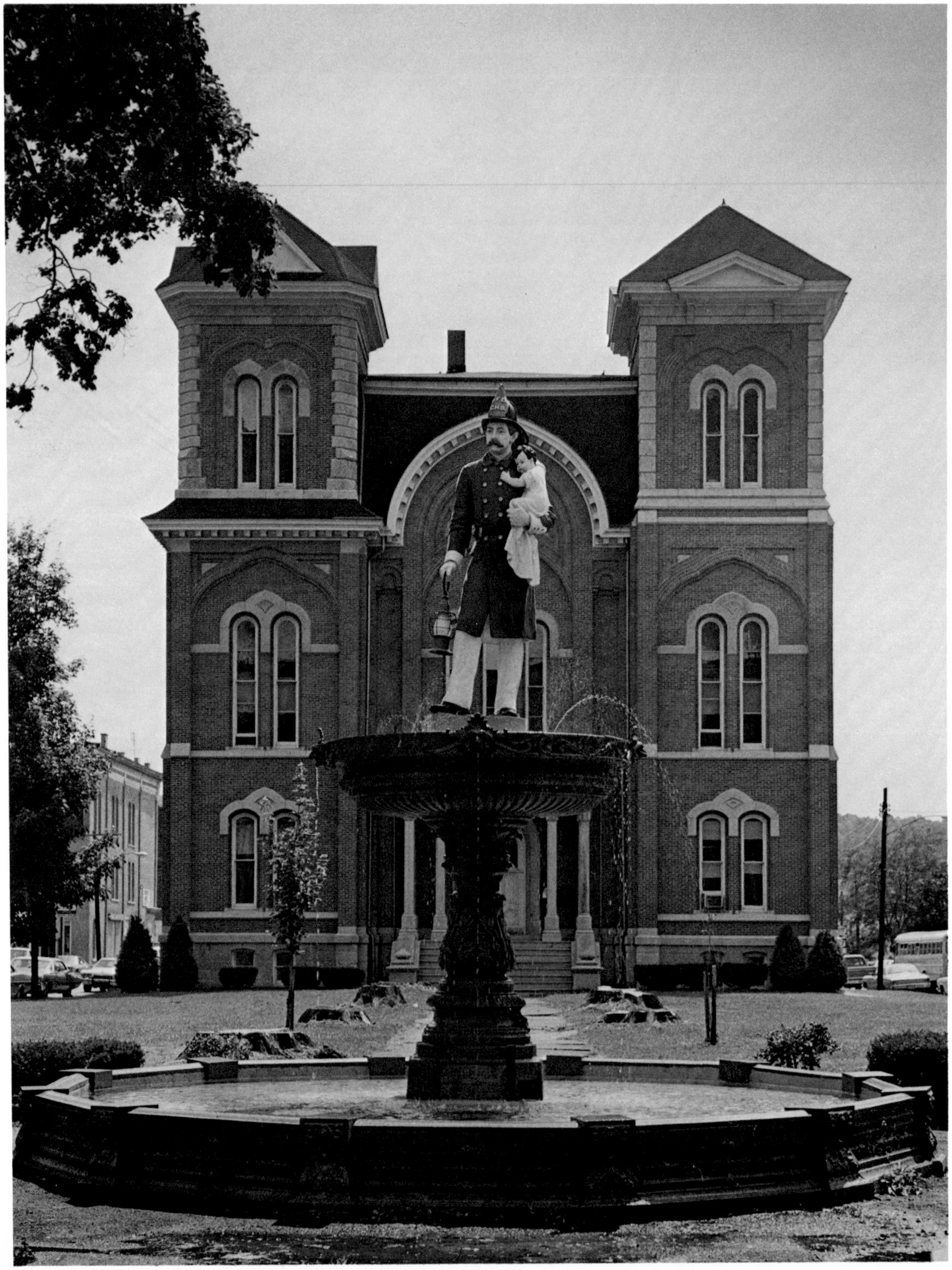

The Tioga County Courthouse at Owego is one of the two best examples of red-brick courthouses of the late nineteenth century (the other: the Delaware County Courthouse at Delhi). The county did not act entirely of its own free will in building the handsome structure with its twin towers; a grand jury had forced its construction by presenting an indictment against its predecessor as inconvenient, unsuitable, and little short of a health hazard.

Tioga County was established in 1791 and for a good number of years was half-shired, but the listing of county seats during that period is rather confusing. Newtown (later Elmira) was the seat for the western district for all but a short time until it, with the rest of Chemung County, was detached from Tioga. Chenango Point, Spencer, and Owego were successively county seats for the eastern district until at last, after Tioga County had shrunk with several amputations of territory, Owego became the sole county seat.

Owego's first courthouse was completed in 1823. In 1852 it was repaired and a cupola added, but patchwork could not keep the old building going forever, and in 1868 the grand jury looked the sagging structure over and declared it unfit for further use.

A new courthouse, built at a cost of $65,000, was completed and accepted in November 1873. This building, which still serves Tioga County, has a seventy- by ninety-foot floor plan; two towers rise one hundred and fifteen feet above the village green and are balanced at the back of the building by two smaller towers ninety-two feet high. A contemporary account described the structure as "a combination of the Grecian with the modern design." It is very difficult to find any Greek influence, but the courthouse is nevertheless very attractive with its red-brick walls and Onondaga-limestone trim.

TOMPKINS COUNTY

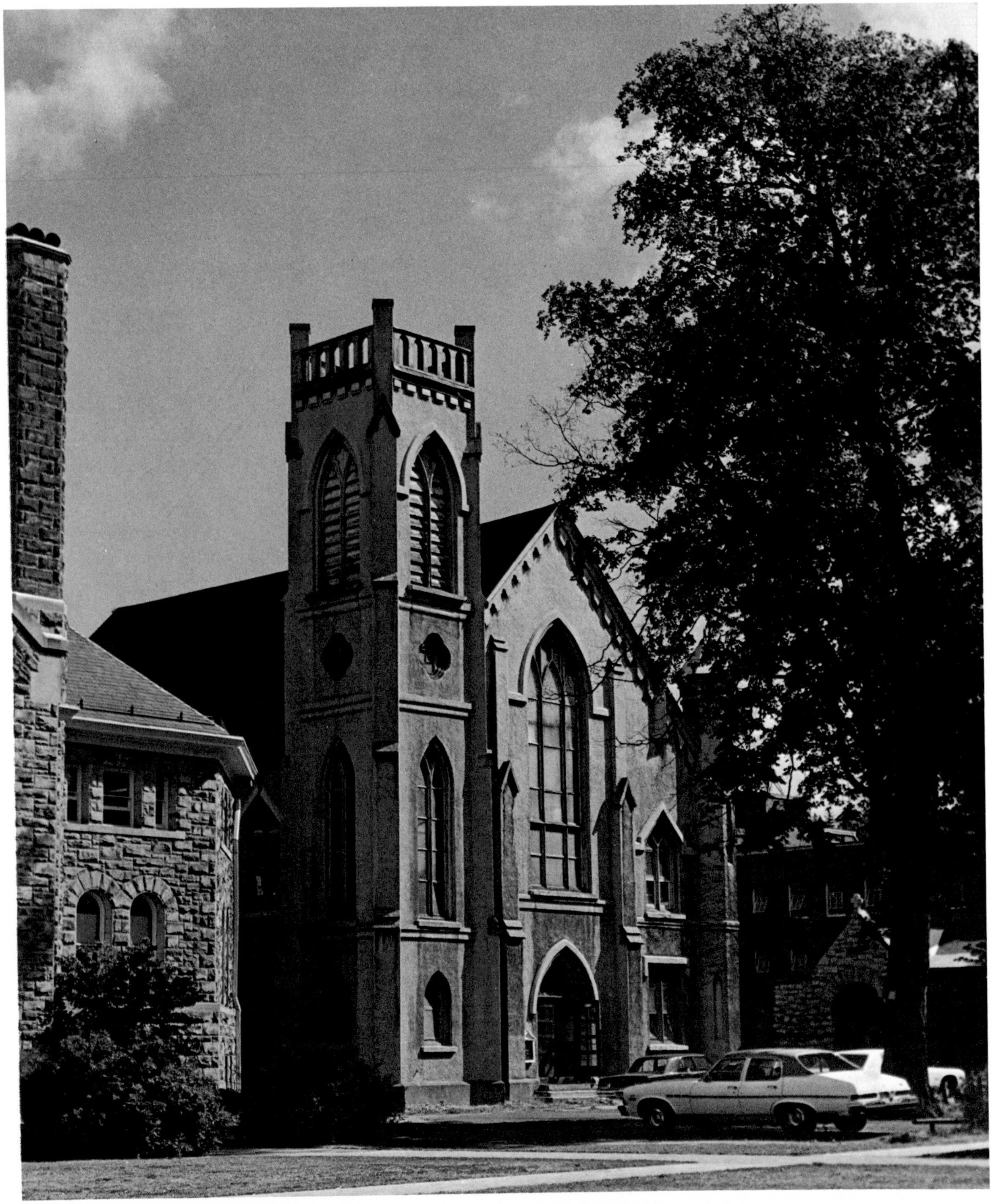

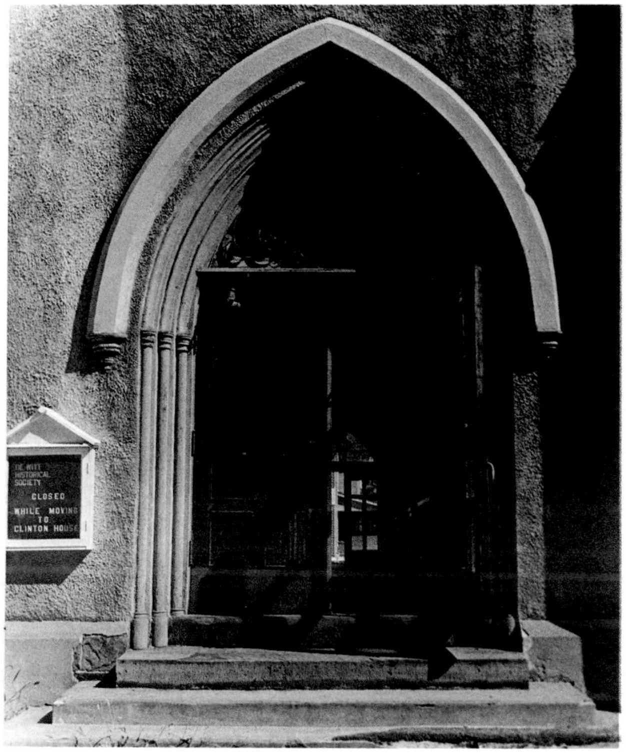
HISTORICAL
SOCIETY
CLOSED
WHILE MOVING
TO
CLINTON HOUSE

When Ithaca became the county seat on the formation of Tompkins County in 1817, it had to pay for the privilege; the legislature designated Ithaca the county seat on the condition that the town provide a site for the county buildings and $7,000. Ithaca fulfilled the conditions, and the next year a building for courthouse and jail was completed.

That first courthouse in time outlived its usefulness, and in 1854–55 a new and more modern structure, the one pictured here, was erected on the same site. Its architecture was not what one thinks of as typical of a courthouse; as the photographs indicate, the building looks more like a church than a place for court sessions. Nevertheless it served well until it, too, became too small for increasing county business and was replaced by a new courthouse in 1894.

The 1855 building was put to other uses in time; until a short while ago it housed a historical society. But very recently it has been put to a use probably unique among replaced and superseded courthouses: court sessions are again being held under its roof (the new courthouse is feeling a space pinch). The old building's return to court use is limited, but nevertheless it is echoing with the sound of a gavel again after more than eighty years.

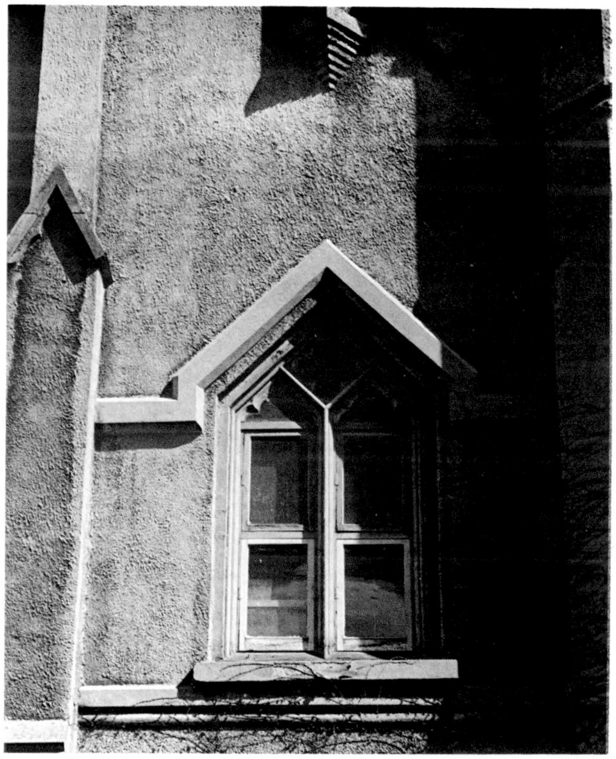

ULSTER COUNTY

Kingston, New York, was once a Dutch colonial town, and the courthouse site was used for judicial purposes a good century before the present 1818 courthouse was built. One early structure that stood on the same spot saw the last sitting of the royal courts, the first term of the New York Supreme Court, and the enactment into law of the 1777 constitution of the state of New York.

During the Revolution, with the British occupying New York City, Kingston was for a time de facto capital of the state, and the courthouse was used by the state government. That courthouse, built in 1773, was short-lived, for in 1777 a party of British troops briefly captured Kingston and put the town to the torch, burning almost every building, including the courthouse. A new courthouse was built within the limits of the walls of the destroyed building, but this expedient left no room for expansion as the county grew. In 1817 the old structure was demolished, along with the historic walls of the 1773 building.

The old records have been lost, so we do not know exactly what the new courthouse—the present one, completed in 1818—looked like originally. However, local historians assure us that the exterior of the gray stone structure is virtually unchanged from the day when it was finished. The interior, though, was very much remodeled during the 1890s, and there is no record of what it once looked like.

The historic building seems secure as a landmark for a long time to come. A new county building just two blocks away removes the kind of pressure for more space that often leads to demolition and "modernization." In addition, we are becoming more aware of the value of our heritage; any attempt to demolish a building as venerable as the Ulster County Courthouse would today rouse a roar of protest.

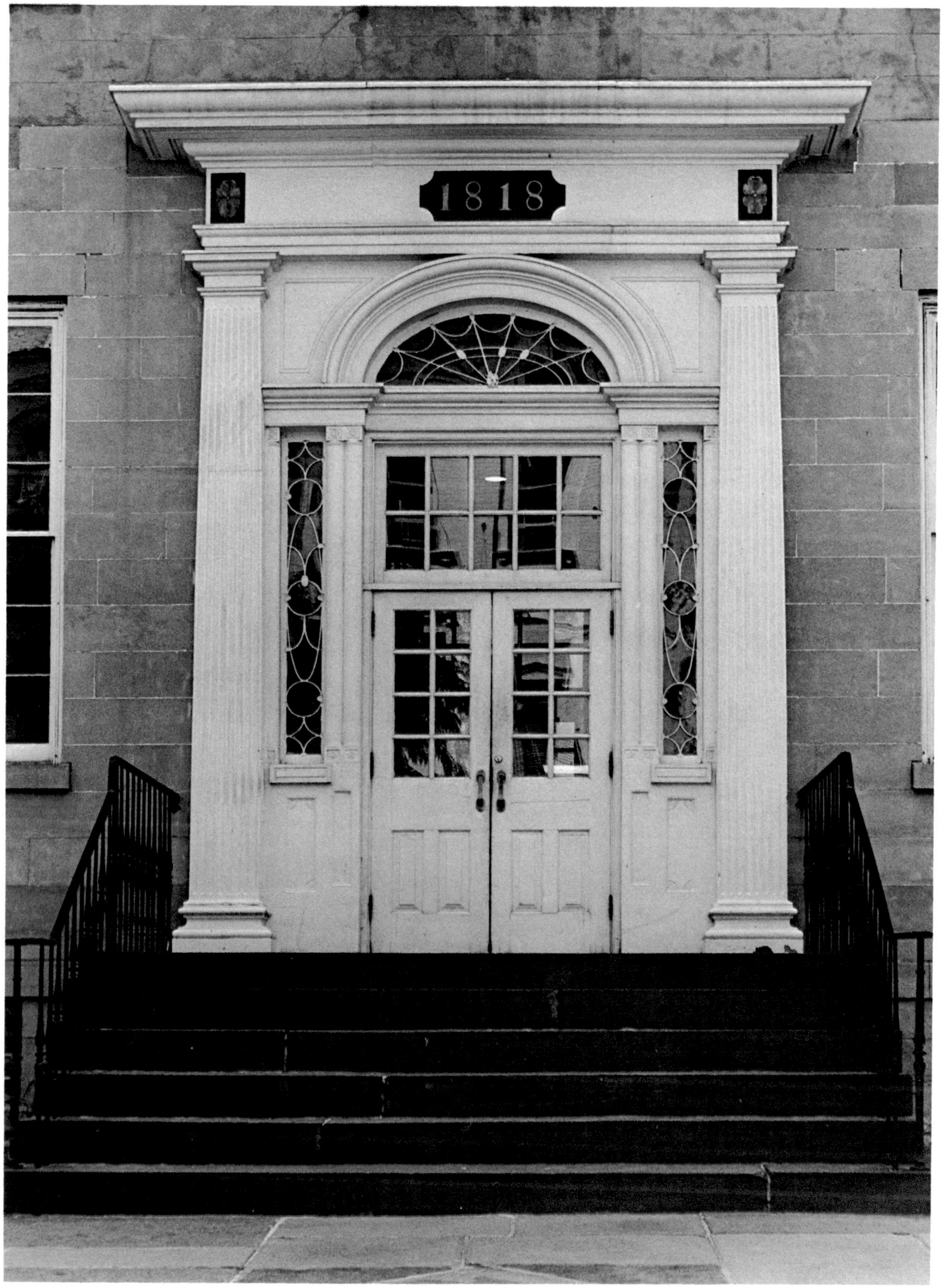
1818

WARREN COUNTY

It seems that the former Warren County Courthouse at Lake George is now safe from the wrecker's ball. After a long battle, preservationists appear to have won over the developers, who looked on the unused building with its Victorian facade only as an occupier of land that could more profitably be used for commercial purposes.

The village of Lake George, at the foot of the lake of the same name, has served as county seat since Warren County was established in 1813. During the first years court sessions were held in the Lake George Coffee House, but court was moved to more traditional quarters when a courthouse was built in 1815 on land donated "for the sole use and benefit of the inhabitants of the County of Warren." Lake George would remain the county seat for almost the next century and a half, in spite of early attempts to move the county seat to Glens Falls, which once contained half the population of the county and two thirds of its taxable income.

The first courthouse was destroyed by fire in 1843 and was replaced with a new building two years later. When the 1845 building in time became inadequate, it was decided to enlarge and renovate it; this program, completed in 1879, gave the courthouse its distinctive tower, among other changes. But as the county and its responsibilities grew, more space was needed than even the enlarged courthouse could provide. Additional space for offices was purchased in Lake George, but as the county continued to grow, this solution became unsatisfactory, and the Warren County Municipal Center, providing a complex of county offices, was built midway between Glens Falls and Lake George and was dedicated in 1963.

This left the old courthouse in Lake George empty and unused. Lake George has always

been a busy resort community, with large hotels along the lake shore, but in recent years it has become a neon strip—lights, signs, motels, and numerous small shops. It is not surprising that in this atmosphere there were many who thought that the old courthouse should be torn down and the land put to profit-producing uses.

The preservationists, who opposed the quick-profit approach, found unexpected allies among motel owners, souvenir sellers, and summer guests, who came to the defense of the building. After a long and complex legal battle, the town of Lake George purchased the old courthouse from the county. The building has been rehabilitated and today is the home of many town offices and of the county's historical association.

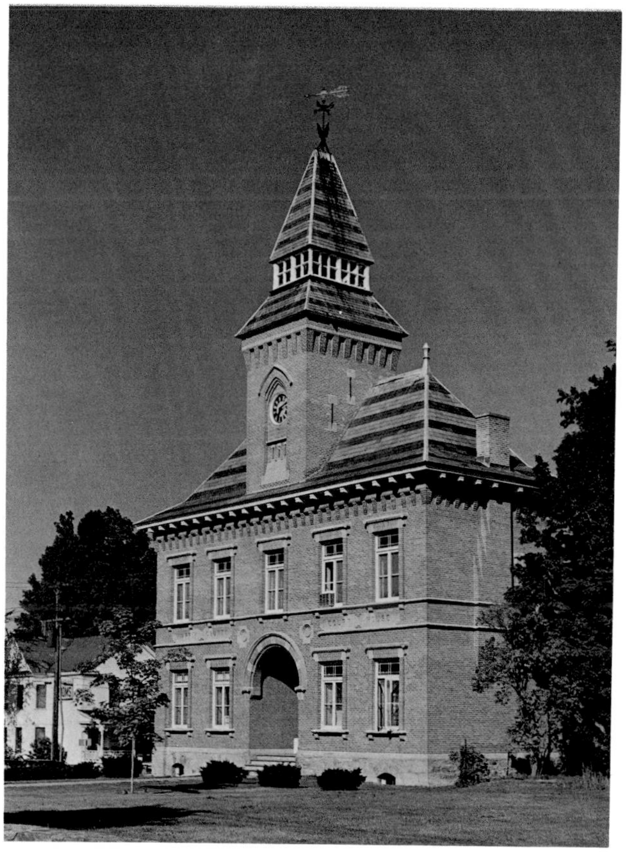

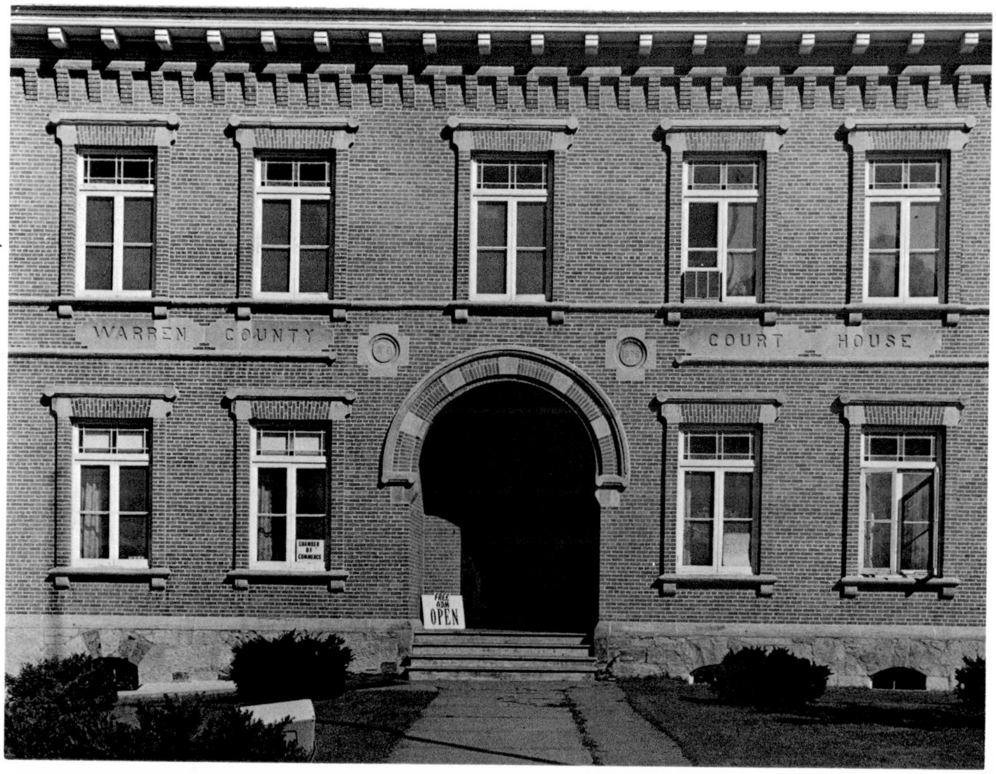
WARREN COUNTY
COURT HOUSE
OPEN

WASHINGTON COUNTY

Washington County is half-shired; Salem and Hudson Falls (formerly named Sandy Hill) have been the two county seats since a few years after the Revolution. There have been the usual moves to shift the county seats to other towns, or to eliminate one of them, but all challenges have been turned back by the two towns —though it took an extravagant pledge of financial support by Sandy Hill in 1872 to keep the present courthouse from being built in

Hudson Falls

Kingsbury and the county seat moved with it.

The courthouse for which the people of Sandy Hill (Hudson Falls) were willing to pay so heavily in order to retain their status as a half-shire seat is still the focal point of the village, just as it was when it was finished in 1873. It is a cut-stone structure, painted white, with a mansard roof, and boasts some excellent interior mosaic-tile work. All in all, its general design is more sophisticated than one would expect from that period in an Adirondack county.

By contrast, the 1871 courthouse at Salem, in the eastern shire near the Vermont border, is a simple structure. It was designed by architect M. F. Cummings, and once had a bell tower over the entrance; the tower has since been removed and today the courthouse looks like a number of private homes in Salem.

Hudson Falls

163

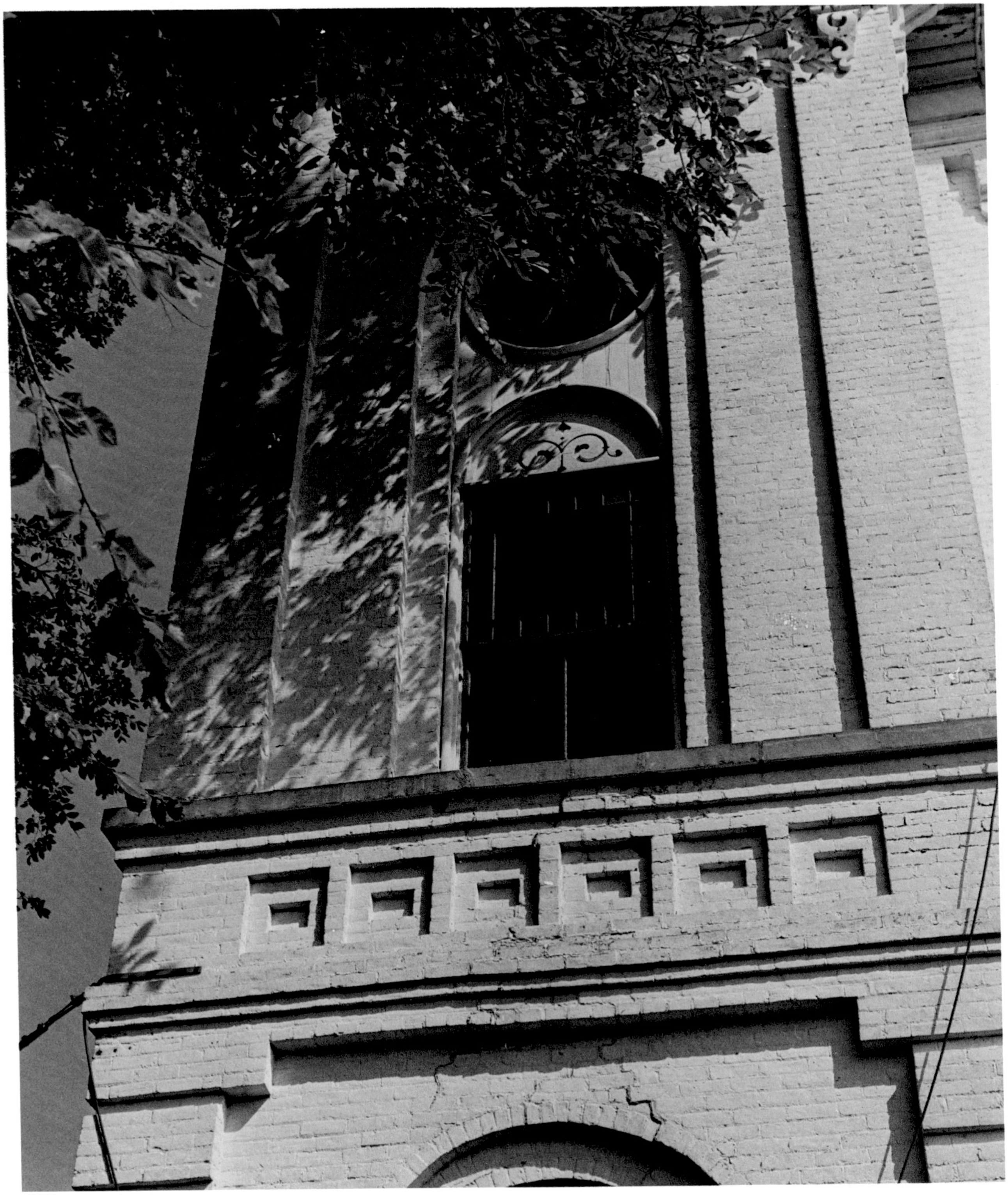

Salem

Salem

Salem

WAYNE COUNTY

The 1854 courthouse at Lyons is only the second courthouse to be built in Wayne County, for Wayne is not only relatively young as New York counties go, but its commissioners have tended to be careful in making building expenditures. The first courthouse, also at Lyons, was put up in 1823, the year Wayne County was organized.

That first court building was destroyed by fire, and the board of supervisors hesitated so long at the cost of a new structure that Lyons almost lost the courthouse, and the county seat with it, to Newark. It was decided to keep things as they were only after the town of Lyons donated a piece of land on the public square for court purposes. The new courthouse was built there, a brick structure with a large dome and an Ionic portico, completed in 1854.

The handsome building that had been the pride of Wayne County at its completion suffered the inevitable deterioration of time and neglect over the years, and by 1896 was in such decrepit condition that Newark made another attempt to take over the county seat, by offering to pay a large part of the cost of a new courthouse. However, the board of supervisors decided to repair the 1854 building, even though an investigating committee found it in deplorable condition: no chambers for the judge, no room for lawyers attending the court, no ladies' room in the entire building, the men's room in

the basement "unhealthy and offensive," and no trial-jury room. By March of 1898 these faults had been corrected and the entire building repainted.

Today the courthouse stands substantially as built in 1854 and repaired in 1898, except that county offices have been added to the rear of the building. The courtroom, for the most part, retains its original appearance, and much of the original woodwork remains, but the windows on one wall have been filled in.

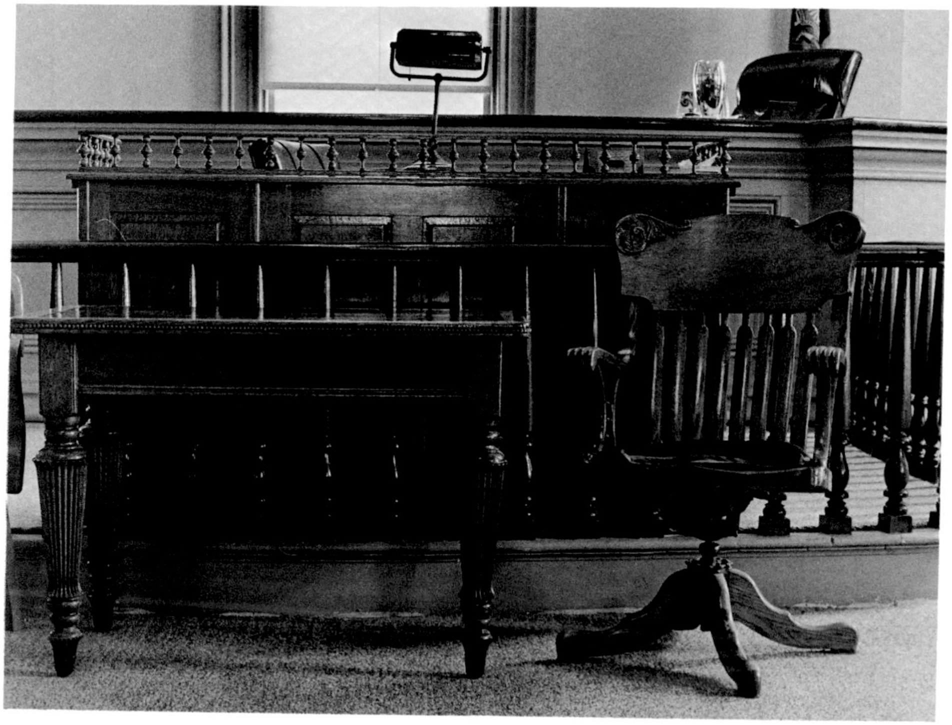

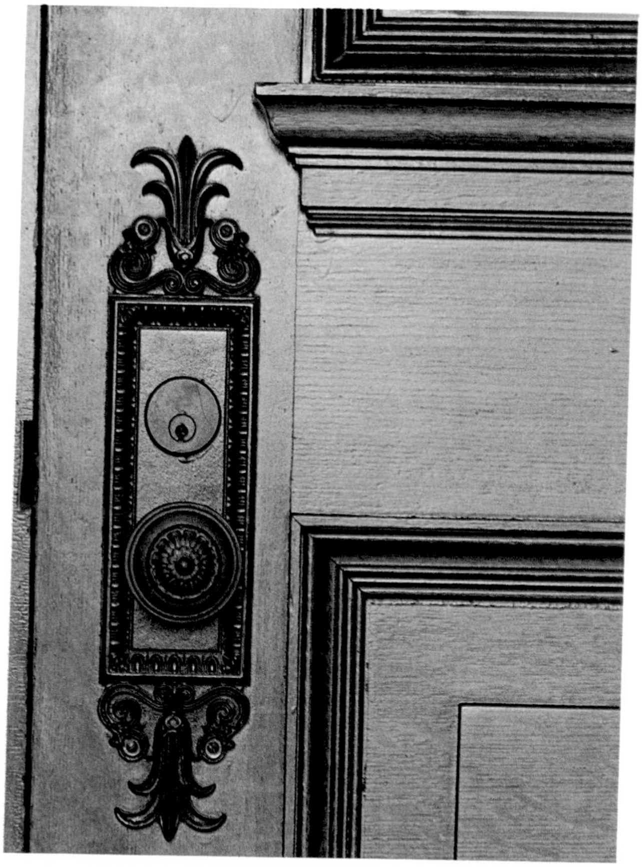

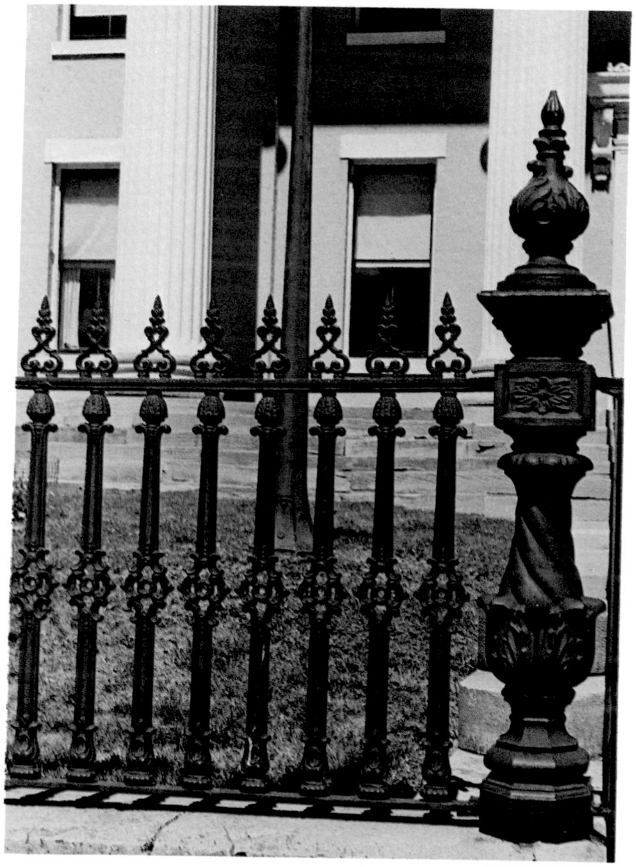

WESTCHESTER COUNTY

The courthouse at Bedford, which once served northern Westchester County, saw its last judicial business conducted more than a century ago. There has been no county court there since; the old building and a mass of fading records are the only evidence now that Bedford ever was a half-shire town—and an important one—in Westchester County.

Most of the proceedings reported in those records are as dry as the old paper they are written on, but now and then one comes alive. Such a one is the 1834 arraignment of Robert Matthews, also known as Matthias the Prophet, on charges of murder. The circumstances that brought Matthews to the bar of justice were far from ordinary, and began in 1832 when he met one Elijah Pierson of Ossining and told Pierson that he was Matthias, the apostle chosen to succeed Judas, risen from the dead. Moreover, besides being the resurrected Apostle Matthias, the spirit of Jesus of Nazareth and of God the Father were also within him. This exuberance of spirituality, Matthews claimed, enabled him to grant forgiveness of sins and to send the Holy Ghost to those who truly believed in him. During the next two years Matthews, through a combination of sleight-of-hand and suggestion, convinced Pierson that he was divine; Pierson then took the self-proclaimed Matthias the Prophet into his Ossining home to live, where

they were aided in meeting expenses by Benjamin Folger of New York City, another convert to belief in Matthews's divinity.

Using threats of godly vengeance, Matthews was able to enhance his worldly wealth at the expense of that of his two followers. By October 1833 he had prevailed on Pierson to convey title of his Ossining house to the Prophet, and at the same time both Folger and Pierson agreed to devote their fortunes to supporting Matthews. This they did until Pierson died in August 1834, when Matthews moved in with Folger's family in New York. But by now Folger was becoming disillusioned; in September, after only a month of cohabitation, he asked his guest to leave. Yet Matthews, even while he was getting ready to leave, still had ability to intimidate sufficient to bully Folger into giving him six hundred thirty dollars in cash.

Matthews was also able to talk the maid into poisoning the Folgers' coffee the morning after he left, to revenge himself very satisfactorily for Folger's apostasy. Folger and his entire family became quite ill, but the maid had not followed Matthews's instructions and the dosage was not fatal. This murder attempt, together with his suspicions about the death of Elijah Pierson, caused Folger to swear out a warrant for Matthews's arrest.

The authorities had other reasons for suspect-

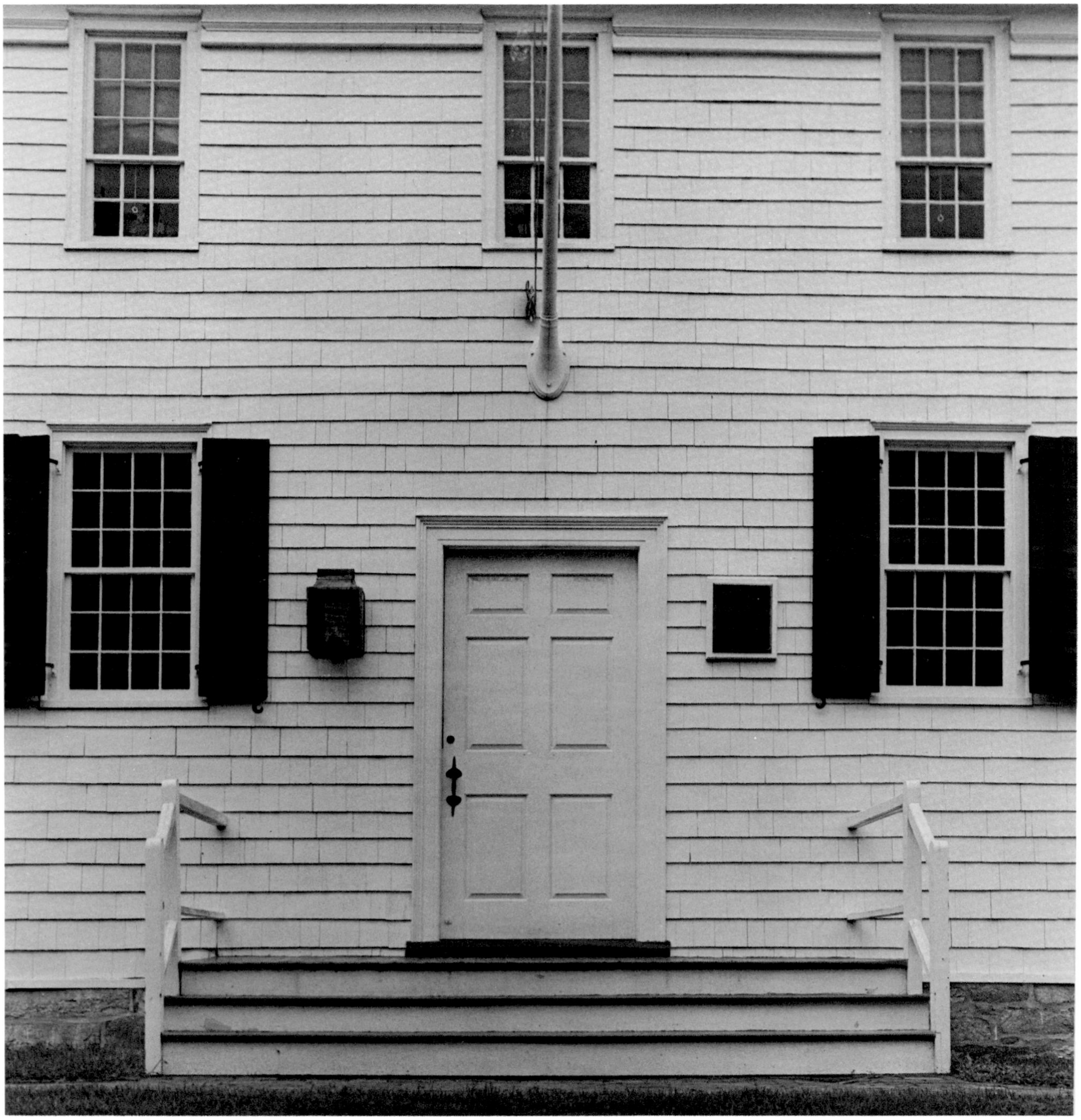

ing Matthews of murder. A Mrs. Rosetta Drach, whom the newspapers referred to as a "long and intimate acquaintance of Pierson," had called on Pierson just before his death and had been refused entry by Matthews, who had assured her that he was caring for Pierson and that, with his divine powers, he certainly would not permit Pierson to die. After Pierson's death, Mrs. Drach went to the authorities, and a post mortem revealed that the man had died with some virulent poison in his stomach.

Matthews was apprehended in Albany on September 21, and taken to Bridewell Jail in New York City to await arraignment. When arrested he had his solid-gold key to the gates of Jerusalem and some money, but most of what he got from Folger and Pierson seems to have been spent on clothes. He had several fine linen shirts with lace cuffs, a pair of kid gloves, a gold-mounted three-cornered hat, an olive-colored cloak lined with velvet and silk, a brown frock coat heavily embroidered with silver stars and suns, and two nightcaps in the form of bishops' mitres. Both nightcaps had the inscription "Jesus Matthias" in front; one was decorated in the rear with the names of the twelve apostles, the other with those of the twelve tribes of Israel. Matthews also had a sword, the actual sword of Gideon preserved for his use, he claimed, although it was inscribed *E pluribus unum*. Publicity attendant on his arrest revealed that he had left an impoverished wife and daughter in Albany while he wandered about the country.

The Bedford courtroom in which Matthews was arraigned and where he pleaded not guilty was in the wooden gambrel-roofed courthouse built for the northern part of Westchester County in the 1780s. The building was still in good condition when Matthews had his brief moment in court. Extensive repairs had been undertaken in 1817: the foundation reinforced, window frames and sashes replaced, the courtroom painted, the belfry repaired, and the exterior siding replaced. During this time a jail room had been installed on the second floor of the courthouse — probably the same room pointed out today as the former jail.

Anyone familiar with Westchester County may find it hard to believe that Bedford in 1790 had a population almost twice that of White Plains and double that of Yonkers. This was in large part because southern Westchester had been a continual battleground during the Revolution; actions, major and guerrilla, had been fought there so often that many of the residents had moved to less disturbed areas. As a result, county government had been established at Bedford during the first two years of the war and moved even farther north for a time to upper Salem. When peace came, all county court sessions were again held at Bedford, usually at the Presbyterian meetinghouse, until 1786, when two jury districts were authorized for Westchester County, and Bedford and White Plains were designated as the half-shire seats. The legislative enabling act of May 1786 authorized £1,800 for the Bedford and White Plains courthouses; Bedford got the small share of this appropriation, £400, though additional money was needed to complete both buildings.

Work went slowly. The Westchester County Court of Common Pleas did hold its first sittings in the Bedford courthouse in September 1787, when the building was far from completed, but not until 1790 did the board of supervisors feel that the courtroom was well enough along for them to use it for their meetings. And it was another six years—June 1796—before the building committee was willing to report that the courthouse was finally finished.

It was in this building—brought up to date with the inclusion of the second-floor jail room and perhaps some other minor changes—that Robert Matthews, a.k.a. Matthias the Prophet, was arraigned at the first sitting of the November 1834 term of the Westchester County Court of General Sessions in the Bedford courthouse. Matthews did not disappoint. He wore a large purple cloak into the courtroom and removed it before seating himself. Under the cloak was a light, claret-colored frock coat, embroidered with seven silver stars on each breast. He had lace ruffles at his wrists, a red silk sash at his waist, green cashmere trousers, and what were described as "fashionable boots."

There was, plainly, more than enough evidence to hold Matthews for trial on suspicion of murder. But the people in and around Bedford were in for a disappointment. They had come in from the farms for the bizarre arraignment—and then, after the self-styled Prophet was ready to be brought to trial, they were cheated of the end of the drama. Matthews was to have been tried in the Bedford courthouse, but the circuit of the Supreme Court was unable to hold its November 1834 meeting there because the circuit justice was absent. So Matthews was moved to the White Plains jail, where he passed the time as best he could while various legal maneuvers postponed his trial from January to April, 1835.

When he did appear in court, Matthews was as flamboyantly dressed as before, and just as certain—or pretending to be—that he spoke with the voice of angels. When a supporter tried to shake his hand, he drew back haughtily, saying, "Know ye not, 'tis written, touch not the Prophet of the Lord." After this rather bad misquotation of I Chronicles 16:22, Matthews went into the prisoner's box and listened quietly to the preliminary proceedings. But the next day the judge expelled him from the courtroom because he persisted in howling and making loud comments while the jurors were being impaneled. The defense entered a plea of insanity, and after the evidence was taken, the question of sanity was submitted to the jury, which decided that Matthews was indeed sane.

But after hearing evidence concerning the crime itself, the jury, to the surprise of the court and most of the spectators, returned a verdict of not guilty without even leaving the room. It appears that fear working on superstitious minds may have been the cause of this precipitous verdict, brought without even considering the strong evidence against Matthews. A newspaper comment reveals what may have motivated this fear: "It is a lamentable instance of the weakness of human nature that many of the people in the neighborhood of White Plains should still place implicit faith in the outrageous impostor. He lately issued a decree from the jail ordering all farmers to lay down their plows [until his release from bondage]. He has also prophesied that if he be found guilty, White Plains should be destroyed by an earthquake, and not an inhabitant left to tell the tale of its destruction."

Thus, it appears, the farmers and villagers who sat on that jury in 1835 did not see Matthews as the eccentric and charlatan he appears to us today; if they did not quite believe that he was the reincarnation of Matthias the

Apostle, they at least were ready to give him the benefit of the doubt rather than risk divine retribution. Another jury, however, was not so easily intimidated and found Matthews guilty of an assault and battery upon his daughter, for which he was sentenced to a month in prison, and another conviction, for contempt of court, added three more months to his time behind bars. After serving his sentence Matthews seems to have disappeared from sight completely.

The old courthouse was formally turned over to the town of Bedford by the county in 1870. By that time there was no need for a northern shire, since the population center of Westchester County had begun its shift southward as early as the 1840s; Bedford had ceased to grow, and its courthouse had become an unnecessary appendage to the more modern structure at White Plains. For a few years the old building was used as a town hall, then stood empty and unused until the front wall above the porch began to bulge out alarmingly and it seemed probable that a severe wind-storm might collapse the whole structure.

In 1966 the Bedford Historical Society took over the courthouse and commenced rescue operations; the society has now turned it into a museum. The building has a colorful and significant history; among those who practiced there were Aaron Burr and Robert Troup, the jurist and land agent who played an important role in opening western New York. It has many associations with John Jay, Revolutionary diplomat and first chief justice, whose retirement homestead is a few miles from Bedford village. Jay's son William presided as a judge in the Bedford courtroom, and his nephew Peter Jay Munro was a frequent practitioner before the courts meeting there.

The Bedford building is not what one thinks of as usual courthouse architecture. With its rectangular shape and gambrel roof it resembles—except for its porch—a midwestern barn with an oversize cupola rather than a typical courthouse. Nonetheless, it is the third oldest surviving courthouse in the state, and a relic of a day when men built to suit their abilities and materials and not some preconceived model.

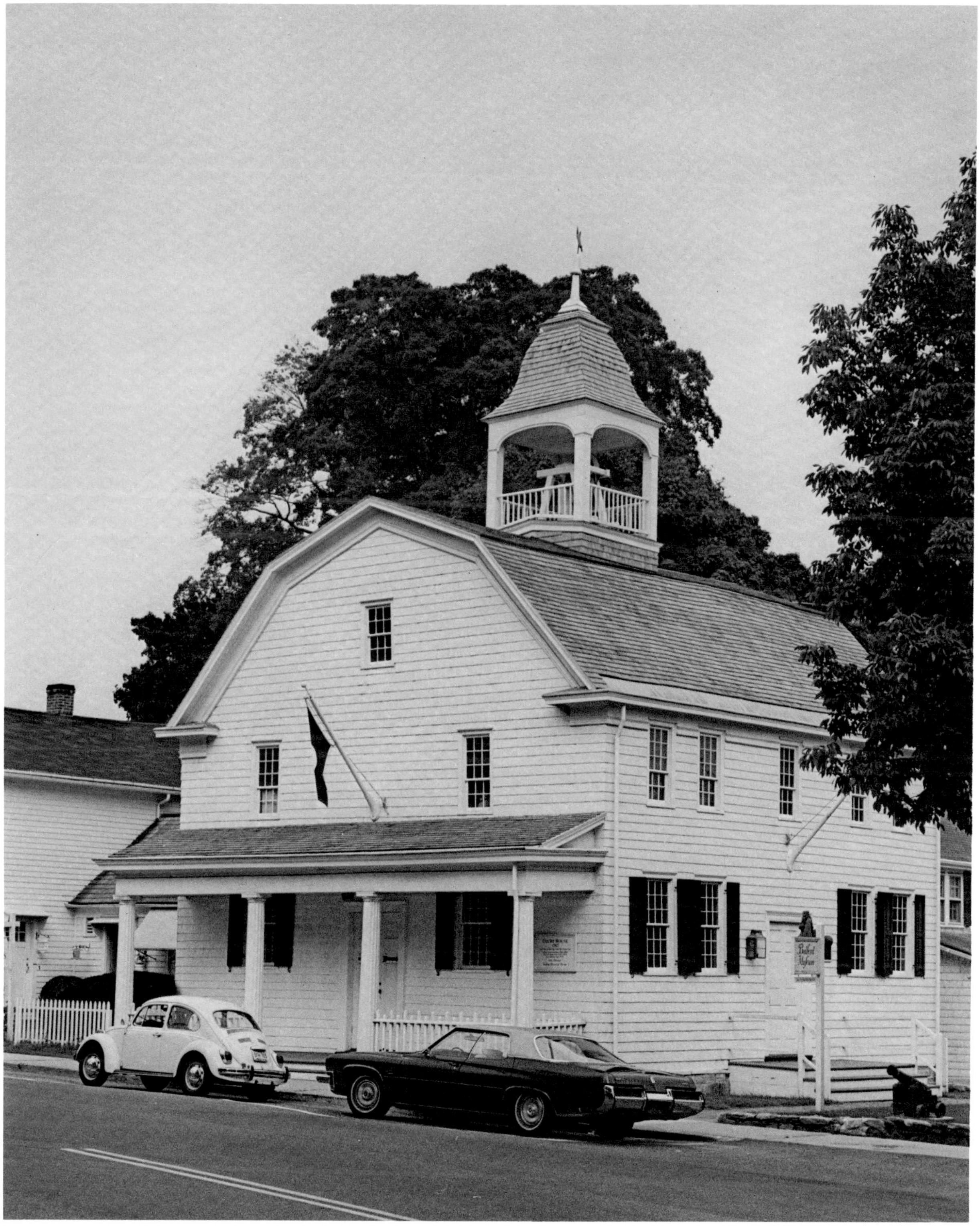
COURT HOUSE
Bedford Museum

YATES COUNTY

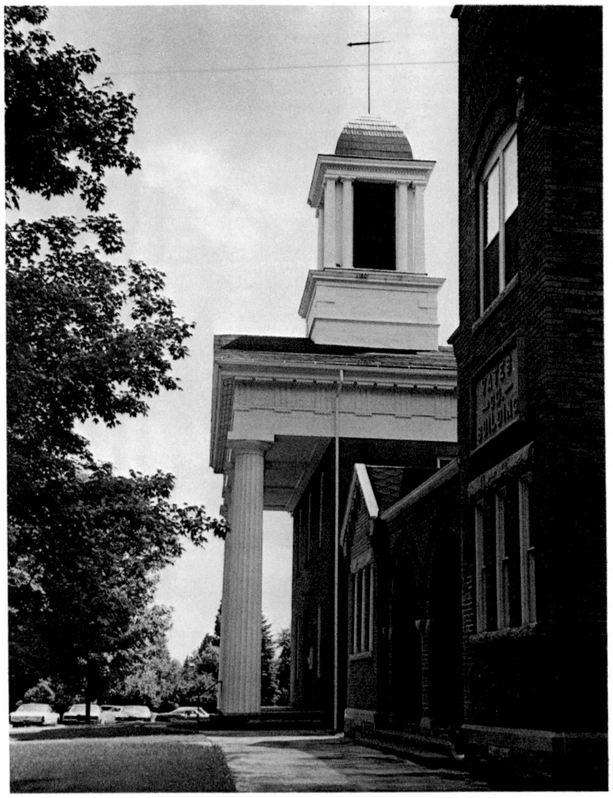
YATES
BUILDING

The Yates County Courthouse at Penn Yan is another historical building whose story has been obscured because the documents that tell of its history have been lost or destroyed. Fortunately, other sources provide enough information to let us sketch in the background of the old courthouse.

Yates County was a part of Ontario County until 1823; for a time thereafter court was held in the home of one Asa Cole, in the village of Penn Yan, while the legislature was making up its mind about a county seat. The legislature soon settled on Penn Yan, and a courthouse was built there about 1825 or 1826. That first courthouse, according to early reminiscences, was a plain, substantial brick building, similar to, though smaller than, the one that replaced it—the replacement that still serves Yates County, the courthouse pictured here.

Sometime about 1834—the exact date is not known—fire swept through the first courthouse and destroyed it. A new one, larger and more comfortable, was erected on the ruins of the old, and was completed in 1835. The new building had the county offices on the lower floor and courtrooms on the second; the county jail was in a separate building (it had been contained within the first courthouse).

That second courthouse has undergone basic repairs since 1835, but otherwise it has remained unchanged for almost a century and a half. The venerable Greek-Revival building sits on a large public square in Penn Yan, a center of architectural interest as well as of legal activity for the village.

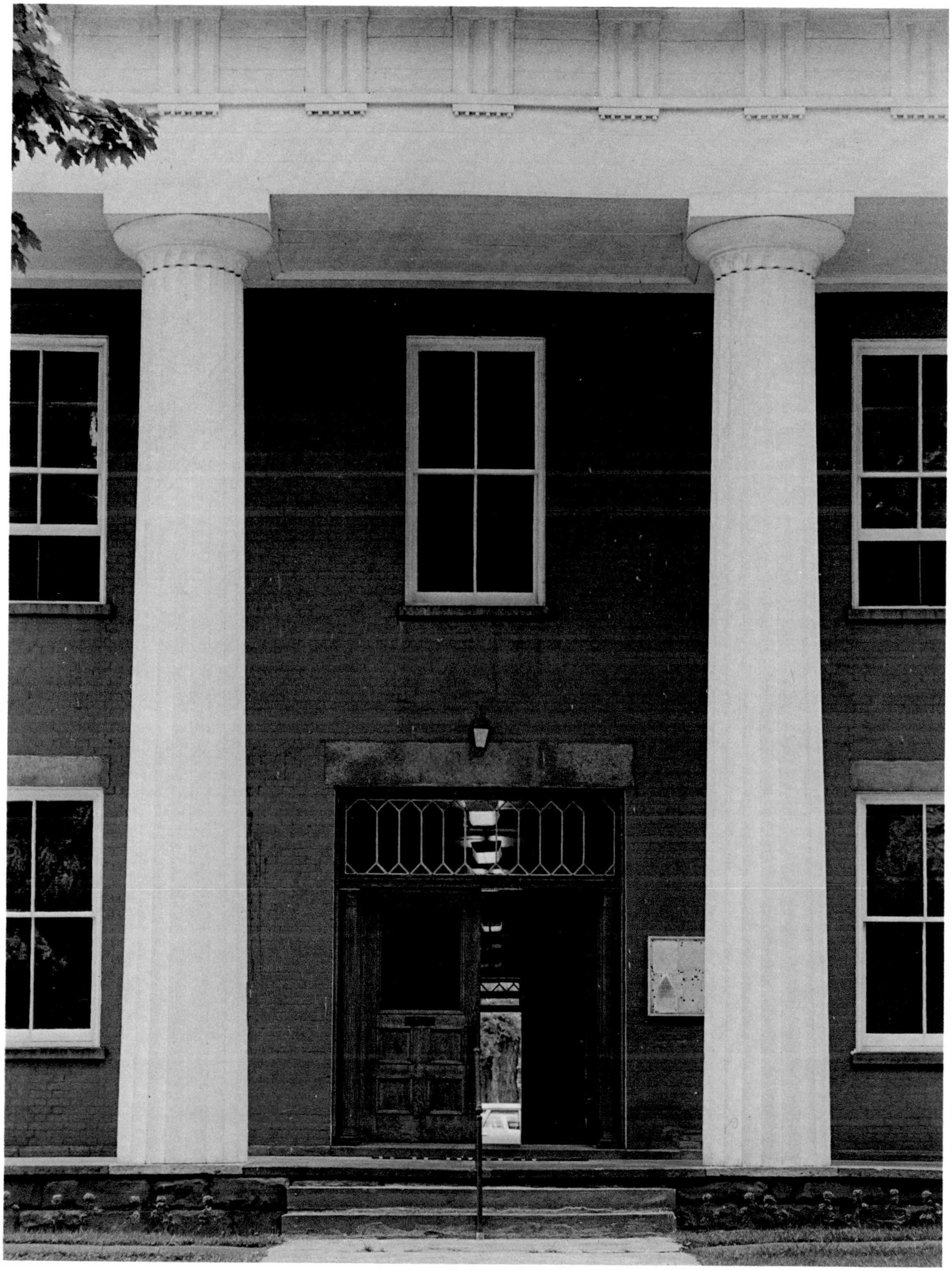